Graphic Design School

The Principles and Practice of Graphic Design

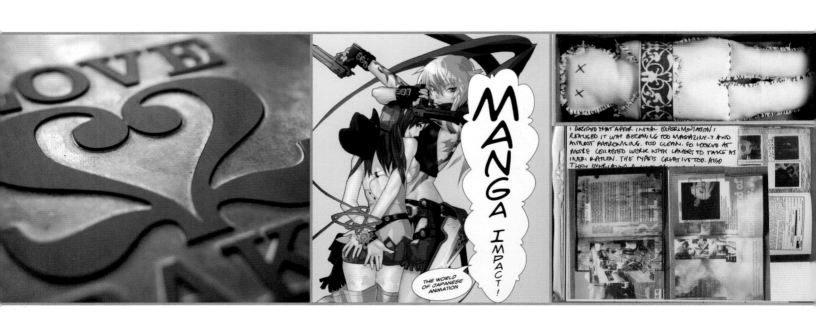

WILEY

Graphic Design School

The Principles and Practice of Graphic Design

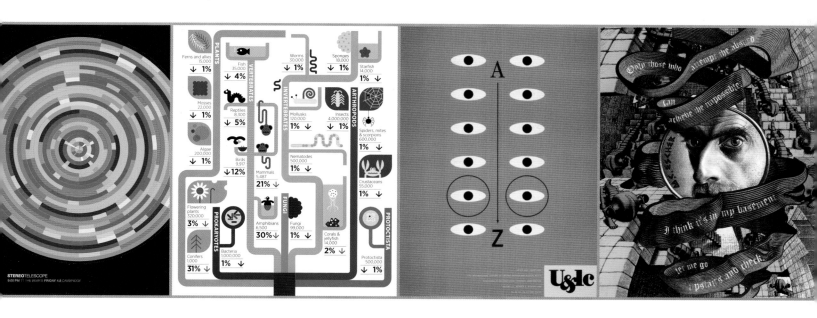

David Dabner • Sandra Stewart • Eric Zempol

A QUARTO BOOK

For general information about our other products and services, please contact our Customer Care Department within the United States at (800) 762-2974, outside the United States at +1 (317) 572-3993 or fax +1 (317) 572-4002.

Wiley publishes in a variety of print and electronic formats and by print-on-demand. Some material included with standard print versions of this book may not be included in e-books or in print-on-demand. If this book refers to media such as a CD or DVD that is not included in the version you purchased, you may download this material at http://booksupport.wiley.com. For more information about Wiley products, visit www.wiley.com.

Library of Congress Cataloging-in-Publication Data
Dabner, David.
The new graphic design : a foundation course in principles and practice / David Dabner. -- 5th edition.
pages cm
Originally published: Graphic design school. 1991.
"A quarto book."
Includes index.
ISBN 978-1-118-13441-2 (pbk.)
1. Graphic arts. 2. Commercial art. I. Swann, Alan, 1946- Graphic design school. II. Title.
NC845.D33 2013
741.6--dc23
2013018920

ISBN: 978-1-118-13441-2
10 9 8 7 6 5 4 3 2 1

QUAR.GRS5

Conceived, designed, and produced by
Quarto Publishing plc.
The Old Brewery
6 Blundell Street
London N7 9BH

Senior editor: Katie Crous
Co-editor: Ruth Patrick
Copy editor: Claire Waite Brown
Art editor and designer: Jacqueline Palmer
Art director: Caroline Guest
Picture researcher: Sarah Bell
Proofreader: Sarah Hoggett
Indexer: Helen Snaith
Cover Design: Michael Rutkowski
Cover Art: © Bogusław Mazur/Alamy

Creative director: Moira Clinch
Publisher: Paul Carslake

Color separation in China by Modern Age Pte Ltd
Printed in China by 1010 Printing International Ltd

Contents

345678

Introduction

This book is written with the intent of providing an introduction to the underlying principles of good graphic design, whether it is print-based, web and interactive, or environmental. The content has been constructed to mirror, in part, how the subject is taught in college design programs, and the illustrations, which are a mixture of student projects and professional design work, have been carefully chosen to illuminate specific teaching points. Many of the sections contain step-by-step exercises and assignments, offer practical advice, and point toward further resources.

The first part of the book, Principles, supports the idea that a thorough understanding of design principles should support the process of creating design works in response to specific briefs and problems,

while allowing room for self-authored experimentation and visual freedom. As you are introduced to the basics of research, typography, color, photography, and composition, you will learn to become visually aware and able to articulate these design principles into your future works. You will also gain some understanding that these principles cross disciplines and are the vocabulary of visual literacy.

In the second part of the book, Practice, you will be introduced to invaluable practical skills that are important support systems to the skills sets in research and creative process you have read about in Part One. They do not replace them, but serve as methods and practices for developing critical problem-solving skills, and learning to manage complex projects. Designers need the whole range of skills to

be truly successful, and expertise will come with continued study and practice in both areas. Unless you learn the practical skills and technology of design production, including how to manage images, create digital files for specific media, and build and structure a website, you will be unable to bring your brilliant concepts to life.

None of these visual skills can be viewed in isolation from the context in which design happens and its larger role in society and the world. Designers are visual communicators, often giving visual voice to new and provocative ideas. They create images that can inform, persuade, and entertain millions of people. This comes with great responsibility, and it is crucial to be aware of the role of design in shaping the world we live in, and changes in the discipline that transcend trends or the latest software. While any kind of comprehensive account of these topics stands outside the scope of this book, becoming visually literate and technically skilled should go hand in hand with an understanding of such issues as communication theories, global audiences, systems theory, sustainable issues in design, and the changing role of technology.

Finally, design education is a lifelong experience that can bring great personal satisfaction and reward. With this book as a gateway, a new way of seeing the world may lead you to a career path that will be a constant source of surprise and delight.

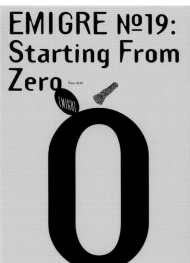

Principles

The first part of this book is concerned with design principles, the building blocks that connect the basics of all good design. Every discipline has its own sets of rules, methods, specialized technologies, and technical requirements. Each one is rooted in the interactions of its history, theory, and practice, but unlike learning law or biology, the language of design is visual. It involves the need for a highly developed awareness of visual relationships, proportion, the perceptions of visual principles, and of the modern world and its complex events and practices. A good designer can filter this information and create relevant, engaging, visually eloquent design that responds to multiple problems, needs, and contexts. While a design student needs to develop the research, concept-development, compositional,

and organizational skills associated with design, he or she also needs to be engaged with the world, and interested, aware, and sensitive to the changing contexts in which design plays a part.

Unit 1 introduces the primary and secondary research skills needed by designers, followed by an introduction to theories of image, the importance of audience, and of organizing your work and time. In Unit 2, the idea of form is spotlighted. Form involves composition of the fundamentals of design (text, image, proportion, space, color, scale) and requires an understanding of the visual dynamics created by combining them with intent. Understanding form comes from the ability to see intrinsic and subtle qualities in the various design elements, and the observation of, and sensitivity to, the changing relationships between

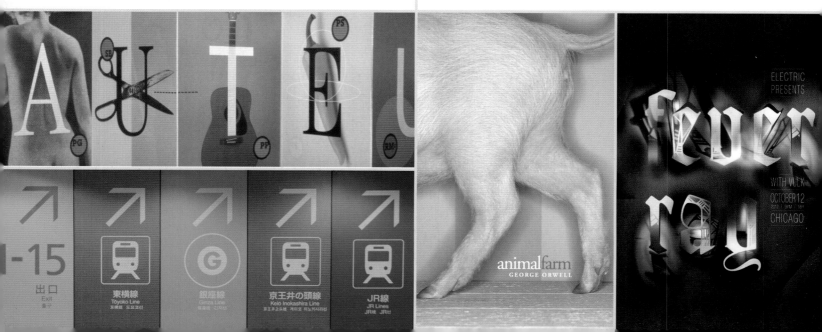

PART 1

them. Unit 3 introduces typography, a core skill for all designers that is layered with complexity, and cannot be understated for its beauty, history, versatility, and ability to influence an audience. Developing a deep understanding of typography is of critical importance. Unit 4 introduces color as one of the primary tools in the language of design, including theory, terminology, associations, issues of legibility, and emotional response. Managing color and its ability to communicate is a skill that also evolves with greater understanding of its influences. Whatever design discipline you ultimately pursue, from editorial art direction to web and motion graphics, these basic principles will give you a solid foundation and serve as the groundwork for further exploration and understanding of design and the role of the designer.

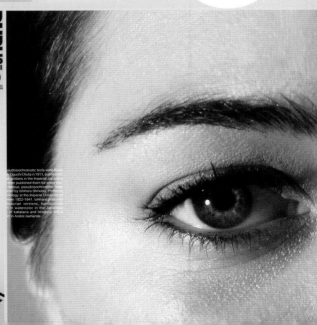

1 RESEARCH AND CONCEPTS

The first step toward becoming interesting is to be interested. The best artists of all kinds—painters, designers, writers, sculptors, musicians, playwrights—make the world their inspiration, and draw ideas and content from both experience and research. They make it a priority to stay aware of what is happening, not only within the world of design, but in the world in general, and this level of engagement enriches their work.

> **❝What you see and hear depends a good deal on where you are standing; it also depends on what kind of a person you are❞**
> *C. S. Lewis*

➡ Observe and collect

Research should be specific to each project, but the process of observation and recording your impressions should be ongoing, and should become a part of your daily routine. When something catches your eye, document it; capture an image and put it into your notebook/sketchbook/device for reference later. Everything you come in contact with can inform your work, so make sure you have a great collection of objects and impressions for inspiration.

PART 1	PRINCIPLES
UNIT1	RESEARCH AND CONCEPTS
MODULE 1	**Basics of research**

Modern media demands an increasing amount of visual information to illustrate its content in print, packaging, and motion graphics, in the built environment or online. Graphic designers are the conduits for all types of communications from multiple sources to specific audiences, and to be successful they must be well-informed, accomplished researchers with inquisitive natures.

Broaden your outlook

Designers who seek information from the greatest range of references are those who successfully communicate with people of all ages, professions, and lifestyles, and who properly contextualize their design work.

• Read about events from multiple sources. Change your sources daily, or read from several sources and compare stories, noting how information about the same events changes, how the language is used to target various audiences, and what type of imagery is used to support the text. Never rely solely on editable web postings for accuracy if you are reading facts. Check your sources!

• You can never read enough books, but don't limit

yourself to the kind you usually read. Reading only about graphic design can be particularly dangerous: although extremely useful for information and guidance, this may turn you into an armchair expert; you want to be an original practitioner. Expand your reading to include novels and plays, and books on sculpture, architecture, art history, cooking, sports, archeology, travel, and math—it really doesn't matter, as long as they provide you with a broad spectrum of knowledge.

• Be open to new experiences. Visit, galleries, clubs, retail environments, and museums you've never been to, listen to music you've not heard before, and eat food you've never tried before. Travel whenever you can, and learn about global issues and cultural treasures.

• Share ideas and listen to people. Whatever language they use, there is always a way to establish communication, if you try. Pay attention to what inspires them, and learn from others while also sharing your insights.

• Be responsible. Remember that the beauty of the world is the inspiration that touches the artist's soul, and it belongs to all of us.

⬆ Experimentation reveals possibilities The journey from a posted process board to a final design is always different, but the process itself is the teaching tool of design. In these images, you can follow the evolution of the designer's process and see how variation leads to discovery.

⬇ Look closely at details Through the simplification of the forms, the enlargement of the dot screen pattern, and the placement of layers, the enlarged and cropped letterforms become fluid, artistic subjects that are vibrant with color.

RESEARCH TECHNIQUES

Primary sources/ Factual research	Secondary sources/ Factual research
• Previous knowledge/opinion/ memory • Observation • Conversation • Analysis • Role-play • Interviews: in person or by email, online chat, or phone • Questionnaires • Focus groups • Commissioned video/written diaries (first hand) • Ethnographic research ("deep hanging out")	• Museums, archives, collections • Newspapers, magazines, journal articles • Published interviews • Films, TV broadcasts, theater • Transcripts/recordings of film, TV, radio • Books • Music • Internet: blogs, websites, forums, magazines • Surveys • Statistics • Organizations, agencies, gatekeepers • Lectures, public debates, conferences

Primary sources/ Visual research	Secondary sources/ Visual research
• Photography • Drawing/sketching • Media experimentation: 2D and 3D • Rubbings/casts • Typographic experimentation • Compositional experimentation • Image manipulation • Photocopying • Video recording • Audio recording • Writing	• Exhibitions • Images/photographs from magazines, books, leaflets, Internet, billboards • Work by other designers/artists • Printed maps/diagrams • Ephemera (e.g. tickets, receipts, packaging) • Found or bought photographs, postcards, posters, drawings • Imagery taken from films, video, performances • Architecture

Other general work practices/approaches
• Put your own point of view into the subject
• Work in groups and respond to feedback from others
• Develop ideas by generating a number of visuals in response to one idea
• Explore the full capacity of your visual language

Record it all

Constant, direct observation is one of the most important tools a designer uses, and learning to look at anything as a designer requires attention to minute detail, and the inclusion of all things that surround the object of your focus. Consider your way of seeing as a kind of inner zoom lens that draws you in and away from a point of observation. As you learn to see with a designer's eye, ordinary things you may have seen before can become amazing sources of inspiration. It can be as simple as a pattern of lace juxtaposed against flat, wide stripes, or as unexpected as the geometry revealed by light and shadow in an architectural setting. Textures, patterns, colors, and visual relationships will begin to have a profound effect on the way you think about your design process.

With this in mind, every practicing designer should carry some form of recording device, such as a sketchbook, camera, smartphone, video camera, or whatever works best for you. Make time for observation and research, taking it seriously as an integral part of your work. Designers, artists, writers, and illustrators all frequently keep scrapbooks/sketchbooks/collections of material that interests them. These bits of inspiration need not have a clear purpose when collected, but the material will become an archive of ideas and inspiration from which to draw on at a later date.

If something commands your attention, sketch it, write about it, photograph it, upload it, or file it away immediately. Collect ideas and build upon initial thoughts by writing, drawing, or sketching. Not only will your drawing and research skills improve by doing this consistently, but over time you will have built yourself a "catalog of inspiration" that can be drawn upon at any point in your career, and will become especially useful when you are short of ideas. This kind of practiced research helps you to begin defining your own outlook, and to develop a distinctive visual voice.

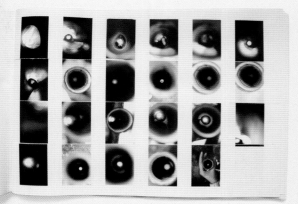

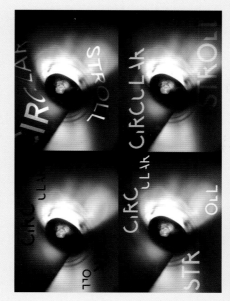

Multiply the possibilities Collect multiple images of every subject, and vary your techniques as you photograph. Each of these pictures captures a slightly different sensibility in light, color, shadow, and composition. When they are combined with deconstructed typography that echoes the abstract forms revealed in the photos, the results are striking.

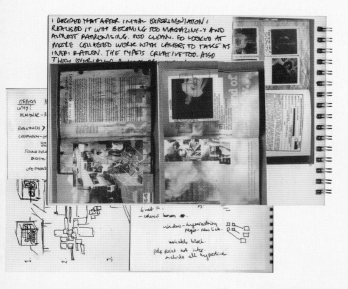

Ideas are organic They can grow from a single phrase, the sum of a series of images, or a combination of both. Record the evolution of your thinking process in whatever manner is meaningful for you. When you reference the sequence of your observations, they can become visualized as layers in a composition or simply lead you to the most relevant point in image or text.

PART 1	PRINCIPLES
UNIT 1	RESEARCH AND CONCEPTS
MODULE 2	**Linear reasoning/lateral thinking**

In the initial stages of concept development, the two main ways to approach a design brief are to use linear reasoning and lateral thinking. These are virtually opposites—the first focused and methodical, the second diffuse and expansive—but both are equally useful as research and development tools.

Linear reasoning implies a strategic thought process, using step-by-step logic, and follows a specific trajectory. This kind of reasoning frequently involves a predetermined idea or concept that is then worked toward in stages. Generally, this will involve splitting the idea up into manageable components, considering color, type, composition, and scale, and working each through to finalize the form to fit the concept.

Lateral thinking involves indirect exploration, generating ideas less readily available by linear reasoning (or hidden by the linear process, so that less obvious associations aren't readily seen or generated). The emphasis is on indirect, creative forms of research. Edward de Bono coined the term in 1967.

Brainstorming, or sketching in a non-linear diagrammatic way, approaches problems by exploring each component in as much depth and breadth as possible, finding connections and associations that work to strengthen the concept. This process aims to push achievable boundaries. Think of it as if it were a walk through a city. You may set out knowing exactly where you are going, focused on the end goal: reaching your destination. Alternatively, you could just stroll along the streets without any predetermined destination in mind. Each will provide very different experiences; in the non-predetermined form, you may notice things along the way that are not obvious if your sights are set only on reaching your destination.

You might consider beginning with a lateral thinking session—where you brainstorm as many ideas as possible—in order to generate your initial ideas, then move to a more linear process at a later stage. The two are not necessarily mutually exclusive, but often complementary ways of researching a design problem.

⊕ **SEE ALSO:** BASICS OF RESEARCH, P10

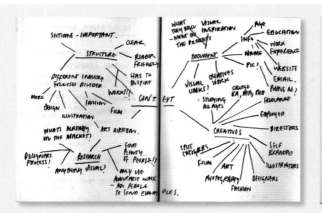

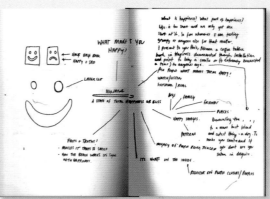

EXAMPLE—GETTING STARTED

Your first brainstorming sessions can be intimidating, so it will help, initially, to work with familiar tools and to combine linear and lateral thinking. Until you are able to think in pictures, begin with words. Make a list of absolutely everything that comes to mind when you consider your brief. Then, make a secondary list of things associated with each item on your first list.

Brief

Design a logo for the Folklore Museum. It should be elegant, lighthearted, and whimsical enough to attract families, but sophisticated enough to appeal to researchers and scholars of folklore.

1 Once you have determined the usage of the logo and the type of audience the client would like to reach, you can begin your descriptive lists, drilling down to as many levels as you need to bring images to mind. Discard nothing at this stage; just allow your mind to make associations freely. There's no such thing as a bad idea in creative process, there are only some that are more appropriate than others.

2 When your lists are lengthy enough to allow you to visualize individual items from your columns, you can combine two or more thoughts from different columns into one image, and you are ready to begin sketching. One idea will always lead to another, so never settle for just one, and save all of your ideas as you work through the process. You may find the seed of something brilliant hidden in an idea you nearly discarded.

Folklore
magic ➜ wand, sorcerer
prince/princess ➜ crown, castle
good/evil ➜ light/dark
homespun ➜ cottage
nature ➜
  animals ➜ frogs, goats, birds
  plants ➜ lilypads

Museum
display ➜ exhibits signage
Information sources ➜ books,
  objects, antiquities
objects ➜ natural, invented

⬆ **Thematic variation** All three of these logos are drawn from the associations recorded first in words, and everything about the design work is influenced by those ideas, from the choice of image to the selection of the typeface.

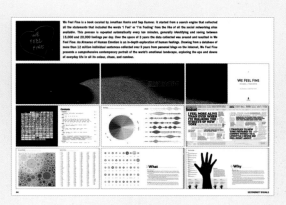

⬅ **Lateral or linear?**
Whether your process unfolds in an orderly sequence or a random scatter of thoughts, the process of discovery and the sequential development of an idea are exciting parts of the design process. Relax, examine your recorded research, and let the ideas flow. The more experience you have using these methods, the faster you will generate ideas.

PART 1	PRINCIPLES
UNIT 1	RESEARCH AND CONCEPTS
MODULE 3	**Exploratory drawing**

Exploratory drawing is a means of translating the outside world and of giving concrete form to abstract ideas. Sketching and drawing engage you in a constant process of observation, and help you understand the world around you. Whereas computer technology is another tool for the development of ideas, you should treat drawing as the basis of expression that underpins your design decisions.

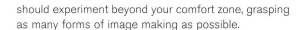

Representational, or observational, drawing (drawing used to document) allows you to see the subject as a shape or a series of shapes, and color as tones and hues. It teaches you to understand and manipulate perspective, to understand how an object exists in space, and to create the illusion of space and depth, and shows you how to convey texture and density. Non-representational, or non-observational, drawing, where your expression is freed from the need to represent what is seen and the result is a gestural abstraction, can generate valuable expressive drawn responses, and is widely used.

In representational drawing, train your eye to see diverse subject matter in detail. Studies of still life and life drawing train your eye to observe static objects in detail from a series of points of view, and evaluate the relationship of the surrounding space to the objects of study. These alternate views and perspectives will stimulate a variety of moving and static subject matter, which in turn changes how you draw. You can work directly in a sketchbook, or photograph your subjects for reference for more finished drawings at a later date. It is important to familiarize yourself with as many diverse aspects of form as possible.

You can always develop your drawing, regardless of how good you feel you already are. Continual practice is the key, and drawing should be a lifelong activity. You should experiment beyond your comfort zone, grasping as many forms of image making as possible.

Understanding tools
Experiment with a variety of media, to determine and affect your created image. Whether charcoal or pencil, crayon or brush, each tool you use requires some understanding of its specific effects and mark-making qualities. For example, pencils allow tonal control, detailed modeling, and a strong line, whereas ink and brush will generate an entirely different mark. Try not to limit yourself to conventional media; other implements, such as a toothbrush for a spatter effect, a piece of string, or even a sewing machine, can create interesting images. The aim is not merely to interpret the objects pictorially (representing them as they look) but to interpret the image in your own way. All forms of drawing have their value and purpose, and should be treated as equally valid.

Understanding form
There are no lines around an object. It consists of its own solid form, defined by the light and shadow that illuminate and surround it. Creating black-and-white drawings, or studies, is the best way to begin to understand form. As you render your study from real life, you are translating the language of color into a tonal gray-

Thinking in pictures Tight contour line drawings are used to explore the relationships between new and supplied elements in these studies for elaborate Nike packaging. Each study is carefully composed to fit within a particular space on the package and on the product before the color is assigned. See also the finished artwork on page 55.

scale, substituting monochromatic values for the spectrum in the existing object.

Be as direct and spontaneous as is possible. For immediacy, do several studies in a short space of time. Use materials to describe form and mass as areas of color, replacing a monochromatic scheme, while using an outline only as a guide to subsequent layers. Concentrate not on an end product, but on the process of a rich description of forms.

Figurative drawing from observation can produce beautiful studies, but it is also the tool that will sharpen your sketching abilities, and will eventually help generate ideas as you work through a design problem. As you draw, you will notice that what you choose to include and what you choose to exclude are equally important. As an object exists in space, so your drawing lives within the finite boundary of a page, and the relationship of the study to the page is part of the image.

When you complete a study, consider recreating the same subject with different media, eliminating all but the most necessary of descriptive marks. A gradual abstraction of the figurative image will help you discover more about structure, form, and spatial relationships as you work.

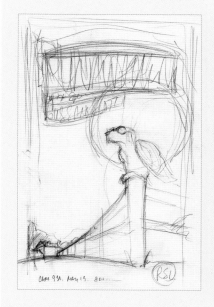

Options Multiple studies are roughed in and considered during the creative process. Promotional material for the band Runaway Dorothy is shown in stages of development. The position the display typography might occupy is considered as a shape in the composition before any style selections are made, and changes in perspective and scale are incorporated in the final illustration of the dog.

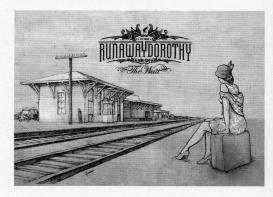

Early sketches for second study show the development of the concept and the changes in viewpoint that made it more moody in the final illustration.

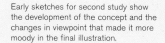

PART 1	PRINCIPLES
UNIT 1	RESEARCH AND CONCEPTS
MODULE 4	**Visualizing ideas**

All designers need to develop the skill of putting ideas down on paper. This involves preparing rough visuals/design sketches—thumbnails, scamps, or roughs. Students often tend to bypass this process and set about producing ideas directly on screen. This practice can inhibit the development of ideas, because you may restrict yourself to only those images you are capable of producing with the available technology. It's better to think freely at first, and to produce as many ideas as you can sketch.

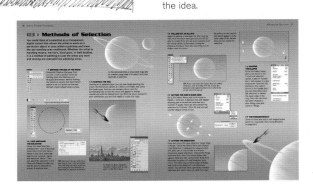

Visualize and organize
Your first sketches can be loose and expressive. Try variations, and do as many thumbnails as you can think of before you begin to finalize the idea.

Initial ideas are generated more quickly and prolifically if you do a bit of brainstorming, recording your thoughts rapidly using various diagrammatic methods or other ways to structure information.

Start with your word lists, and as you begin to think in pictures, move on to sketching directly. In this process, coordination between brain, eye, and hand can be amazingly fast, and by working quickly you can generate many diverse (and sometimes unexpected) ideas, concepts, and associations. Your mind starts flowing and loosening up, and becomes open to the diverse aspects of the project, swiftly moving the thought process forward. Literal and non-literal, lateral and non-lateral forms of thinking are used to maximum effect in these early sketches.

Roughs and thumbnails
There is no predetermined size for rough drawings. Thumbnails are, as the term suggests, small. Designers usually begin with thumbnails, a series of rapidly drawn,

Putting it all together Looking spontaneous takes time. Finished artwork may be the result of experiments in various media and techniques, and it may be the sum of many successful combinations. Once you have the concept and the general proportions in mind, consider the best way to execute the style you want to communicate. Then, determine the right tool for the right job, and use as many as you need to get the right visual language for your message. For this poster promoting an exhibition of rock 'n' roll music posters, the artist wanted an image that expressed the concept of "art at 1000 decibels," a part of the copy line on the poster.

First, a sans-serif typeface was selected and type treatments were designed on computer in several variations, then printed in black and white. The result felt too static.

The printed type was placed on a copy machine and the paper copy was moved during the copying process to blur the image. Several versions were scanned back into the computer, and the best were combined and cropped. The balloon form was added.

The bird was hand drawn with pen and ink, and the hands were drawn separately.

stamp-sized compositions that block out the general structure and content of a design. Thumbnails should be spontaneous and prolific; they are the recorded thought process of developing ideas and should move as rapidly as you can think. Obviously, this can leave no time for the inclusion of any detail or refinement. These will be considered in the final stages of design development. Thumbnails that have the most interesting potential are selected and a rough, larger, loose drawing with more detail but as yet still unfinished, is created that further develops the composition and placement on the page.

Drawing by hand

Although roughs require a certain degree of drawing skill, these will be learned easily for this kind of work, where the generation of ideas is the focus, not drawing as an end in itself. This is unlike observational drawing, or drawing as documentation, which needs to be precise. Hand-drawn ideas can be vague and leave a lot to the imagination, which can be a good thing. Excluding detail from the sketch will allow you to leave your options open for more deliberate decisions at a later point in concept development. Remember, the "big idea" is the most important part of the process at this stage.

Once you have a number of ideas sketched out, you can step back and make judgments regarding their value, and potential for development, without having committed to any design in detail. This allows maximum flexibility and fluidity in the design process.

An important advantage of developing the ability to produce quick, effective roughs is that when presenting ideas to clients, alternatives can be quickly sketched out, keeping your approach fresh and relatively unrestricted. This, in turn, gives clients confidence in your willingness to be flexible and open-minded, while showing your design abilities.

Computers and visualization

Roughs are usually generated on a sketchpad. When generated on a computer, roughs tend to look too fixed and polished, and students can be reluctant to change or refine them. Wait until you have a sketch that excites you, then scan it and look at it on screen.

Once you have chosen an idea or shortlist of ideas that you feel may have potential, computers come into their own, because they enable you to produce as many alternate versions of your ideas as you wish, changing colors, typefaces, line weights, and images. Typefaces and grid measurements become fluid decisions when you are working digitally, and you don't need to commit immediately. In fact, it may be better not to. It's fast and easy to change these on screen.

➕ **SEE ALSO:** LINEAR REASONING/LATERAL THINKING, P14

The artist added a washy ink texture to the background, and added a bit more onto the top of the artwork by taping it to the top. All the elements were scanned into the computer and assembled electronically.

When all of the additional typography was complete, the artist explored several color variations (above) until they were pleased. Two different color versions were printed: the magenta one (right), and a predominantly cyan version (not pictured).

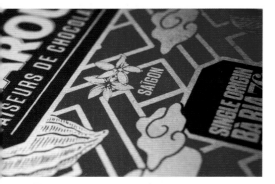

PART 1	PRINCIPLES
UNIT 1	RESEARCH AND CONCEPTS
MODULE 5	**Theories of image and text**

The success of visual communication depends on the ability to reach a targeted audience and elicit a desired response. Sometimes the response is an immediate call to action and a clear, concise message with little open to interpretation. Most often, visual imagery is used to evoke an emotional state that will put the viewer in the appropriately receptive frame of mind to receive the message targeted at them.

Designers influence the message through the development of provocative imagery that may persuade, shock, entertain, and provoke with purpose. In order for designers to speak clearly and visually say exactly what they mean, they need to develop a clear and strong visual language.

Rhetoric

With its origins attributed to ancient public speaking in Greece and Rome, rhetoric is a skill of persuasion most often associated with politics and public speaking. To construct a strong rhetorical speech, ancient philosophers used something kindred to contemporary design thinking to define and refine the categories of invention, arrangement, style, memory, and delivery within a compelling dialogue. If we examine these subjects as design vocabulary, the same can be said for the construction of a successful and equally compelling visual. In visual communication, the concept of visual rhetoric usually describes the visual tone of voice chosen for a given communication task.

⬆ **Make an impression** Each of these approaches to package design has a distinct message. The chocolates packages are as rich in color as they are in content. With luxurious metallics, deep saturated color, and intricate graphics, they invite elegant indulgence with every design decision. The clean simplicity of the die-cut labels on the bottles allows the actual ingredients to become the vibrant color in the artwork, promising freshness and the visual implication of "nothing added."

↗ **Didactics** Information graphics should be beautiful in addition to delivering a body of information in a clear and immediate way. Economical use of space and carefully considered typography are essential for clear communication.

→ Universal messages
The pictograms used in the 1972 Munich Olympics set the standard for subsequent Olympic designs. Each sporting event is clearly represented through an economy of line and shape, yet each symbol is visually strong enough for signage and promotional use at any size.

↑ Dependable artwork International symbols transcend language and communicate instantly. The appearance of a symbol can vary greatly in style through line weights and positive/negative balance, as long as the symbol is easily understood. Symbols like these in public places play a part in public safely.

Semiotics, signs, and symbols

Ferdinand de Saussure is generally acknowledged as the father of semiotics. His theory divides signs, or all things that represent meaning, into two categories: the signifier and the signified. The signifier is the symbol that represents something from which meaning can be extracted; the signified is the actual object or meaning it represents. For example, the universal symbol, or signifier, for a male or female restroom has instant recognition that transcends languages, and the signified is the actual restroom. This type of non-verbal vocabulary of signs has increasing relevance in the global reach of contemporary communications and, when designed well, can command instant recognition.

Didactics

The term "didactics" refers to clear, pragmatically delivered information and instruction with unambiguous meaning. Airport signage, road signs, and warnings are prime examples of didactic information. It is important to note that nuance can be added to most visuals, even in the strictest definition of category: didactic panels in museum exhibitions must deliver clear information, but can be associated with the subject matter in inventive visual ways.

Symbol style

Signs can be simple or complex, depending on the accompanying message. A denotative sign denotes exactly what it pictures and should be visually direct, but can convey secondary information through the use of a particular style. A connotative sign will be single-minded and may convey a range of associated messages that are to be interpreted by the viewer. Symbols and signs can have rich layers of associated meaning.

The Olympic symbols are prime examples of design defining attitude. The symbol for swimming usually doesn't change much in content, but the designer may assign an element of playfulness, structure, and discipline, or reference other time periods through the use of line weight, drawing style, or color. The five interlocking rings of the Olympic symbol itself represent five continents or major geographical areas of the world that participate in the games. Exposure to the Olympic symbol, over time, has elevated it to iconic stature and it may now evoke an emotional response in some through its association with the actual events.

Symbol families

Complex systems and extended families of symbols usually share common essential criteria. They have clarity and are easily recognizable with a simple message. All symbols in the system share a look, with similar treatment in line, style, weight, and scale. They are easy to reproduce in any size and will retain clarity, and are flexible enough to be combined with other elements, and will still remain distinctive.

⌃ Identity to icon The first Apple Computer, Inc. logo was designed by Ron Wayne, a co-founder of Apple Computer. The original was illustrative and included a full image of Sir Isaac Newton sitting under an apple tree with type in a traditional banner arrangement as an integrated border. That logo was replaced in 1977 by graphic designer Rob Janoff, with an image of a rainbow-striped apple with a bite taken out of it. The bite was added for scale, so that the image would not be mistakenly identified as a cherry. This monochrome version was adapted in 1999.

⬆ Abstract icon The Nike "Swoosh" was designed in 1971 by Carolyn Davidson. Originally, it appeared with the word NIKE above it. As the brand's recognition grew, the trademark was gradually streamlined.

Metaphors

Signs and symbols are primary sources in the design and development of logos and trademarks, and are essential in the development of the visual metaphor, an image that will trigger associations to other meanings or signifiers, and is connotative in nature. A visual metaphor might be as obvious as a lightbulb to signify an idea, a heart to signify love, or a book to represent learning. Logos become metaphors for the business, goods, or service they represent through association, and some become so memorable, that they need no words to explain them.

Carolyn Davidson designed the Nike "Swoosh" in 1971. Originally, it appeared accompanied by the word "NIKE." As the brand grew, the trademark was streamlined to the positive, checkmark/wing of the current version.

Poetics

Some of the most involving design work can deliberately engage the viewer for much longer periods of time. With current media, the attention span of a target audience is shortened by the number of competing stimuli encountered daily, and by the availability of viewing options, handheld and environmental. They can pull your audience in too many directions to concentrate on your message. If you can engage your audience members, they are more likely to remember what you have told them or to associate your message with a visual style that can be revisited.

Poetic forms of work have much less immediately accessible meaning, and the message is deliberately left open to interpretation. Graphic designers make

⬆ Metaphors and media The use of toy soldiers as a metaphor for a combative childhood experience provides a thought-provoking image for this *Lord of the Flies* book cover. The unusual color enhances the feeling of discomfort, as does the placement of the title typography in a deliberately challenging sight line between toy opponents.

⬆ Mood and matter The unlikely combination of images in this delicate illustration for *The Orange Tree* sends simultaneous messages of conquest, beauty, vulnerability, and history through the use of line, color, and composition.

⬆ Concept Without using the obvious tool of a dramatic change in scale, photography and illustration combine to portray the altered reality of Gulliver's world in a refreshing way.

conscious decisions to leave the work open to provoke thoughtful responses, to stir controversy, or to tease. Ad campaigns, posters, and book and publication design are examples of media that can support more complex visual allegory, and the illustrative and graphic works that support them are often produced though a range of media and stand as works of art in their own right. Poetic work can be seen as the polar opposite of didactic, but all graphic design is visual communication, and the decision to use one or the other is part of the designer's problem-solving process.

GLOSSARY

Didactic: A pragmatic and unambiguous method of giving clear information.

Metaphor: Word or image that sets up associations; for example, a "piece of cake" is a metaphor for easy.

Poetic: A style that is less clear, but more artistic, more open to interpretation.

Rhetoric: A style of arguing, persuading, or engaging in dialogue. For a designer, it is a way of engaging the targeted audience.

Semiotics: A system that links objects, words, and images to meanings through signs and signifiers.

Symbolism: A way of representing an object or word through an image, sound, or another word; for example, a crossed knife and fork on a road sign means a café is ahead.

⊕ **SEE ALSO:** AUDIENCES, MARKETS, AND CONCEPTS, P24

ANIMAL COLLECTIVE

FRIDAY MARCH 23 - 7PM
First Unitarian Church
2125 Chestnut Street Philadelphia, PA

STEREOTELESCOPE
8:00 PM TT THE BEAR'S FRIDAY 4.8 CAMBRIDGE

◀ **Poetic ambiguity**

These poetic images use color and composition to imply and suggest, but leave conclusions to the viewer. The suggestion of telescoping movement is accomplished through a series of color blocks carefully placed to move the eye around the graphic, and maximizes the placement of complementary colors.

◀ **Softer suggestion**

A painterly loose wash of color in a cascade design might express animal markings, the bars of a cage, liquid, or simply set a mood, depending on how the viewer interprets the imagery. These images are deliberately ambiguous, and invite a longer examination.

PART 1	PRINCIPLES
UNIT 1	RESEARCH AND CONCEPTS

MODULE 6 | Audiences, markets, and concepts

Good graphic design is not simply the result of brilliant execution or technique. It is the strong expression of clever, well-formulated ideas, drawn from an ongoing engagement with research and an interest in the world at large. In professional practice, as in school, extensive exploratory research is invariably the key to the most successful projects, and research into audiences is a primary tool of effective design.

It is vital to remember that everything you design will be seen by other people: designers are visual communicators and do not work in a vacuum. Therefore, it is part of your job to discover everything you can about the intended viewer. Before designing, think about the people who will be looking at your design work. What is the target market? What do you know about them? What can you/should you find out about them? Can you imagine how they might interpret a particular visual message? Think about the age of the viewer, their geographic and cultural influences, and the level of their education and experience. The more you discover about your audience, the better informed your work will be, increasing its potential effectiveness.

The Internet has reinvented the communication timeline, and what you post will be seen around the world with amazing speed. To complicate things further, viewers now have shorter attention spans and may split their concentration as they multitask with different electronic devices. Graphic designers have only a few seconds to grab the attention of any potential audience before they turn a page, click to the next website, or jump to the next broadcast with a remote control.

If your preliminary research is thorough, you will be able to speak a visual language that your target audience understands, relates to, and responds to, thus increasing the odds that your visual communication will hit its mark.

Think globally

It is the designer's job to deliver a message, and as we communicate globally, accurate information transfer becomes increasingly complex. Be aware that different cultures may react differently to colors, images, and language. The color red is used as a warning in some countries, yet is considered lucky in China. An image that appears delightfully contemporary in one culture can be offensive in another. Do your homework before you begin brainstorming, and pay attention to brands that advertise globally. Are there different versions of the same advertisement in different countries? What brands have instant recognition internationally, and how has the brand been developed? What type of image does it communicate?

Market research

Large companies have whole departments devoted to what is formally called market research. These people spend their time conducting surveys into their customers' needs and preferences. They do this by a variety of means, including questionnaires, surveys, and focus groups where people carefully selected as representative of the target audience are brought together to discuss a product or campaign before it is launched into the public domain. If, however, you are the only team member on the project, you can still do some research. Modern communications make a large part of the world accessible. Use the Internet, libraries, museums, and

⊕ Entertain and inform

A complete direct mail campaign reinterprets the word "EATS" in many different ways, and keeps the message lightheartedly urban and wittily childlike. Strong use of typography and color carry the clever messages and keep the system unified.

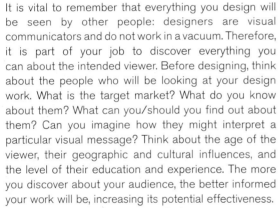

GLOSSARY

Audience: In its broadest sense, the consumers, voyeurs, and occasionally participants of design work.

Customer profile/profiling: The process of creating a series of parameters or set of information that defines the desires, trends, or interests of a demographic so that designs can be pitched or marketed to them.

Market research: The process of collecting and collating data from questionnaires, interviews, and comments from the public regarding a concern, a problem, or a possible solution.

any other appropriate research venue at your disposal to do your market research, and find out as much as you can about your client and your audience.

You can still find out a great deal about your target and determine a reasonable approach to communications without a staff at your disposal. Identify and research potential competitors and see what type of brand image they are projecting. Define your target audience with your client by age, gender, level of education, income, marital status, and location. Develop a questionnaire, or have a series of questions ready to ask, and visit people in the target group firsthand. Use your developed powers of observation to note various trends/habits/practices/attitudes of your target audience and record your impressions. Read as much information about the buying practices of consumers in your brand category as you can. When you have collected some information, imagine your target in as much rich detail as you can, and try to put yourself in their place. How would you respond to the ideas you are proposing? Bring your concepts right to the source and ask people what they think of them. You can create a small, informal focus group made up of friends, relatives, and colleagues. Smart, informed design always begins with information.

Make contact

Talking about things often sparks other avenues of thought. Learning to articulate your concepts is the first stage in developing great presentation techniques, and explaining your ideas to others can help you really understand what you are trying to achieve. Be prepared to listen to opinions offered. Remember, you do not have to act on them if you think they aren't relevant or helpful. Try not to take any criticism personally. Use it constructively to uncover which aspects of your ideas aren't working and what you can do to improve them. You will often have to listen to comments about your work, and they will not always be positive. Try to remember that your work should never really be all about you, unless it's an introspective artist's piece. Good design is about perception, and about accurate information transfer.

➡ **Bring the audience closer** The clever concept of a tomb-shaped personal voodoo kit entices the audience to come closer and investigate the product through clever packaging with an unusual shape, and subtle, moody typography and texture that remains consistent throughout the packaged materials.

ELIMINATION PROCESS

Explore your ideas visually to see which have the most potential. Do not be too precious about detail; concentrate on expressing your ideas.

1 Make quick sketches to determine which ideas work well and have immediate impact. Use color if it helps, but don't get involved in the subtleties.
2 Discard any sketches that are too complex or rely on tired visual clichés. Getting rid of the bad ideas quickly will help you focus on the good ones.
3 Select the strongest idea, then put together a presentation visual that demonstrates why your idea is so brilliant.
4 Now you can start working on the detail. The best ideas are often the simplest, but you need to show that careful thought and preparation have gone into your work. Consider how you will explain your idea to your client. You might need to "sell" it to them, so think about what you would say to support your images.

➕ **SEE ALSO:** BASICS OF RESEARCH, P10

LINEAR REASONING/ LATERAL THINKING, P14

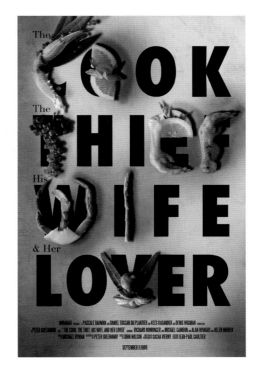

⬆ **Make them curious** Strong typography juxtaposed with photographic images of food combine to send a sophisticated message that grabs the audience's attention immediately. It invites a closer look at the formally presented foods that double as letterforms, and intrigues the audience by being both bold and suggestive.

⬇ **Macro** Look at the big picture. Preliminary ideas shown in a flat plan of a book or a magazine from start to finish will help you determine how the mass of information is divided, and allow you to plan the rhythm and flow of images and text throughout the entire publication. Now you can set your design and production deadlines accordingly.

Assign a different color to each chapter or section.

If it becomes necessary to delete or rearrange content, a flatplan will help you to keep track of the changes.

The Beauty Book

Half Title 1	Title 2		3	Contents 4		5	Introduction 6		7	SKIN 8		9	Creams & Cleansers 10		11
Buttermilk 12	Strawberry 13	Exfoliators 14		15	Skin complaints 16		17	Sun protection 18	Safe tanning tips / Lavender 19	Lime / Papaya 20	Visible capillaries and veins 21	Wrinkles 22		23
Cellulite 24		25	HAIR 26		27	Cleansing and drying 28		29	Detox 30	Wash and go 31	Conditioning 32		33	Natural colour 34		35
cont. 36		37	Dandruff 38	Hair growth 39	Sun protection 40	Scalp problems 41	HANDS AND NAILS 42		43	Hand Care and Creams 44		45	Winter protection / Sun protection 46		47
Manicure Basics	Tips for perfect nails	Nail Art		Nail Wraps, Acrylics and Gels	Nail problems	Brittle nails / Flaking nails	Pedicures		

PART 1 | PRINCIPLES

UNIT 1 | RESEARCH AND CONCEPTS

MODULE 7 | **Scheduling, organizing, and finalizing**

Creativity, talent, and originality are all expected, but if a design project can't be delivered on time, those first three attributes may not matter in the long run. Organized thinking is the key to understanding how to manage a big project. All design projects begin with the broadest of ideas and must be broken down into smaller, manageable parts.

Read the design brief carefully, and ask questions if you need more information. Design briefs always involve interpretation by the designer. Some clients have little idea of what they need, and they look to the designer for clear analysis of, and a solution to, the problem. Other clients may have a clear idea of what they want, and these ideas need to be considered and respected—but also questioned if they are inappropriate. For example, green may be a favorite color of one member of a group of clients, but it may be the wrong choice for the project. Similarly, it's important to recognize that clients have valuable insight into the workings of their organization and its needs, and although they may not have the design skills, or the language, to implement their ideas, their input on these matters is crucial. Be open and flexible, but stand your ground when you know you are right.

Check it
There are as many different solutions to the same problem as there are designers. Your job is to choose

Micro At the micro level, you can begin to decipher the details. Generate your thumbnails and carefully consider the pace and placement of every element in your page design. Determine how your sketches support an overall system, and still add enough variety to keep it interesting.

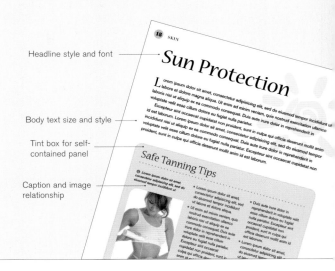

Headline style and font

Body text size and style

Tint box for self-contained panel

Caption and image relationship

the solution that you think is the most appropriate. This decision-making isn't subjective; it comes from informed judgment. It's a good idea to set a series of checkpoint meetings/approvals with your client as you work through the design process. It's a better practice to have the client approve or reject an approach at the early stages, at which point you can adjust your design thinking accordingly.

Think macro and micro

Good design works both at a macro scale (the large, overview structure, as though viewed from "above"), and at a micro scale, where the tiniest details are important, down to letter spacing. Often you will have to give the information order and structure (hierarchy) as well as visual form. You will need to make micro decisions such as type size, individual page layouts, and color choices, and these will need to be balanced and related to the macro scale: the whole design needs to appear considered, as does every part of the project. In the case of a print or package design, every aspect of the project should be designed, including the selection or creation of additional materials for closures, bindings, and fastenings. If you can see it, your audience can, too. Make sure all the details are included in your design thinking.

Scheduling and organization

Time management and organization are crucial aspects of a design practice, and their significance cannot be overstated. Organize your time, and plot out the progress of each project, from start to end, allocating time to each aspect of the design process. To help you do this, make a schematic diagram to identify how long certain aspects of the job will take to complete. If you are working on a project with numerous applications and different elements, it will help immeasurably. It's easy to be swept away on a wave of creative thinking, and aspects of your process can take longer than you think they will. If you are new to the practice, allocate reasonable time, then pad each aspect a little to allow yourself time for unplanned discovery.

PERSONAL DEADLINES

Set intermediate deadlines for yourself. If you break down the process into manageable steps, you can set your calendar accordingly. A breakdown of the process might read:

Research
Sketches/concept development
Presentation sketches/roughs
Client meeting
Refined comprehensive concepts (comps)
Revisions
Client meeting
Finished files

⬇ Plan ahead

Keep track of your process hours and plan ahead to make your deadlines.

⬆ Development

Research and concept development following the client brief to develop two interlinking logos for sister companies—Cintros for IT solutions and Cintsafe for safe file storage.

⬆ Refinement

When the concept is developed, sketches with proposed color treatments are presented.

❶ Remember

- Write everything down. Don't rely on memory.
- Without a relevant concept, your visualization has no meaning.
- Try creating a flowchart/spider diagram with routes for different ideas.
- Look for professional criticism and use it constructively.
- Talk about your work. Learn to be articulate, and explain your intentions, influences, and solutions.

Over longer jobs there may be only one deadline per week (for example, interim presentations to the client); on shorter jobs this may be two deadlines per day (for example, multiple proof stages). One way to organize ideas into sequence is to write everything down on self-adhesive reminder notes and put them in a logical order. Job jackets, envelopes with deadline lists, approvals, and everything else related to the job, help keep track of multiple projects.

If you'd rather do it all electronically, software programs such as Excel can be invaluable in plotting job progress and in maintaining an overview. Organize your digital files logically, making sure everyone working on the project knows the system, and back up your files regularly. You can create a timetable with each checkpoint assigned a date (see above). Include all of the subcategories you need to cover until they become second nature.

Many good designers miss the importance of time management and organization, and their work and client relationships suffer as a result. Get into the habit of good time management, now!

Comps (comprehensive sketches)

Comps are the most finished approximation of an actual product and often look exactly like the real thing. They will evidence all design considerations, including final colors, tints and halftones, all typographic considerations, textures, and paper finishes and weights. If a project has many parts, comps for the extended system may be produced at different stages. After a client approves the comps, a production designer can take over the job, if needed, and match all aspects of the production to the designer's choices.

Page plans/flat plans

There has to be a logical visual (and conceptual) sequence in any design project. A magazine or a book illustrates this point well. Magazines and books are

↑ **Presentation and production**
Comprehensive designs that simulate the finished product are presented for approval before the artwork is sent into production.

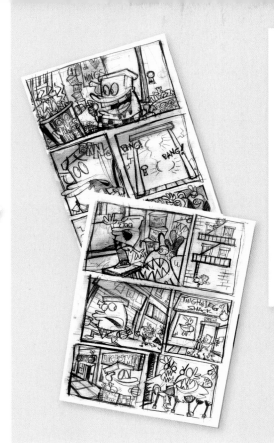

← **Storyboards** Motion graphics or film and video can be expensive to produce, especially if animation and effects are involved, so be clear about your intentions. Storyboards clarify the concept by showing the progression of the idea and the transitions from scene to scene. An expert storyboard may even serve as a shooting guide on the set.

normally laid out in miniature on a page plan several times before full-size layouts are started. The page plan may consist of no more than the article title, but can be much more specific, including a list of all the page elements or a thumbnail drawing of the layout with text blocks and artwork sketched in. The page plan is intended to clarify logical sequence, distribution of color, change of pace, and so on.

Storyboards

Storyboards give the client or production person enough information to allow them to begin to design their assigned spreads or pages of the final product. As well as in multimedia design, storyboards are commonly employed in films, comic strips, animation, and TV commercials. The storyboard contains a sketch of the visual aspect of the screen, information that will be present, descriptions of animations, interactions (for example, dialog boxes), sounds, and any other media.

Although storyboards were originally linear (for film), non-linear elements are incorporated. Storyboards are also used in web design to plan individual pages or sequences before engaging a web designer.

Website flowcharts show how pages link up in a logical order (see page 158). The organization of a website reflects the actual body for which the site is designed. It is important to get the structure right before designing the look of the pages.

⊘ **Timescale**
Research can be very time-consuming, so bear in mind that there has to be a cut-off point at which you have to start generating your visual concepts. "Design" is a verb as much as it is a noun: it's about doing things, so jump right in. One idea will always lead to the next.

see page 158

GLOSSARY

Comps: Comprehensive sketch, a close approximation of the printed product.

Page plan/Flat plan: A document with a series of numbered thumbnails set out in an ordered grid that represents each page in a book.

Storyboard: A document similar to a flat plan, but with a sequence of thumbnails that specifically lays out the narrative for a comic strip or film.

UNIT 1: ASSIGNMENTS

⊙ RESEARCH: OBSERVE AND RECORD

With your sketchbook and camera in hand, take a walking tour of your neighborhood, or walk to a location that provides you an interesting route, or even one you might take every day. As you walk, really look carefully at your surroundings and record your observations using photography, sound recordings, handwritten notes, sketches, and collected ephemera. You should try to see things differently and be very sensitive to light, shadow, textures, patterns, and random relationships of objects and colors. Zooming in on the sidewalk, a wall, or a streetlight can reveal subtle textures and color variants you may have missed, so crop your images creatively. Shoot some images from several points of view and at different exposures. Record your own impressions of what you see, and transcribe any chance conversations you have along the way. Sketch various points of view at different spots along the way. Primary and secondary research for a particular project can take weeks, and the process is an important influence on the final outcome.

⊙ APPLY YOUR OBSERVATIONS: YOUR JOURNEY AS IMAGE

1 Carry out the assignment at left, then begin to consider images that can recreate a portion of your journey, and convey the personality of the location and your impressions of it. Continue to add to your research by adding secondary sources.
• Consult library archives for historic images of the same locations
• Read histories of the neighborhood
• Interview residents and shop owners.

2 Think about who might be most interested in the area, decide how you would best catch their attention, and how your story should unfold. Consider your state of mind as you made your observations in the first assignment.
• Was the area you observed alive with activity or quiet and reflective? Noisy or peaceful?
• Was the weather bright or murky?
• Did time pass slowly or quickly?

3 Using your collected research, create sketches for a poster that recreates your journey from beginning to end. The emphasis of this assignment is on the creative process, not on the final project, so use your skills in observation and research as expansively as possible, and consider all of the possible interpretations of your research before you commit to a single idea. Create a storyboard or a spider diagram to organize your thinking, then generate as many thumbnail drawings as you can imagine. Use words, images, and collage materials you may have collected. When you have five thumbnails you really like, enlarge them, either by drawing them again or by using a copier, and clarify your intentions by writing a short descriptive paragraph on each one.

⊙ DRAWING: OBJECTIFY AND ABSTRACT

1 Choose an everyday object you are familiar with: a spoon, a cup, a pen, a shoe, a phone, anything at all. Place the object in good light and look at the form carefully from above and below and around all sides. Choose a point of view and draw the complete object three times using three different techniques. Your drawings should be at least 8in (20cm) square.

Drawing techniques you might try include:
• Descriptive/rendered line: draw the object in pencil as representationally as you can, shading in light and shadow.

• Contour line: draw the object in a figurative, descriptive way, using only thick and thin outlines to describe light and shadow.
• Gestural line: draw the object using quick expressive strokes and try to capture the essence of the form.

2 Choose your favorite of the three drawings and zoom in on an area that is only 2in (5cm) square, but that still describes the object in some way. Enlarge this area and draw it at 8in (20cm) square using any technique. Can you convey the essence of the object by just showing a portion of it?

● ANALYZE AND VISUALIZE

1 Find three different logos and analyze them in detail. Determine whether they are didactic or poetic, and identify what techniques they use to communicate their meanings. Pay close attention to the point of view the mark expresses. Is it steadfast and reliable or lighthearted and fun? Does it look elegant or casual? Is it easy to understand or does it require a second, more careful, examination? Analysis of existing work is an important step in learning about effective graphic communication. It will help you learn to deconstruct and improve your own work.

2 Record your critique, then choose one of the logos you think might benefit from a new design. Share your observations with another design student, another designer, or someone with an appreciation of design.

● MARKET RESEARCH

Conduct your own market research on the company whose logo you redesigned in the previous assignment. Write up your findings in a report you might present to the client at one of your preliminary meetings.

- Learn everything you can about the company.
- Determine who the competition is and look at their communication tools.
- Create your own survey.
- Speak to current customers, and to non-customers, about how they perceive the company.
- Use the product/service yourself.
- Look at the target market, researching who they are, what they do, and how they spend their time.
- Read market reports online or in the library.
- Determine the usage of the logo. Will it be in print, on the side of a truck, on a website, animated for TV, or all of the above?

Further Reading:

Meredith Davis, *Graphic Design Theory*, Thames and Hudson, 2012

Alina Wheeler, *Designing Brand Identity*, Wiley, 2012

Ellen Lupton and Jennifer Cole Phillips, *Graphic Design Thinking: Beyond Brainstorming*, Princeton Architectural Press, 2011

Bo Borgstron and Laurence King, *Essentials of Visual Communication*, Laurence King Publishing, 2009

Steven Heller and Veronique Vienne, *100 Ideas That Changed Graphic Design*, Laurence King Publishing, 2012

● CONCEPT DEVELOPMENT

Based on the target audience you want to reach, and using the findings of the research report from the previous assignment, determine if the new logo should be pictorial (using a representational drawing), typographic, or abstract, and explain your decision.

1 Begin the brainstorming process by associating as many words as you can with the ideas, values, services and/or products your company represents.

2 Set up a spider chart or flow chart to record your word process, and connect ideas that help you generate images.

3 Generate thumbnails, eliminating any visual clichés or derivative ideas, and allow the ideas to flow very freely. Discard the ones with limited potential and choose the best three. Think about how the message they communicate might be enhanced through a particular drawing style, line weight, or color treatment.

4 Begin working on the details and develop your thumbnails into clean comps. Consider how the finished product will work in various applications, such as corporate identity components (business cards, letterheads, folders, and so on) direct mail, websites, and animations.

● BUILD A SCHEDULE

Using the concept from the previous assignment, think about all of the elements you may need to design in order for your client to launch their new identity, and create a hypothetical work chart that keeps track of all of it: you can use spreadsheet software, such as Excel, or do it by hand. Listing your workload and prioritizing your schedule will help you keep track and budget your time accordingly.

2 FUNDAMENTALS OF COMPOSITION

Good composition is an essential element of all art forms, graphic or otherwise, and should be considered the foundation of visual communication. Successful graphic designers are masters of the fundamentals that underlie all aspects of design. Elements on a page or on the web, in motion or in three dimensions, should always be led by concern for spacing, visual organization, style, and the size and format of the finished work.

Graphic design projects use text and image in concert, with consideration for the relationships established between each of the elements. These compositions should also establish a visual hierarchy that directs the viewer's eye through a deliberate visual sequence.

> **"** Visual literacy also is an ability to view any image as an abstraction, to understand what is happening in purely visual terms as well as knowing and understanding visual terminology. It involves training the eyes to see minute detail and being sensitive to color, shape, form, and line. It has little or nothing to do with content or style" **"**
>
> *Rob Roy Kelly*

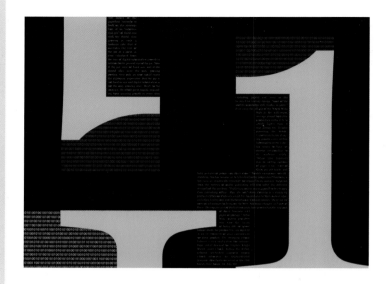

PART 1 | PRINCIPLES

UNIT 2 | FUNDAMENTALS OF COMPOSITION

MODULE 1 | **Basics of composition**

Composition refers to the visual structure and organization of elements within a design. It concerns the process of combining distinct parts or elements to form a whole. Composition involves seeing the whole as greater than its parts, and is just as important as the individual elements that make up a design.

Designers organize images and text—each with their own shapes, sizes, colors, and textures—in many different media and in a wide range of formats; from two- and three-dimensional black-and-white design through full-color work to web-based and time-based (moving) imagery. A practical understanding and exploration of composition is crucial for effective visual communication: it is the most significant tool in guiding the viewer through the complexity of visuals to the intended message. To create effective design work, no matter which medium you are working in, you must understand the principles of good composition.

⊃ **Building a composition**
In this series, horizontal and vertical lines gradually translate into lines of typography to illustrate a concept. The same principles of placement and relationship apply to the placement of body text and headline, and the hierarchy should be examined carefully to ensure typography is read in the proper sequence.

Carefully placed vertical lines of varying weights show a gradually imposed order as they begin to form a grid.

The substitution of typography for lines, using the word "structure," reinforces the concept and identifies the relationship between typographic point sizes and line weights.

The structure of the series continues to build with layers of typographic lines working in concert to suggest heavier masses of line.

The final composition adds closely locked forms of typographic lines to create an architectural composition where each weighted area is visually supported.

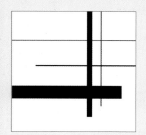

⬆ **Negative space** Placement on the page is critical. In the first composition, the shapes appear to be aggressively competing for space. When the objects are reduced in size and placed in the lower corner of the page, they appear to be racing to exit the image.

⬆ **Organized chaos** In the initial composition, the placement of the circles creates tension though asymmetry and cropped edges. As the second and third compositions develop, the same principles are in play, using texture to create mass, and repetition and variation in placement.

⬉ **Shape and space** By using simple forms like dots and lines or geometric forms, you can control the dynamics of the composition through the placement of each object. The relationship between positive and negative space, the strength of horizontal or vertical forms, the dominance of variations in scale and value, and the space between the objects will all work together to attract and direct the viewers' attention.

Theories of composition

Throughout the history of the visual arts, different theories of composition have been advanced. Vitruvius, the Roman architect and engineer, devised a mathematical formula for the division of space within a picture. His solution, known as the golden section, the golden mean, or golden rectangle, was based on a set ratio between the longer and shorter sides of a rectangle. This principle profoundly affected theories in mathematics, architecture, painting, graphic design, and industrial design regarding the use of spatial composition. The French painter Henri Matisse (1869–1954) put greater emphasis on inspiration, maintaining that composition is the art of arranging elements to express feelings.

Most contemporary theories have acknowledged the following elements as important considerations in composition: balance (the deliberate distribution of elements on a page); consistency or harmony (similarities in visual objects); contrast (obvious differences in visual elements); proximity (the relationships in the placement of the elements in play); repetition with variation; and white space (the deliberate open areas in a composition that give the viewer the ability to focus on everything else).

Form and space

Positive space is a form or object that, to the eye, appears to exist. This can be a solid shape of any size, a line, or simply a texture. Negative space is everything around or within an object, the "empty" space that helps to define the borders of the positive image. It is important to learn to effectively control the relationship

The space around the rice-shaped white shape in the black box is repeated in the relationship of the typography in the square above it, and in the placement of the whole object on the page in the brochure.

Expanded space The perfect placement of a single white mark in a black square establishes the relationships for a greater extended system. Repetition with variation is demonstrated by the placement of the word treatment above the rice/box, reversing the angle of the rice by creating a triangle in the white space and enforcing the figure—ground reversal of the squares.

The packaging and display add texture in the choice of photography and in the use of the product itself.

The placement of the double box mark at the juncture of white space and image on the page echoes the packaging.

Letters, dots, and lines Strong horizontal lines suggest blinds on a window when they are used as interruptions in this strong typographic treatment. The two black dots—the only circular forms on the page—placed asymmetrically in the composition draw the eye and suggest binoculars peering through the blinds. This typographic image supports and suggests the subject matter of the film it promotes.

Make it new Simple shapes, lines, and circles suggest machines that defined an industrial society in this graphic illustration about the Modernist movement in arts and culture.

Creative composition These three images show how the relationship of composition in photography can translate to graphic images and, in this case, to the development of a logo.

between positive and negative space, and to explore this in basic compositional studies, before moving on to more complex designs. In general, negative space works to support the positive "image" in any given area (also called the picture plane). To create a more considered and effective composition, control the relationship between positive and negative elements, and recognize the effect each has on the other.

White space can create tension or contrast, or can add the welcome open space needed to reflect on complex, visually active, and textural images. You can easily see the effects of open space on the overall feel

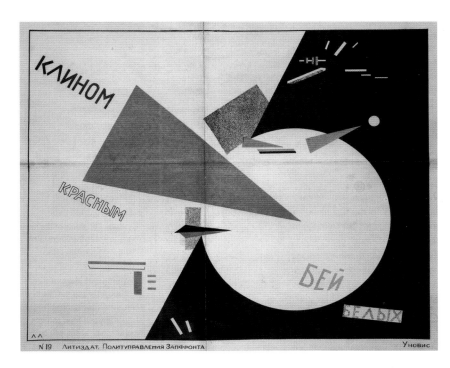

← **Symbolism** Dots, lines, and shapes can be used as powerful symbols in the right context. Artist El Lissitzky combined geometric shapes and a bold red, white, and black palette to create a strong political statement in *Beat the Whites with the Red Wedge*, 1919. The sharp red triangle of the Bolshevik army is invading and dividing the white circle in this graphic statement on the Russian Civil War.

GLOSSARY

Balance: The deliberate placement of objects on a page.

Composition: The arrangement of elements or parts of a design (text, images) on the page.

Consistency: The considered selection of design elements that have similar attributes.

Contrast: Obvious differences in elements in a composition; size, form, color, and weight.

Element: One small part of a composition, such as a point or line, an image, a letter, or a word.

Line: A continuous form of connection between two points ("___").

Negative space: The white or colored area around an element—for example, a margin of a page.

Point: A dot on a page, such as a period (.).

Positive space: A form, image, or word printed or formed on the page.

Proximity: The relationship of one object to another.

Repetition: The repeated use of select design elements within the same composition.

Repetition with variation: The alteration of selected aspects of a repeated element.

White space: The open space surrounding a positive image that defines shape and directs hierarchy.

⊕ **SEE ALSO:** FORM AND SPACE, P36

---

of a composition by altering the ratio of positive to negative. If you place a single dot in the center of a relatively large square of white, far from disappearing, the dot becomes more important. This is because the expanse of white space highlights and focuses attention on the dot itself. You can also actively encourage ambiguity between picture elements and background. For example, a particular group of forms can come together to support each other and compete in such a way that the (normally negative) space is given form by the positive elements, as in figure–ground relationships (see page 36).

Dots and lines

A dot exists as a mark, on its own, as a point in space, and it can also be the start of a line. Many points together start to set up a rhythm or a pattern that, depending on uniformity, repetitiveness, scale, or quantity, can suggest regularity or variation, and can express tense or relaxed sensibilities.

A line is a pathway between any two points. It can be straight, curved, thick, thin, horizontal, diagonal, jagged, solid, gestural, or broken. Soft, sensuous lines imply tranquility and harmony, whereas sharp, zigzagged lines invoke discordance and tension. Two converging lines might imply a point disappearing in the distance, and can suggest the illusion of three dimensions in a two-dimensional space. Horizontal lines suggest open planes; vertical lines can suggest power and strength. Lines are elegant tools that imply motion, momentum, rhythm, and upward or downward movement, and are primary aids in establishing visual hierarchies and closure. Simply put, closure is the ability of the human brain to observe an incomplete circle and to perceive it as complete in our imaginations.

Look at the expressive qualities of the artist Franz Kline's strong, emphatic painted line, or Cy Twombly's wandering, fragile drawn and painted lines. Examine Wolfgang Weingart's use of line in typography as a way to structure information or Russian Constructivist Alexander Rodchenko's powerful use of red and black line. El Lizzitsky and Piet Zwart also used lines emphatically and expressively in their work.

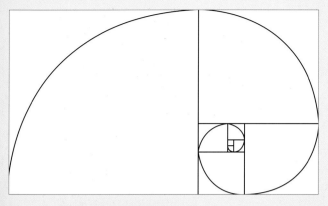

⬆ Fibonacci spiral
Each time a square is taken from the section, a smaller rectangle remains with the same proportions as the original. The spiral (also known as the golden ratio) can be used to create a proportional and harmonious composition.

⬇ Tricks on the eye Figure–ground relationships produce different effects that confuse the eye. For example, the Rubin vase (top left) relies upon a visual confusion between figure and ground, so that the eye sees either faces or a vase.

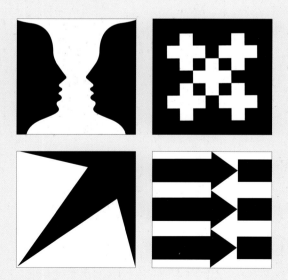

In learning to create meaningful compositions, it is important to understand the role of visual perception (the way our eyes and brains make sense of what we see) and its role in visual communication.

Whether consciously or not, our eyes are constantly supplying information to our brain, which processes and makes sense of that visual input. Being able to control that process and understand how it works is crucial. Good design thinking requires an understanding of how the relationship between visual elements affects the way we perceive them, as well as an understanding of how to control and exploit them.

Figure and ground

A form is always experienced in relation to the space it occupies and to other forms that may be present in the format. We call this the figure–ground relationship (where "figure" refers to any object in a given space and "ground" refers to the background, or space in which that object is seen). Another way to talk about this relationship is in terms of negative and positive space. Visual elements are always seen in relation to a visual field, background, or frame. In other words, every form is seen in context and cannot be totally isolated.

Generally speaking, a form is considered to be positive and the space around it negative. The space within a format (the ground) is an important element of any design and not just something left over once a form is placed on it: it matters within the overall design, since the ground affects the form and vice versa. Usually, we tend to notice the form before we see the ground, or what is placed in a space before we see the space itself. However, a well-known example of where this relationship becomes confused is drawn from Gestalt psychology. "Gestalt" is a German word meaning "essence or shape of an entity's complete form." Look at the Rubin vase (left), where the effect depends on whether we see the form as the white element, with the ground as the black, or see the black shapes as the form.

Closure: The ability of the human brain to observe an incomplete circle and to perceive it as complete.

Gestalt psychology: A theory that suggests that the mind perceives and organizes holistically and finds patterns in that which appears to be unconnected.

Ground: The page, surface, or area in which the design will be placed.

Law of closure: The mind creates a solid object on the page from suggestions of shapes and placement and proximity of elements.

The law of closure

Another phenomena drawn from Gestalt psychology is the law of closure, which argues that we tend to "close" or complete lines or objects that are not, in fact, closed. This can be a useful device in design, and is related to figure and ground, since it relies on our ability to collapse the space between foreground and background. It is also a primary tool in directing a viewer's eye through a composition in the designer's intended sequence.

The rule of thirds

The rule of thirds says that most compositions become more dynamic when divided into thirds vertically and/or horizontally, with important elements placed within those thirds. Dividing a composition in half will halt the closure and keep the viewer's eye centered on the halfway point, especially if an object is placed at the exact center point. The rule of thirds ensures movement on the page, and actively engages positive and negative space in the visual dialogue. The rule of thirds applies to graphic design for print, web, and motion graphics and applies equally to framing for photography, film, and video.

Gestalt law of closure

Examples of the law of closure demonstrate the ability of the brain to complete incomplete forms and, consequently, continue to move around the complete form. In page design, or any composition, it will keep the viewer's attention on the design at hand and move the eye around a page, package, poster or sign.

Negative as positive

Using principles of negative space and figure–ground reversal, typographer John Langdon's painting directs the viewer's eye to decode two words in one, "you" and "me."

WOMEN
OF ART
AND ROCK

STEREO TELESCOPE
CASEY DESMOND
RHIANNA LAROCQUE
AMY LUNDSTROM
TOFUSQUIRREL

Live Music & Art
Sept. 12th, 7:30–11:30PM
@ afterHours
NU Student + 1 Guest FREE

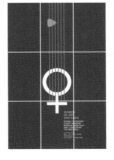

Thirds Beautifully placed, simple geometrics and lines send a message of music in this dynamic example of the rule of thirds. The composition divides horizontally and vertically, with the placement of the most critical imagery right in the center. Accent color in the upper and lower thirds keeps the viewer moving between the two spots, lengthening the observation time.

PART 1	PRINCIPLES
UNIT 2	FUNDAMENTALS OF COMPOSITION
MODULE 3	**Symmetry/asymmetry**

Symmetry in design refers to a spatial relationship between elements, and specifically to a situation where the elements in a layout are centered, having equal space to the left and right or above and below them, a mirror image on either side. The second meaning of symmetry is more general, and refers to a sense of harmony, or balance, which in turn is seen to reflect beauty. Symmetry carries associations of perfection, tradition, order, and rationality and peace.

Designing without symmetry

In asymmetrical design (without symmetry), elements are not centered, but utilize the whole format, creating dynamic compositions that play with scale, contrast, space, and tension between elements. Negative space is usually less passive in asymmetrical design, and becomes easily evident as a part of the design. Asymmetry is generally associated with fewer rules and limits, and more expressive possibilities. However, each kind of composition has its place, and the important thing is to learn how to identify when it is appropriate to use one or the other. While asymmetrical design may seem less rigid, it is crucial to spend time learning how asymmetry activates elements in a given space, and to carefully control the effects you want to achieve rather than randomly placing elements in a design.

Choosing symmetry or asymmetry

Similar questions arise in any design you undertake. How should the space be divided? How should the subject matter occupy the space? Each decision you make on placement will affect the emotion of the design. A symmetrical composition makes for a calmer, more peaceful work, while something more dynamic can be achieved if the elements are arranged asymmetrically. Symmetry tends toward balance, and lack of movement, while asymmetry injects movement and spatial tension into a design.

⬧ In harmony The ancient Chinese duality symbol for "yin" (black) and "yang" (white) is the perhaps the most famous example of perfect symmetry, each shape a reversed mirror of the other.

⬆ Typographic symmetry Beautifully mirrored hand-drawn letterforms produce this symmetrical ambigram, which reveals the word "excellence" the exact same way when the book is turned upside down.

Testing the theory

In these examples, various effects are achieved by simple variation of the position of the square within a stable frame.

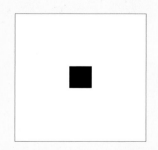

1 Balance
The centered square is stable or static, as the space around the square is equal on all sides.

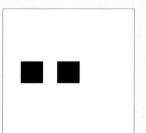

2 Movement to the left
When a second square is introduced, visual forces develop. There is a sense that the squares are moving left.

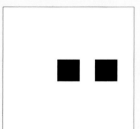

3 Movement to the right
Changing the position of the two squares suggests movement to the right.

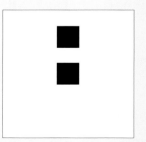

4 Upward movement
The position of the two squares hints at movement upward.

Asymmetry: A composition where elements are juxtaposed and do not mirror the other forms on the page.

Symmetry: A composition where elements are balanced or mirrored on a page.

Asymmetry

Placement of the image slightly to the right on the package is balanced nicely by the ghosted graphic on the lower left, providing balance and adding a bit of motion.

Symmetry

Perfect symmetry is in place on the smaller packages, with a nod toward the motion associated with asymmetry addressed in the placement of spot color in the photos.

Different but equal

Equal weight is represented on opposite sides of this clean publication design composition. Both are aligned to the far edge of their respective sides, and the primary information on either side occupies about the same amount of space.

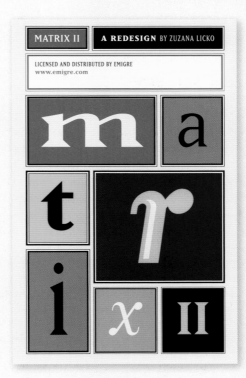

Symmetry in asymmetry

Perfectly centered letterforms create symmetry within an active asymmetrical composition. The contrasts in placement and color create visual rhythm in this dynamic composition.

Zang Tumb Tumb,

by F. T. Marinetti in 1919, uses creative asymmetrical typography to express the sounds of battle. In typography, "onomatopeia" refers to the use of type to express sounds in a literal way.

PART 1	PRINCIPLES
UNIT 2	FUNDAMENTALS OF COMPOSITION
MODULE 4	**Basic principles of design layout**

The term "layout" refers to the organization of disparate material that makes up the content of a design. Well-designed visual communications present information in a logical, coherent way, and make the important elements stand out. Basic principles of good composition are of the upmost importance in the process, and a thoughtful approach to the delivery of the material is, as always, the designer's first consideration.

The use of a grid system and consistently styled design elements helps the reader to absorb information in a visually pleasing way, and enhances the communication of the content. Good composition in layout design is dependent on the grid, and there are many configurations to choose from.

Practical factors
There are three basic stages in beginning any graphic design project. First, the designer receives a brief from the client, usually establishing what material should be included and the format for the project. This involves a combination of text, or copy (main text, display copy [headings], boxes or sidebars, captions) and images (photographs, illustrations, maps, diagrams). The brief should also indicate the desired look or "feel" of the work, which in turn will depend on the target audience. Should the layout look authoritative? Should it be densely packed with information? Does the message warrant a lean and structured design, with lots of white space? If the brief is vague, schedule time with your client to ask the right questions and help define the goals of the design. Should it shock the viewer, relax them, or make them smile?

Second, you will need to consider the format and budget. If there are many pictures and extensive copy for a small space, this will affect the look of the layout. Agreement should be reached on hierarchies within the copy; an editor may already have labeled their headings "A," "B," "C," and so on, to indicate their relative importance. Such elements can be indicated typographically for emphasis, through differences in type size, weight, form, and choice of color. Determine how many colors will be used. Beautiful design work can be created with a limited palette or with a full range of inks and effects. The number of colors used will affect a print production budget, so find out before you begin to conceptualize a project for press. If the project is hosted online, your palette is free, but certain colors are easier to read on screen than others. For website design, see pages 142–185.

Grids
The third stage involves organization. In print-based work and web design this means developing a grid system, in which various elements can be placed within a ready-made structure that underpins the entire design. The grid enables the layout of columns, margins, and areas for text and image. A well-designed grid allows for some flexibility of placement on individual pages while providing an underlying system that gives visual coherence across a series of pages. This is obviously crucial in any kind of editorial work, including books and magazines, but certainly applies to well-designed website pages, where some elements stay the same and others change. Of course, working within a structured format will also offer many excellent opportunities to break the rules, but it's best to learn them first.

Divide and conquer Organizing information on a page meaningfully is critical to the information transfer, especially when handling large amounts of text. There are many ways to divide the page and the choice should be a consideration of the type of design work, the viewing platform, and the amount of information to be presented on each page or sub-division.

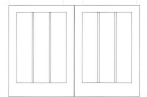

Individual units of equal size, separated by equal margins top and bottom, form a system perfect for compositions with many images. The units can be combined in any number for larger images or columns of text.

Three columns works well for mid-range amounts of text. The designer can use any given column in any system for added white space and can divide the page asymmetrically with text and image in this three-column system.

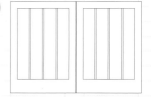

A four-column system begins to add more flexibility for variation in placement. The symmetrical division will add order, if desired, and added control in the overall system.

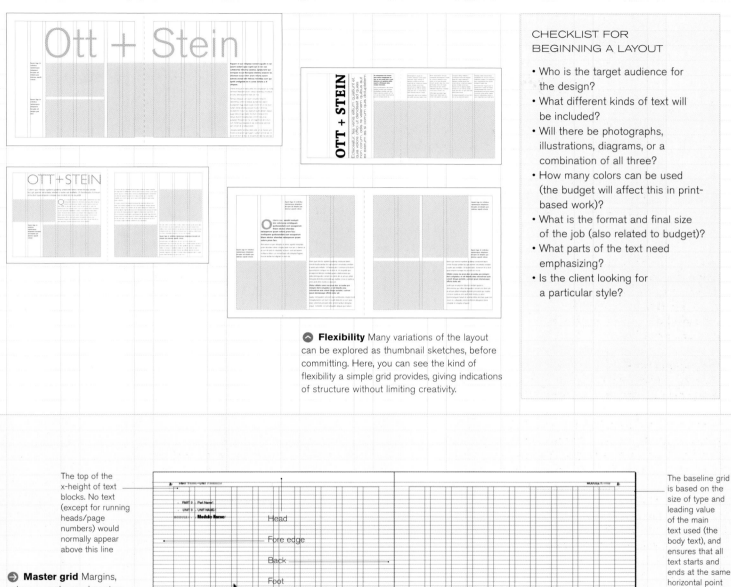

CHECKLIST FOR BEGINNING A LAYOUT

- Who is the target audience for the design?
- What different kinds of text will be included?
- Will there be photographs, illustrations, diagrams, or a combination of all three?
- How many colors can be used (the budget will affect this in print-based work)?
- What is the format and final size of the job (also related to budget)?
- What parts of the text need emphasizing?
- Is the client looking for a particular style?

Flexibility Many variations of the layout can be explored as thumbnail sketches, before committing. Here, you can see the kind of flexibility a simple grid provides, giving indications of structure without limiting creativity.

The top of the x-height of text blocks. No text (except for running heads/page numbers) would normally appear above this line

Master grid Margins, columns, and non-changing typographic elements such as page numbers and running heads can all be placed on the master grid, which provides the design template. The grids have been printed over this module to show how they structure the design.

Head
Fore edge
Back
Foot

The baseline grid is based on the size of type and leading value of the main text used (the body text), and ensures that all text starts and ends at the same horizontal point

Here you can set the number of columns per page and the space (gutter) between each

Margins and Columns

Margins
Top: 14 mm
Bottom: 17.7 mm
Inside: 14 mm
Outside: 19 mm

Columns
Number: 10
Gutter: 5 mm

OK
Cancel
☑ Preview

What flowers are
found in tropical
rain forests?

⬆ **Natural order** This tight, modular grid
system shows the expressive freedom that
comes with control. A wonderful range of
shapes and sizes is available to showcase
photography and text with this six-column
format, and you can sustain the viewer's
interest in larger publications.

Margins, grids, and structure

For any form of publication design you should begin by formatting a double-page spread that can then be applied to the entire publication. This is important because you need to see how the verso (left-hand page) relates to the recto (right-hand page) and judge how well they balance. Established practice in book design suggests that the back (inner margin) should be half the fore edge (outside margin), and the foot (bottom margin) greater than the head (top margin). These rules should ensure a balance, with the type area sitting comfortably in the format. Remember that the eye will need to move from one page to another, so the gap, or gutter (the two back edges combined), should not be too large.

When establishing page margins, consider the material, the client, and the reader. For example, paperbacks tend to have tight margins to keep page numbers—and therefore costs—down, whereas heavily illustrated publications have generous margins and use white space effectively. Economic considerations play a part: brochures and promotional materials tend to have bigger budgets, so even more white space is possible.

The grid shows the layout of columns, margins, and areas for main text, captions, and images; it also shows the position of repeating heads (running heads) and page

⬇ **Variation** Spreads
from the same publication
showcase the system's
flexibility, adding blocks of
color, half-page photography,
translucent color overlays, and
highlighted inserts, all while
remaining faithful to the
boundaries of the grid system.

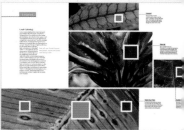

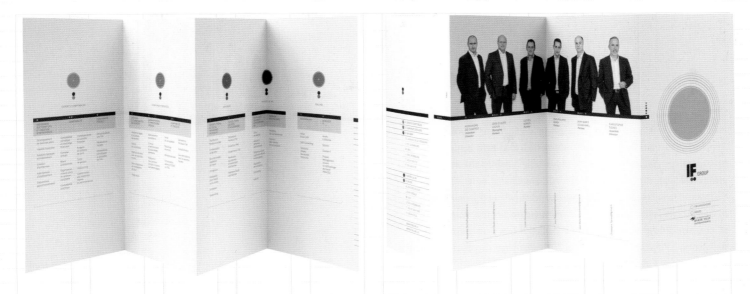

numbers. These elements normally stay the same over a series of pages.

After drawing your double-page spread, you can prepare some layout roughs: these can be small thumbnails or half-sized visuals in which your first ideas are sketched out. This preliminary thinking time is key in the page-design process; it's where you make important decisions about the composition of pages and the organization of material. Preliminary sketches can then be transferred to the computer and several variations quickly produced, based on the main grid. It takes less time to sketch ideas than to create designs directly on screen. Remember, the computer is simply a tool; it cannot think for you, nor can it generate ideas. With initial sketches, the imaginative designer can fully explore ideas and options before moving to the production phase.

Using a grid

The grid divides the available type area into proportioned units, providing an overall visual structure and helping to unite all visual elements. The most basic grid structure—used primarily for text-based material such as business reports or novels—is that of a single column. The width should relate to legibility. With complex layouts, in which text, images, diagrams, and captions must be integrated, a more sophisticated

horizontal and vertical grid is needed. Grid systems comprising between three and six columns enable you to use all kinds of elements. The more units used, the more flexibility you have to accommodate smaller pieces of copy such as captions, longer measures such as section openers, and displayed material. Never simply follow your computer's default settings for columns, but decide on your own.

Ideally, a grid should have some vertical controls, both for structure down the page and for order to the overall design. Give headings, subheadings, captions, and page numbers set positions for continuity. Finally, be flexible. After two or three spreads the grid may seem too rigid, so adjust it. Grids should not be restrictive, but provide structure while giving rich compositional variations to spreads.

Form and function

Consider the format style and the user experience when you select a grid system. If the content information can be neatly divided into components, it may suggest the use of a particular fold that will help to display the information in a logical sequence. The tall, slender accordion fold on the brochure above adds elegant white space and repeats the form in the photo.

SEE ALSO: AUDIENCES, MARKETS, AND CONCEPTS, P24

STYLES OF LAYOUT, P44

PACE AND CONTRAST, P46

SIZE AND FORMAT, P50

TYPOGRAPHIC EMPHASIS AND HIERARCHY, P78

PART 1	PRINCIPLES
UNIT 2	FUNDAMENTALS OF COMPOSITION
MODULE 5	**Styles of layout**

In simple terms, page design, or layout, can be divided into two basic styles: symmetrical and asymmetrical. In broad terms, symmetrical style is a traditional approach in which design is structured around a central axis. This type of layout has its origins in the earliest printed books, which, in turn, borrowed their layout from handwritten manuscripts of the medieval era. Asymmetrical style is non-centered, dynamic, and associated with 20th-century modernism and contemporary design.

Symmetrical style

Traditionally, symmetrical layouts are most commonly seen on title pages of books, where each line of type is centered above the others. Part of the tradition is also the use of serif typefaces, often set in letter-spaced capitals with, perhaps, the addition of an ornament or printer's flower.

Decorative borders and the addition of decorative elements became more popular in the 15th and 16th centuries, but until the 1920s most publications were designed with symmetrical formats. Achieving a balanced-looking composition within a symmetrical design is not as easy as it sounds. Type size must be carefully judged, and spacing between each line considered, since certain information belongs in the same typographic unit and should be grouped accordingly. Fine-tuning horizontal line space is critical. These judgments must be made while maintaining balance and beautiful composition. For superb examples of symmetrical typography, see the work of Aldus Manutius, the Dolphin Press, and the Venetian printers from the late 15th century.

The asymmetrical revolution

Asymmetrical layouts can be traced back to the 1920s and 1930s, in particular to the German school, the Bauhaus. Artists such as Kurt Schwitters and Theo van Doesburg experimented with layouts based on an off-centered axis, creating tension and dynamism. In this style, type is primarily ragged left; ragged-right setting is kept to a few lines, as Western cultures read left to right. Other predominant designers to note are Armin Hofmann, Herbert Bayer, Wim Crouwel, and the work of Josef Müller-Brockmann.

The modernist movement also rejected ornament, and sans-serif typefaces, with their clean lines and modernity, were the popular faces of the school. The work of the Bauhaus and their stylistic descendents, such as the Swiss typographers of the 1950s and 1960s, favors sans-serif faces and often completely

⬆ Asymmetrical page design Justified blocks of text are important design elements of the modular grid system in this asymmetrical page design. The unusual division of the photographic image elevates the grid system itself to a central design element and, as the margins become lines, shows the influence of the Constructivist movement.

⬅ Balance The symmetrical design system of these pages allows large display typography in different styles, both sans serif and serif, to divide the pages and play a central part as design elements in the compositions.

lowercase headlines. Rules, in a number of weights, are used as distinctive features in color and in black and white, adding dynamic movement to the compositions.

Another amazing typographer, whose work over a long career shows both styles well, is Jan Tschichold. Early on he was heavily influenced by the modernist philosophy of the Bauhaus, and is considered a pioneer of the asymmetric revolution. He later changed direction, rejecting the hard-line approach advocated in his book *Asymmetric Typography*. Tschichold returned to the frequent use of centered, serif typography, but continued working in both styles.

Integrating styles

Contemporary designers often integrate both theories of spatial arrangement and select the style to suit the project. Contemporary typographers, like Philippe Apeloig, also use both in their search for visual solutions. As a designer you need to understand both styles, and their historical precedents and contexts, so that your selections and design decisions are based on knowledge rather than guesswork. Read as much about graphic design history as you can, and follow the philosophy of Jan Tschichold: use both styles, but understand that mixing them needs to be undertaken with caution. Research and experimentation will be your best guides. Keep your options open, and be flexible and fearless in reaching appropriate solutions.

⊕ **SEE ALSO:** SYMMETRY/ ASYMMETRY, P38

BASIC PRINCIPLES OF DESIGN LAYOUT, P40

SIZE AND FORMAT, P50

⬇ **Classically centered**
The *Hypnerotomachia Poliphili*, printed by Aldus Manutius's Dolphin Press, Venice, in 1499, is an example of the highest art of Renaissance printing. Its symmetrical typography harmonizes with the wood-engraved illustrations.

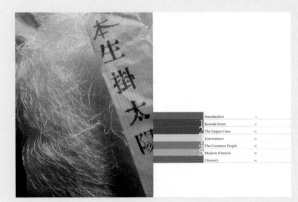

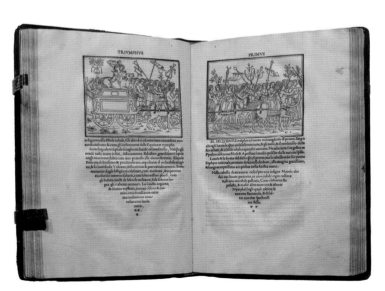

Combining styles
Inserts, short pages, and fold-outs create symmetrical and asymmetrical page designs and work in concert to evidence the decorative nature of pattern design in this book on the history of kimonos. The unusual combination is influenced by asymmetry in traditional Japanese art.

PART 1	PRINCIPLES
UNIT 2	FUNDAMENTALS OF COMPOSITION
MODULE 6	**Pace and contrast**

Pace and contrast are vital qualities for catching and maintaining a reader's interest in graphic design: they provide variety, and set the rhythm and the mood. This is particularly evident in magazines and image-heavy books, where it is critical to be able to direct the eye to different pieces of information in a particular sequence. Think in cinematic terms: the audience should be given different experiences, have different reactions, and enjoy the complete experience from beginning to end. The digital age has created a world of multitasking citizens, and holding their attention over time can be a challenge.

In continuous text, the reader takes more time to cover information and is primed to read every word. In a highly integrated design—with panels, pictures, captions, quotes, and so on—there is more competition for the reader's attention. An article may be skimmed over, some pages will be scanned for pictures, or the reader might be seeking only a specific piece of information.

The pace of a publication will be dictated by the content and space available. Contrast is closely linked to pace and is an excellent tool for controlling the pace

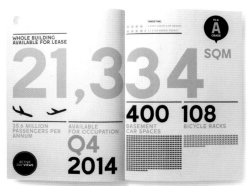

◐ **Controlling the pace**
The same principles of design apply to any platform, whether it is web, print, motion, or environmental. The system shown on-screen at right maintains common elements in the titling and hierarchy and varies the pace of the content pages with colorful full-bleed images and pages with smaller insets. The viewer has more options to zoom and link to new pages online than in print, so visuals should be planned out as a fully extended system.

◐ **Momentum** The publication *Gateway 241* neatly divides spreads with a strong landscape/horizontal image and provides enough variety of form to keep it interesting. Pace is varied through contrast in scale, fine use of white space, large bleed photography, handsome display type and infographics that cross the gutters, and a landscape double-foldout image.

of an extended design system. You can create visual emphasis with large type and imagery, unusual cropping, sidebar information graphics, and full bleeds of image or color. Alternatively, you can create a quiet interval by having text-only spreads and open areas of white space.

Planning for pace

In order to achieve good pacing, with contrast and visual rhythm over a succession of pages, an overall plan is needed. Too much visual complexity can be counterproductive, but a succession of similar-looking spreads will become boring and you may lose your audience. One technique is to construct a flat plan showing the total number of pages in the publication. The flat plan can be drawn small (thumbnail size) in double-page spreads. It should contain page numbers, titles, and content. A quick survey of this plan gives you a broad overview of how your material will unfold (see page 28).

When you begin your design process, don't become too dependent on the images you create on screen. If the final result is meant to be in print, print your document often during the process and view your pages at the actual size of the finished product. Type sizes and weights, image quality and scale, and the rhythm, pacing, and transition from one spread to the next should be evaluated in the same format as the end user would see it. Check your pacing throughout the process and be flexible enough to initiate change where it is needed.

Creating momentum and rhythm

At the beginning of an article, or section of a book, create momentum and rhythm and set the mood for a receptive reader using all the composition skills you have learned. You can use pictures as a frieze, in a narrow sequence of images running along the top of the spreads that moves the reader across the pages. You can create various mosaic arrangements on the grid, using one large picture and a series of smaller ones. You can break out of the grid at strategic points. Depending on picture content, you can create vertical movement with narrow vertical images. Conversely, with landscape-format pictures you can create a strong sense of horizontal movement.

You can control the pace by juxtaposing black-and-white images with bright spots of color, or black-and-white with duotones, tritones, and specialty inks. Variation between narrow and wide text measures will add pace to your pages, and using your grid system creatively is essential. Strong background colors or reversed-out type at specific points can also create a sense of movement to change the speed and vary the rhythm. Be deliberate in your decisions and interpret your subject matter thoughtfully. Keep it quiet if the material calls for introspection, or pick up the pace and build excitement if appropriate.

Printed publications

In publication design, pace and contrast are fundamental. There are more types of magazines—print or

↑ Color and contrast

Color is a valuable asset in controlling the pace. Full-color photography juxtaposes monochromatic images to illustrate the history of masks. A mask-on-mask belly-band surrounds the book with a muted image that reveals a full color subject when removed.

⊕ SEE ALSO: BASIC PRINCIPLES OF DESIGN LAYOUT, P40

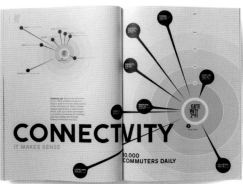

CONNECTIVITY
IT MAKES SENSE
10,000 COMMUTERS DAILY

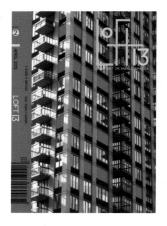

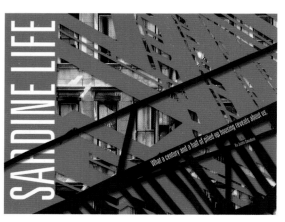

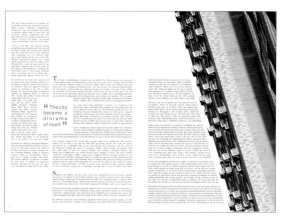

electronic—than any other category of design. They range from highbrow, political, economic, or philosophical journals to sporting, arts, satirical, and leisure and lifestyle titles. Each publication will require different solutions to the pacing, depending on content and readership. Magazine readers differ from book readers because they view the product in unpredictable ways and in differing environments. Some will be led by the cover images to the contents page, where they will select their articles in an ordered way; others will dip in and out of any part of the magazine; while others will always read certain sections in a peculiarly personal order. Magazine readers may view the publication at home, in a relaxed environment with no distractions, or they may pick up an issue in a waiting room or a public place. Engaged, entertained readers become loyal subscribers, so the visual should work with the content to transport the reader, like any good book. For a design to be memorable, visual interest should be present on every page and the editorial personality of the magazine

↑ Form follows content
A combination of techniques and decidedly constructivist page design combine to create a feeling of urban crowding in this article on small-apartment dwelling. The designer used a combination of photography and cut paper to create a vibrant electronic collage, then supported the system with enclosed pull quotes encased in a tight grid system.

should be evident at every turn. If the publication is trendy and edgy, designers use every tool, including pagination and way-finding marks, to reinforce the style and mood. A true master of magazine layout is the American designer Alexey Brodovich, who worked primarily in the 1940s and 1950s. Bradbury Thompson also understood the importance of pace and contrast.

In illustrated books, change of pace is also required. Generally, readers behave in a relatively logical way, moving through the publication from start to finish. They, too, will dive in and out, but not to the same extent as magazine readers. In book design, economic factors also play a part. If plenty of pages are available, then you can introduce section openers and use lots of white space to create drama with headings and placement. Each book design should have a strong visual identity. If the spreads are too diverse, it can have a hazardous effect on the book and become confusing to the reader.

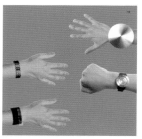

◀ Simple lines
Showcased products become the composition in this series of spreads. Interesting image placement adds rhythm and horizontal and vertical motion to the compositions, with little or no distraction from the clean design of the products themselves.

Digital publications

Electronic magazines require different strategies; type and images interact much more immediately on screen. Imagery is much easier to manipulate and adapt to a variety of purposes and device formats. Some of the principles of print-based work may not apply directly to screen-based designs: one obvious difference is that, instead of turning pages, viewers scroll up and down for consecutive views of "spreads." Instead of using weight, style, or position for emphasis, type might move or a static image may click through to a video presentation. Page structure and the placement of graphic elements must reflect the function of the site.

A new aesthetic continues to develop hand in hand with emerging digital technology that ties form and function. Ultimately, though, basic issues of pace and contrast for print still apply, in part, for screen. The designer must still navigate the viewer through the maze of available information and present the appropriate markers for way-finding. Learning the basics of layout design from the model of print design is a stepping stone to the development of new ways of working in digital environments. The rules of good design should always be considered, regardless of format or media, and the designer should be able to apply them appropriately.

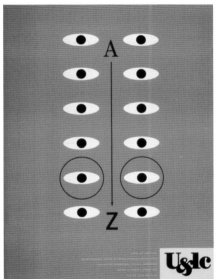

⬆ **Sophisticated wit** With humor and a touch of surrealism, Carin Goldberg's beautiful, iconic magazine covers for the *New York Times* and the typography magazine *U&lc* reflect contemporary culture through the designer's playful eye.

➡ **Complex systems** Digital publications have complex systems that offer multiple options and need to be considered in depth by the designer. Well-designed digital publications should have all the excitement and visual narrative skills of the printed page. *TLQ* magazine presents expert editorial art direction at every swipe, scroll, or zoom, and provides the pacing and detail needed when the viewer can easily alter the pace.

⬆ **Purposeful shapes**
The inspiration for this project was an old-fashioned ice-cream van, and the die-cut cover conceals a traditionally shaped booklet inside.

PART 1	PRINCIPLES
UNIT 2	FUNDAMENTALS OF COMPOSITION
MODULE 7	**Size and format**

Size and format are important considerations in any printed design. They are affected by budget, practical restraints such as mailing costs, and by the needs of the job. The experience the end user has while interacting with the materials will affect the type of response the material evokes. Print is an intimate medium that's meant to be viewed close to the body. The tactile qualities of printed media are evidenced by weight, surface texture, binding, gloss, matte, or metallic inks, foil stamps, and die-cut surfaces, all of which play a part in the personality of the product.

Primary considerations

In deciding on format, the designer is often limited by external factors. Certain elements in a corporate identity package, such as letterheads, envelopes, and official forms, are usually a standard size; other factors, however, may also have to be considered. Cost issues loom large: can the size selected for printing be cut economically from a bigger sheet of paper or will there be unnecessary expensive waste? Carefully evaluate the sheet size with the number of copies required. Will the finished work have to be mailed out? If so, weigh a mock-up to estimate postage costs: a larger format may prove to be too expensive to send by post if you are printing thousands of impressions. Can the job be folded economically in relation to the grain of the paper? Work with your printer to find the most economical and environmentally sound solution, and determine your size and scale before you begin your design process.

Content determines format

In book design, format should be determined by purpose or nature, with the user in mind. Text-only books pose fewer problems than books with a heavy concentration of photographic or illustrative subjects. For continuous reading, a good point size on a readable, attractive font with adequate margins in play can help to determine the format as either portrait or landscape, and in paperbacks, which need to be both cheap and portable, point size is typically small. In illustrated books, the images should resonate the mood of the subject and a larger format book is appropriate—but check your size in a mock-up version before you begin, to ensure the book won't become unwieldy. Illustrations and photographs do not necessarily lose information value if they are smaller than first anticipated, and there are benefits in making a product easier for the reader to handle. The largest

⬆ **Book art** Unusual formats can transform a simple design into conceptual art. An alternative binding can enhance the tactile user experience and reinforce the content in subtle ways.

◀ **Dramatic landscapes**
The horizon line in the two-page bleed photographic image determined the typographic sight line on the preceding page, and adds drama to the page design.

Vertical orientation
Stacked vertical columns of text, supported by vertically oriented typographic illustrations, add height and drama in this text-as-image approach to page design.

Nostalgic The clever accordion fold was produced to celebrate and commemorate a community arts project run by artist Mark Storor in the seaside town of Jaywick. The concept design and format mimicked a vintage-style folded postcard.

GLOSSARY

Concertina folds: Folds in alternate directions.

French folds: Sheets of paper are folded in half, so that they are double thickness. The two folds are at right angles to each other and then bound on the edge.

Gatefold: A way of folding paper so that the outer quarters of a page are folded to meet in the center. The result works like symmetrical doors that open onto an inner page.

Paper grain: The direction of wood fibers that make up a piece of paper.

Perfect binding: Method similar to paperback binding, where loose sheets are encased in a heavier paper cover, then glued to the book spine. Edges are trimmed to be flush with each other.

Rollover folds: A way of folding a page so that successive folds turn in on themselves and the page is folded into a roll.

Saddle stitching: Binding method where sheets of paper are folded in the center, stitched together along the fold, then glued into the cover spine.

formats are generally reserved for art and design subjects and museum catalogs, in which excellent-quality illustrations are central to the book's success.

Whenever possible, content should determine format. Think about your subject matter and examine all available materials for inclusion before you determine the final format. If there are beautiful panoramic landscape views to be featured in the book, a horizontal format may be your obvious choice. Experiment in your initial layout sketches and determine the best way to showcase your materials to the greatest effect. If the subject matter calls for white space to be part of the design, be sure to anticipate the additional dimensions for your margins and gutters. Multilingual publications pose their own set of problems. It is probably best to try to accommodate two or three languages side by side to achieve a consistent flow of text and, if illustrated, to ensure that text references are on the same page as pictures.

Although international standardization in paper sizes helps keep prices down, the same old formats can become boring. There are several inventive solutions, but be sure they fit the design concept of the publication. By folding sheets differently, you can effect simple changes: fold on the short side for an elegant long format, or trim standard sizes for unfamiliar shapes at no extra cost. Add gatefolds to portrait formats for an unexpected horizontal image, or add short pages to a horizontal format and add interest by providing a layered, textural interlude.

Folds and binding

With smaller publications and brochures, folds can play a big part in enticing the reader into the subject matter. The aesthetically pleasing square format is simply achieved by folding the sheet in a different way. Organizing copy to follow folds—whether rolling folds or concertina folds—creates a sense of fun and is an excellent way to entice the reader into the publication.

Simple binding ideas can also enhance the appeal of smaller publications and can be used inventively to add to the way-finding of the content. You might consider trimming each spread a little shorter than the preceding one, giving the area at the end of the page a space for information graphics or subheads. An untrimmed fore edge makes for an attractively handcrafted feel, as does visible colored thread for the stitching. These ideas are easy to implement; they don't necessarily cost a lot and can make your designs different and memorable. Be sure to consider all aspects of the project as part of your design process from the very beginning: changing one or two elements will affect your other decisions as well, and may cause you to back up the process and redesign certain elements. Part of the fun of design work is in the discovery of inventive solutions, new materials, and new combinations of tried and true techniques. Take the time to consider the importance of your choices and remember that if you can see something, your client can, too. Every aspect of the project should be evaluated with a designer's eye, down to the smallest detail.

SEE ALSO: BASIC PRINCIPLES OF DESIGN LAYOUT, P40

STYLES OF LAYOUT, P44

PHOTOGRAPHY AND ILLUSTRATION, P56

PART 1	PRINCIPLES
UNIT 2	FUNDAMENTALS OF COMPOSITION
MODULE 8	**Identity and extended systems**

Few things are designed to work as stand-alone pieces. Look at a successful branding: the logos and corporate identity, advertising campaigns, direct-mail campaigns, annual reports, websites, and social-media presence all have common design elements, binding them together and identifying them as part of the same brand. Look at the total content of any magazine or newspaper: the information changes, yet the publication looks consistent, issue after issue, and at a glance, we can easily and immediately identify our favorites on the shelf.

GLOSSARY

Identity: A unified, identifiable look for a product or organization.

Patch: The space on a bookstore's shelf occupied by spines of books from the same series.

This brand identity is achieved through a coordinated design and effective design strategy that is fluid enough to allow for variation and change, but is consistent throughout. With newspapers and magazines, this can be achieved with strict rules. For example, major headlines will be set in one font and ranged left; secondary headlines in another font and centered; body text in yet another font with fixed point size, leading, and justification; feature articles in a bolder font with looser leading and alternate justification. These rules are never broken, but they should be comprehensive enough to allow for any situation while maintaining a consistent "look."

Authors may write more than one book, and publishers almost always use coordinated designs for their book covers. If a publisher is repackaging the back catalog of a bestselling author, they will use a coordinated strategy for the covers that allows for changes of color, image, and titling, but also enables book buyers to identify the titles as part of a set, or brand. Perhaps the unchanging element is the type, set in the same face, at the same size, and in the same position throughout. Or it could be the style of the photograph used—black and white, full color, abstract—or the illustration—pen and ink, painting, digital, collage. A good

⬇ Rebranded The identity of the Finnish baking company Backers has been redesigned with a concept inspired by research into the client's origin in the seventeenth century. In the resulting branding, the contemporary sans-serif font used for the company name contrasts well with the detailed B. The pennant shapes recall ancient banners from the times when Backers was originally founded.

In the tradition of folk art and woodcarving, the initial B has been detailed with baking and farming symbols that include a decorative wheat pattern.

In the packaging design, the wheat pattern is lifted from inside the B and repeated in a sunray around the dominant circular form.

The mark works equally when used small or greatly enlarged on the side of a truck.

designer ties together all the elements, creating a formula that not only makes each individual piece striking in its own right, but also ensures easy identification with its counterparts.

Creating identifying characteristics

Well thought-out extended systems are the building blocks for all complex design projects. Corporate identity systems will partner clean, easy-to-decode logo designs with supportive graphics or photography that become an extension of the brand and can be used interchangeably on multiple applications. Most will also include a distinct color palette and a particular typographic sensibility that support the content without diluting the brand's original message. These design assets keep the brand fresh and exciting, and enhance the presence of a product, something that motivates all manufacturers and organizations competing for attention in the marketplace whether the product is books, chocolate, a gallery, or an online music service. The next

time you go out shopping, or attend a cultural event, look for this principle and you will notice that many of the products that have the most eye-catching and coordinated identity schemes are those of the most successful businesses and organizations. This is not a coincidence, and the designer who can successfully coordinate a brand or a company will always find their services in demand.

Know the content

Getting to know your brand and your target audience is part of your preliminary research. To speak to your audience accurately, you must also understand the content. In package design the product is usually easy to recognize, sometimes visible through the packaging material, and positioned for attention in the marketplace. The architecture of the package and the details in the design system work together to create an image-aware brand that proclaims itself as expensive, healthy, fashionable, or traditional by the very nature of the design system the artist creates and the materials used in the

◆ Understated elegance
Simple shapes and large fields of color define these elegant design systems by Carin Goldberg. The boxed set of books for New York's School of Visual Arts uses the rectangular form of the books and carefully placed dots to mark volumes one through four in the series, and extends the system of color blocks and simplified and gestural shapes to the inside page designs. The system for the works of Kurt Vonnegut uses bars of color that are reflected in the collective spines of the books.

packaging. It should also lead consumers through the functions of opening, dispensing, and reclosing without making them work too hard to get to the product. In complex packaging, there may be enclosures, hang-tags, and labels to design. The extended design system can enhance the product but should always remain true to the brand. In addition to housing and protecting the product, package design is advertising at the place where the consumer actually makes their purchase, sometimes in large displays that become part of the retail experience. To be really successful, it must communicate the correct message at a glance if singular, or work together in big displays of multiples, if it is to compete with other goods.

Interpretation and detail

In editorial design, the content must be carefully considered for its message and the author's point of view. A book jacket is, in effect, a piece of packaging that advertises both product and publisher. It should be approached in the same way as an advertising campaign, but the imagery can sometimes deliver its message in a more thought-provoking, poetic way.

First, each book must compete with all the others on display, leaping out from the shelf before informing potential buyers as to what the book might be about and why they should buy it. In bookstores with limited space, only the spines will be visible, so how these detailed areas work as small-space designs is

⬇ Restaurant identity

Handsome use of elegant white space and interesting repetition of diagonal lines mark this strong restaurant identity system. Beautiful detail derived from the system is noted in the circular hardware at the top of the menu, a perfect complement to the circles containing icons.

The repetition and variation of the linework, the exchange of positive and negative color, and the use of the diagonal in dividing space crosses over from the printed system to the website design.

important. The same principle of multiples in package display is in effect here, but on a much more economical scale. A series of covers with spines in bold black text on acid colors will create an impressive patch when a dozen or so are stacked along a shelf. The spine should be part of the overall cover image and work as a stand-alone design element when seen in multiples.

Book jackets begin telling the story to the consumer. A concept for a book-jacket design will be influenced by a number of factors, but the concept development should begin by considering the content. Consider whether the book is fiction or non-fiction; consider the genre the book belongs to; the subject matter—is it fun, grave, romantic, or scary; and, most importantly, who the book is targeting for readership. When designing book jackets, good designers make it their business to ask the publisher lots of questions—and to read the book! After all, your jacket design should inspire people to buy the book. Think about how your design might stand out enough to entice curiosity, or be provocative enough to convey information in an intriguing way, and try to create visuals that represent your author and subject matter of the book.

🔽 **Jumpman** Ginger Monkey Design engineered this amazing incorporation of two very different, recognizable, styles into a perfectly married new brand identity for Air Jordan.

🔽 **Added value** Elaborately detailed packaging for Nike Air Jordan Year of the Dragon 2012 limited edition incorporates decorative elements from the extended system at every turn, reinforcing the brand, enhancing the consumer's visual experience, and adding value to the product through the packaging. Small details are revealed as the package is turned and drawers slide open.

The Air Jordan Jumpman logo has been surrounded by mirrored dragons and enclosed in a mortise drawn from traditional Chinese imagery.

Tilted slightly and placed asymmetrically on the shoe, the mark is strong enough to remain active, airborne, and tied to the system—despite the emphatic color change on the product.

PHAIDON

Whether to use photographs, illustrations, or even type as image—or all three together—are important design considerations. A well-coordinated look is a hallmark of good design, and the way you plan, edit, and incorporate images significantly affects the outcome.

Boundaries between photography and illustration are becoming increasingly blurred by digital art; a straightforward choice between a realistic photograph and an illustrator's interpretation is still possible, and digital techniques allow for a merging of the two. Within the three categories are both relatively direct and obscure approaches, so you need to think about how you want your message to be understood and interpreted.

Much will depend on the category in which you are working. Advertising can be obvious or subtle, but it can also be crucial to show the brand your client is endeavoring to sell. Food packaging or car ads often feature beautifully photographed and highly realistic images showing the product in a flattering situation. If you are working on corporate design, the company's ethos is as important as its products or services. In this circumstance, a more abstract or evocative set of images could work.

In magazines and books, the look of the images will have been considered at the initial styling stage, when all the questions about the target audience will have been discussed. A mix of diverse styles—illustrations and photographs—can be used to differentiate between various editorial sections while maintaining the defining image of the publication.

Creative constraints

Some clients will have definite ideas about the types of images selected to represent them. They might send you the pictures they want you to use along with the initial brief, so sometimes the decision has already been made for you. Photography might not always be possible for logistical reasons—distance, budget, or difficulty in gaining permission—in which case commissioning an illustration is the only route.

⊙ Lightly whimsical Choosing the right visual style to tell your story can be difficult. Sometimes a single technique is inadequate to communicate the nuances, so custom combinations are invented. Delicate line art evokes the look of old etchings, but combines offbeat images in unusual parings and colors to make a contemporary statement on these lighthearted wine labels.

⊙ Manga style Versatile styling is displayed in the choice of manga artwork for the cover of a book on the impact of the manga style. Hand-drawn type and a thought balloon reinforce the subject and an arresting composition brings it a fresh perspective.

⊙ Man and beast Photo collage brings an unexpected twist to the back cover of the classic novel, *Animal Farm*. Custom photography of the suited human subject joins seamlessly to the stock image of the pig, creating an image that's memorable and provocative.

Technical manuals, company reports, educational books, or anything that aims to explain how things work, benefit from visualization. This might be a specialized form of technical illustration, in which designer, illustrator, and author/originator must liaise closely. Information graphics, charts, and data representation can be beautiful, inventive, and entertaining. Try to turn every constraint into a creative opportunity. Limitations set you free from certain decisions so you can concentrate more fully on others.

Budget and schedule

Commissioning an intricate illustration, such as a big design of a busy street scene, might not be appropriate if you do not have a large budget, in which case it might be more cost-effective to work with photography or photomontage. Conversely, asking a photographer to set up a full-day shoot involving several models, a makeup artist, a stylist, as well as complicated sets and props, may be outside your project budget, in which case it might be more cost-effective to commission an illustration.

Occasionally you may have to produce something for which there is an impossibly small budget. Don't let this stop your creative energy or curb your enthusiasm for the project—there are always creative possibilities. Contemporary designers should be able to generate imagery, even if there's no budget for a specialist. Inventive, evocative typography can function as illustration, and copyright-free pictures can always be found if you know where to look. Creating a fresh approach using stock images is an exercise in reinvention. Use your newly developed ability to see things differently, and transform the ordinary into something fresh and inventive. Try duotones, tritones, or spots of brilliant color on neutral fields. Think about layers of texture or open space, and fresh typography to pull it all together.

Photographers, illustrators, and libraries

You may be working on a self-initiated project or to a brief; either way, the illustrative approach may be immediately clear, or you may have to work harder to decide on the right style of image. First, ask yourself what would be suitable for the market and the message you are trying to communicate, then consider the scope of your budget and your timeframe as you research your potential sources.

Begin this phase as you begin all others, with research. You may need to create images yourself, or commission a freelance illustrator or photographer. There are many ways of looking at people's work beyond flipping through a portfolio. Look at work on the Internet, at exhibitions and agencies, and in other graphic works and design publications. Professional

↑ **Typography and illustration** The works of film director John Huston are celebrated on a poster illustration created by typing the titles of his filmography and lines from the scripts or novels and assembling them into a beautiful representation of the director's literate filmmaking. The assemblage was created by hand and then photographed.

← **Deconstruction and reassembly** Favorite elements and masterful images from the subject's own works and original illustration are combined to create a fresh composition on this poster celebrating the work of M. C. Escher.

associations have active websites where members often post work and you can view those that win awards for excellence.

There are also several online photographic resources that represent photographers and illustrators: type "picture library" or "illustration agency" into a search engine and you will find plenty. Generally, such companies allow you to use a low-resolution version for rough concepts, either for free or for a small fee. Then, when you have finalized your idea, you can buy the rights to use that picture. Always check what the final fee will be before committing yourself. These sources also now supply downloads, scans, or CDs of royalty-free images (you can use them without paying further fees)—so if you intend to cover a certain subject or style repeatedly, it might make sense to buy one of these. Another source is archival, copyright-free images, which can be useful in a number of ways.

Collect and store

The best way to ensure you have imagery at hand as you need it is to keep an image bank of your own. Most designers keep files of photographers' and illustrators' work. Sometimes you'll receive promotional work that has been sent in speculatively. If you like it, or think it might prove useful in the future, file it away carefully for potential future use. If you have a need for specialty photography, perhaps architectural interiors, food styling, or fashion photography, look for experts with strength in that area.

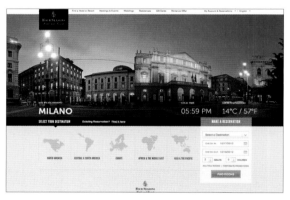

Photographic subjects Strong photography commands attention in this website design. The viewers' close proximity to these rich panoramic location images transports them to their destinations in fine style.

SEE ALSO: THEORIES OF IMAGE AND TEXT, P20

Line art The classic Bicycle playing card is reinvented in this design. Astonishing detail rendered in clean black-and-white line art renews the traditional symbolism in the cards and adds a rewarding layer of surprise in the inventive details encoded in the familiar motif.

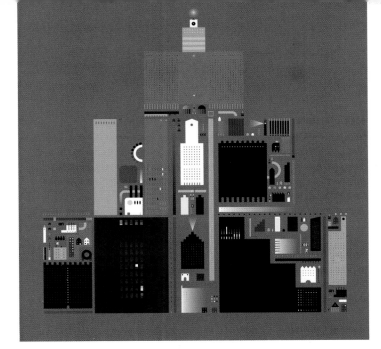

↑ **Vector** Simple shapes can make complex patterns when they are combined in a dynamic composition. These beautifully positioned squares and rectangles create a flattened urban landscape that begs for close inspection.

→ **Background check** Plan your composition, photographic subjects, and text before you photograph your finished subject. Clean, textural slate in neutral gray serves as the perfect backdrop for richly colored images and decorative display type on these menus. Repetition in the composition and variation in type and subject keeps the series inventive.

TIPS AND CHECKLIST FOR SELECTING IMAGES

- **Image, style, and theme** Determine the look before you commit. It's fine to be inspired by images you see in your research, but be sure to resolve the concept before you make a purchase or hire a freelancer.
- **Be contrary** Consider the opposite of what is expected: this will either give you a new angle or help to consolidate your original thoughts.
- **Budget and schedule** Check that your solution is affordable and feasible in the time you have available.
- **Age/gender/socioeconomics of the target audience** Who will see it? The visuals for the horoscope page of a teenage magazine, for example, could certainly be more quirky and abstract than the imagery for a financial company report and accounts.
- **Shelf life** The images in a weekly magazine can be transient, whereas those in an expensive book with a selling potential of ten years or more need to have more lasting resonance.
- **Clarity of information** The images for an editorial design might be deliberately obscure, whereas those for a technical manual must be clear and didactic.
- **Perceived value** This is tricky to pinpoint, since often something that is inexpensive is marketed as valuable through its image, and something that is really expensive can seek to appeal to a mass market through a casual, trendy approach.
- **Design criteria and usage** Do you want a dynamic cut-out shape or a square image bled off the page? Will you use it in black and white or color?

UNIT 2: ASSIGNMENTS

○ BASIC COMPOSITION

This exercise can be done electronically or by hand. Unless you plan to only study web-based design, it is highly recommended that you develop your craft skills and work with traditional media. You can use cut paper, or draw each of the elements with pencil and fill them with black paint, but be precise.

Prepare three white 8-in (20-cm) squares. Using only five black squares positioned within the larger white ones, express the concepts of harmony, chaos, and structure. The black squares can be any size, and you can position them however it feels meaningful to you. Begin by creating 20 thumbnail sketches for each of the three concepts, then select the best one for each final version.

Pay attention to the negative space that is created when you crop squares off the edge of the page or overlap them, and remember that negative space is part of the composition. Think about the effects of symmetry and asymmetry, closure, and field ground as you work.

○ UNDERSTANDING GRIDS

Choose a magazine that you find attractive or compelling and select three different spreads—both right- and left-hand pages. These should include feature editorial spreads and spreads that contain a mixture of multiple images and text.

1 Remove the spreads carefully from the magazine and mount them on boards. Cover each spread with a sheet of tracing paper that will reach from edge to edge.

2 Using a pencil and measuring carefully, identify and trace the grid lines on each of the page designs. Note the column widths and the margins at the top, sides, bottom, and to the left and right of each column. Look carefully for the edges of all the elements placed on the page, some of which may reach over two or three columns, so your lines may cross right through an element on the page. Make sure you look carefully before you draw.

3 When you have finished, identify the system on each page. Is your selection based on a two-column, six-column, or a modular system?

4 Write a brief summary of your findings, and explain why you were attracted to the pages you selected and how you think the grid system supports the design work.

○ PAGE DESIGN

You will need to use a computer to do this exercise, using software that composes pages, such as InDesign or QuarkXPress.

1 Select a short story that you have read in a magazine or in a book and retype the text, including the title and author's name.

2 Develop a simple grid system for a two-page spread, each page 8½ x 11in (21.5 x 28cm), total spread size 11 x 17in (28 x 43cm).

3 Select one typeface, either serif or sans serif, and determine a point size, weight, and leading.

4 Using the same typeface and type presets each time, develop six different dynamic compositions utilizing the same grid system. Remember how symmetry and asymmetry affect composition. Think about placement on the page and test the flexibility of the grid system you have chosen.

5 Repeat the exercise with a more complex grid system and add a photographic subject to each of the compositions.

O DECONSTRUCTING PACE AND CONTRAST

Publication design requires the coordination of carefully placed text and image to lend variety, anticipation, and drama, whether the publication is printed or appears online.

Select a printed magazine, brochure, or book. Identify the design strategies used to vary the pace. How is the white space used? Are there variations in the grid system? Does the placement of type and image vary in size and scale? Is there smart use of contrast and scale? Are certain pages making you pause for a lengthier examination? If so, why?

Now examine an online publication and note the differences and similarities used to set the visual pace as you click through. Can you follow the flow of information? Is there enough variety to keep you interested? Make special note of any tools that might be unique to the online experience.

Further Reading:

Phillip Meggs and Alston W. Purvis, *Meggs' History of Graphic Design*, Wiley, 2011

Steven Heller and Louise Fili, *Stylepedia*, Chronicle Books, 2006

Richard Hollis, *Swiss Design*, Yale, 2006

Timothy Samara, *Making and Breaking the Grid*, Rockport, 2005

Gavin Ambrose and Paul Harris, *Basic Design 07: Grids*, AVA, 2008

Milton Glaser, *Art is Work*, The Elephant's Eye, 2008

Horst Moser, *Surprise Me: Editorial Design*, BATTY, 2003

O EXTENDED SYSTEMS

1 Identify a favorite brand image and examine it closely. Find three examples of the brand used in different applications—for example, printed page, web page, packaging. Make a list of every element that is repeated exactly and of every element that is added to the composition or varied in any way.

2 Select a famous person, fictitious or real, living or dead, and develop a logo for them that reflects their personality. It can be any type of logo you think is appropriate— pictorial, letterform, or abstract. Be sure your logo design can be reduced and enlarged without losing legibility.

3 Design a letterhead and business card that uses the logo in a controlled system. Be sure that the design of the letterhead and card continue to reflect the overall personality of your subject.

4 Add a third element and extend your system. It could be the design of a website, or you might imagine your famous personality has developed a signature product line—for example, clothing, perfume, jewelry, sports equipment. To do this, look carefully at the work you have just completed on the logo, letterhead, and business card. Identify three characteristics that make your system constant on all three designs. Now begin sketching ideas for your third element, using at least two of the three elements, and adding one or more variations.

O PHOTOGRAPHY AND ILLUSTRATION

1 Select a classic novel that you have read and are fairly familiar with. Consider the storyline, the message, and the overall tone of the writing. Make a list of the most influential elements in the novel—for example, characters, circumstances, defining events, time periods. Define the target audience for the novel. Research archival images if you need them and keep them handy as you conceptualize.

2 Sketch three to five ideas that best illustrate your concept for the book's cover. When you have selected the best sketch, begin your final versions by tightening up the composition and clarity of the concept.

3 Develop a more refined version using traditional media—paint, pencil, collage—to determine coloration and value. Consider whether photography or illustration would best suit the concept, or if a combination of both would be most effective.

3 FUNDAMENTALS OF TYPOGRAPHY

Typography is the process of arranging letters, words, and text for almost any context imaginable, and it is among the most important tools a designer masters for effective visual communication. Graphic designers learn the nuances of typography in order to use it creatively, with imagination and a sense of exploration, while maintaining respect for its rules and traditions.

In design, typography is the visual manifestation of language, utilizing all its expressive and practical qualities, and occupies a unique place where art, science, and communications connect. You need only look at work presented by concrete poets, or to various art movements such as Futurism and Dada, to see typography's significance as an aesthetic medium. It also involves the design and selection of type for both legibility and communication of information, and, in some instances, aesthetic experimentation takes a backseat to pragmatic concerns.

Expressive typography and hand-drawn letterforms are a calligraphic art form in their own right With so many interpretative typographic choices, sketching and hands-on experimenting with layouts will help you learn to evaluate the readability and nuance of the message before working onscreen, essential stages that help in learning about the subtleties of type.

New vintage
Hand-drawn letterforms evoke the decorative typography of another century in this beautiful logotype by Tom Lane. The configuration of the letterforms, the overall shape created by the type design, and the selective use of ruled lines for depth and underscoring keep the composition unified. The overall effect is one of tradition and craftsmanship.

PART 1	PRINCIPLES
UNIT 3	FUNDAMENTALS OF TYPOGRAPHY
MODULE 1	**Typography and meaning**

By definition, a typographic message, aside from an intrinsic beauty, must convey a meaning. Meaning, and its expression, is at the core of typographic activity, at the level of both individual words and entire passages of text. This is called linguistic meaning, since it resides in language.

Letters and words have an abstract beauty, seen and appreciated through experiments in type anatomy, which isolate the forms and separate elements of individual letters, and frequently reveal them as shapes, rather than meaningful linguistic objects. However, the instant words materialize on page or on screen, they begin to express ideas and possess this elusive quality we call meaning. Linguistic meaning, an essential element of typography, can be expressed, controlled, and amplified through such typographic variables as size, weight, typeface (or font), placement on the page, and letterspacing.

Sometimes, as in the pages of a book, the visual aspects of typography must take a backseat to the process of understanding. However, designers use such visual techniques all the time, to communicate messages effectively; building confidence in working with text in this way is important, so that linking typographic form to linguistic meaning becomes second nature.

Meaning

But what is "meaning"? An alternative term is "semantics," an important subtopic within all aspects of design, which is worth exploring in more detail. Semantics is the study of meaning and applies to both images and language. "Syntax" (or grammar) refers to the rules that govern the organization of elements of a sentence or paragraph, so that meaning is conveyed. If the syntax is wrong, then language becomes nonsense, or meaningless. In a general sense, to say that something has a meaning (a semantic value) relies upon its ability to present its idea in a form that can be communicated and shared. In linguistic meaning (the language-based meaning that typography participates in), this communicability is based on sets of symbols in the given language, which include letters and words, and also on the space between words, punctuation, and placement of the characters.

Typographers such as Wolfgang Weingart, Willem Sandberg, and H. N. Werkmann pushed the expression of meaning in typography to its very limit and, in so doing, expanded its visual vocabulary and expressive potential by working at the boundary between language and meaning.

Dada and Futurist artists such as Kurt Schwitters and Tristan Tzara, Marinetti, and Wyndham Lewis experimented with the relationship between language and meaning. These historical practitioners are worth studying closely, as are their inspirational typographic experiments. Look at the works of the concrete poets e.e. cummings and Apollinaire, and contemporary designers such as Robert Massin, Johanna Drucker, and Erik Spiekermann. Look at the experimental work of David Carson, who used type as texture in *Ray Gun* magazine, and at Paula Scher's graphic type solutions in poster design and environmental graphics.

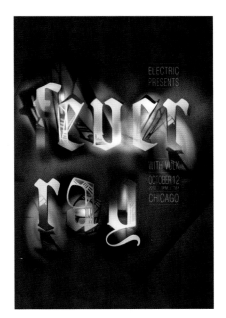

When you look at a city, it's like reading the hopes, aspirations and pride of everyone who built it."
—*Hugh Newell Jacobsen*

⬆ **Word as object** Expressive typography can be used as an image, and the meaning of the words can be linked to the image. Here, the vision of the city is visually expressed by the adjectives that describe it.

⬅ **Constructed letterforms** Dimensional letterforms die-cut with lacy patterns are illuminated to create graphic shadows in the composition. The positive and negative shapes are defined by light and shadow in the delicately half-toned photographic image used in the final poster.

⬋ **Abstract composition** Here, oversized and carefully cropped letters create dynamic abstract forms in a strong composition. Depth is added though variation in scale and texture, and bold color adds to the strong declarative voice.

GLOSSARY

Font: One size, weight, and width of a typeface: Garamond Roman 12pt is a font.

Linguistic: Of, or relating to, language.

Semantics: The study of meaning in language and elsewhere.

Syntax: The study of the rules for the formation of grammatically correct sentences.

Typeface: The set of visual attributes (design or style) of a particular group of letters: Garamond is a typeface.

PART 1	PRINCIPLES
UNIT 3	FUNDAMENTALS OF TYPOGRAPHY
MODULE 2	**The anatomy of type**

Familiarity with the basic structure of letterforms, the anatomy of type, is essential to understanding how typefaces differ and what characteristics they share, and allows the designer to make decisions about selecting and using the multitude of typefaces now available. The most basic element of typography is the letterform, and each typeface has its own unique characteristics, while sharing a basic language that describes its parts.

Common terminology of typefaces includes the size of the x-height, counterform, serif (or sans-) style, and stress of the letter (vertical/oblique). The ability to compare these characteristics between typefaces establishes essential knowledge about the suitability of a particular typeface. By providing valuable information, or "earmarks," about how typefaces relate to classification systems, such as old-style, transitional, humanist, modern, and serif/sans serif, knowledge of type anatomy helps graphic designers to identify and select appropriate typefaces for different purposes.

Technology has accelerated the creation of new faces and produced digital versions of classics. There are so many choices available that selecting an appropriate typeface can be daunting. There are some digital fonts on the market that are of limited use, often downloadable for free. Many don't have much to offer in versatility and lack a timeless quality. An argument can be made that that they do appear different or somewhat experimental, and novelty has its uses in certain circumstances. For general use, especially where readability is a key concern, however, it is better to select classical fonts. Criteria for selection should normally be based on a careful evaluation of the media, the readership, and the design objective.

Key terms
There are over 25 anatomical terms applicable to letterforms. For general typography it's not necessary to know all of them, but some are essential to making visual judgments that aid typeface selection for different situations, and you should be able to describe

Typeface A block of letterpress type, showing the face of the letter, whose surface is inked and printed, giving us the term "typeface." **a** face, **b** body or shank, **c** point size, **d** shoulder, **e** nick, **f** groove, **g** foot.

Oblique, angled stress, associated with old-style typefaces

Semi-oblique stress, associated with transitional typefaces

Vertical stress, associated with modern and sans-serif typefaces

Language of letterforms Each distinct part of a letter has its own name, forming a "language of letterforms."

Identifying characteristics The different stresses of typefaces are essential information in identifying their place within the classification systems, and to locating them within an historical timeline.

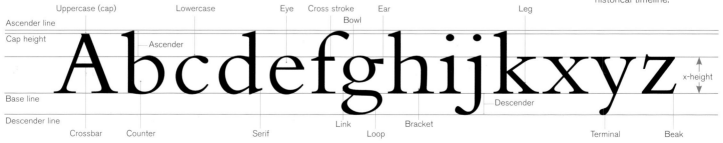

Ascender line · Cap height · Base line · Descender line · Uppercase (cap) · Ascender · Lowercase · Crossbar · Counter · Eye · Cross stroke · Bowl · Serif · Ear · Link · Loop · Bracket · Descender · Leg · Terminal · Beak · x-height

Times New Roman   Bodoni Book   Times New Roman   Bodoni Book

those differences in a technically correct way. For example, you may want to argue for the use of the beautiful 18th-century typeface Bodoni in a particular design. You should be able to state that its characteristics include a vertical stress and a high degree of contrast between thick and thin strokes, and that the humanist quality of the font is appropriate to the readership and message.

Information about the difference between x-heights of typefaces is very helpful, since this allows the designer to choose typefaces that are more or less readable at smaller sizes. The x-height is the size of a lowercase "x" in a given typeface, and the ratio between x-height and the ascenders and descenders of the lowercase letters, such as "g" and "h," define the overall appearance of a font. As with all design decisions, the space around the design elements, type or image, is part of the picture and should be considered. Typefaces that have a large x-height may need more space between the lines (leading), so that they don't appear visually heavy on the page.

Typefaces of the same point size can appear larger or smaller. Futura has a small x-height, and long ascenders/ descenders, whereas most sans-serif typefaces, such as Helvetica, typically have large x-heights. Although a general understanding of the terminology of typefaces is adequate for most designers, if you become interested in designing typefaces you will need to develop an intimate knowledge of type anatomy, in all its nuances, and have an excellent understanding of typeface history and development.

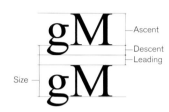

Measuring The point size of type is measured from the baseline of one line of type to the baseline of another. Leading is the vertical space between lines of type, and affects the readability of text.

Impact of x-height The x-height is the height of a lowercase x and determines the visual size of type. The x-height size varies from typeface to typeface: some, like Bodoni, have a small x-height, whereas Times New Roman has a large x-height. However, each type has the same body size. Type with large x-heights tend to have small ascenders and descenders, whereas type with small x-heights have large ones.

Small x-heights
In typefaces with small x-heights, such as Caslon and Futura, there is more white space above and below the lowercase letters. Such type is easier to read, because the eye can travel back and forth along lines without difficulty. Use less leading in these typefaces, or even set them without any additional leading ("solid"), and set them in a larger point size.

Large x-heights
In typefaces with large x-heights, such as Bookman or Helvetica, the lack of white space above and below the lowercase letters, and the larger white spaces within the letters, requires more space between lines. Increase the leading so that text is easier to read, and the overall "color" (another term for density or texture of the type) on the page is less heavy.

GLOSSARY

Baseline: The line on which the lowercase letters sit and below which the descenders fall.

Earmark: Identifying or distinguishing marks or characteristics of a typeface.

Point size/Pica: The relative size of a font. There are 72 points in an inch.

Stress/Axis: The angle of the curved stroke weight change in a typeface. Seen clearly in letters such as "o."

Type anatomy: The language used to describe the various parts of letterforms.

x-height: The height of a lowercase "x" in any typeface.

SEE ALSO: UNDERSTANDING AND SELECTING TYPEFACES, P66

1234567890
1234567890

Numerals Aligning (above, set in Palatino) and non-aligning (or old-style) numbers (below, set in Bembo Expert).

Helvetica   Futura   Bembo

Typefaces of | the same size | look different sizes
| because they | have varying | x-heights |

Bodoni   Bernhard Modern   Times New Roman

PART 1	PRINCIPLES
UNIT 3	FUNDAMENTALS OF TYPOGRAPHY
MODULE 3	**Understanding and selecting typefaces**

Since the introduction of digital typefaces, the number of fonts available has increased exponentially; it is virtually impossible to know them all, or be able to reference all of their attributes. However, it is always advantageous to know a typeface's historical background, since this can help in relating its characteristics to the content of the text. Selecting and understanding typefaces is a complicated business, one that becomes easier with practice.

For example, a sans-serif typeface such as Univers references modernity in a way that a serif font such as Garamond does not. Bodoni, designed in the late 1700s, has certain formal characteristics that, in their own era, were considered modern, including its use of perfectly vertical stress and sharp contrast between thick and thin lines, departing from "old-style" typefaces based on pen-drawn forms. In a modern setting this font is associated with classicism and history. Although it can be used in a contemporary way, it's important to understand Bodoni's history and associations, and to take these into account when considering its use.

Understanding a typeface's historical origins and references, and its associated formal (visual) characteristics, is crucial when it comes to matters of selection. Broadly, contemporary typefaces such as Futura and Univers tend to work in modern contexts, whereas traditional type such as Garamond might be more apt for a literary classic. Of course, all these conventions are there to be played with and broken, but only when you have a full understanding of their significance. Research and read books on graphic design history, since our design past is always influencing the present.

⬆ Newspaper fonts
Sans-serif fonts were first seen in 1786. Shown above is an early use of a sans serif working with serif fonts, in a French newspaper, from 1898. Until this time, all newspaper text and headings were set in serif fonts, and to this day, text setting is usually in serif.

SERIF

oAad
Bembo regular

Humanist Old-Style

Typefaces of the 15th and 16th centuries are based on hand-drawn calligraphic letterforms. They are characterized by having slanted (oblique or diagonal) stress, bracketed serifs, and low contrast between thick and thin strokes. Sabon, designed by Jan Tschichold in 1966, is a contemporary example, based on the 16th-century typeface Garamond.

oAad
Baskerville regular

Transitional

A more vertical axis is visible in these 18th-century typefaces. The sharp contrast between thick and thin strokes was considered controversial at the time. Serifs are still bracketed, but they are moving away from the calligraphic influence. Baskerville is an example of a transitional typeface.

oAad
Bodoni Book

Modern

In the late 18th and early 19th centuries, typefaces became significantly more abstract. Bodoni shows a highly exaggerated contrast between thick and thin strokes, a perfectly vertical stress, and serifs that are no longer bracketed, but straight lines.

oAad
Rockwell regular

Egyptian and Slab Serif

In the early 19th century, in response to the industrial revolution, many new typefaces were designed for use in advertising. Their bold, robust, decorative forms grew from this context. Egyptian typefaces are typical of this period, with their heavy, slab serifs and "industrial" quality.

SANS SERIF

oAad
Gill sans book

Humanist Sans Serif

Sans-serif typefaces originated in the early 19th century but became dominant in the 20th century. Gill Sans, designed in 1928, combined the characteristics of both old-style serif and sans-serif fonts, with its calligraphic qualities but lack of serifs.

oAad
Helvetica regular

Anonymous Sans Serif

Sans-serif fonts were first produced by Caslon in 1816 (in capitals only), and William Thorowgood in 1832 (with lowercase), and they were known as Grotesques, since they were thought to be ugly. Helvetica was designed in 1957 by Max Miedinger, and is one of the best known sans serifs.

oAad
Futura book

Geometric Sans Serif

Typefaces such as Futura (designed by Paul Renner in 1927) are extensions of earlier sans serifs, but have a more geometric design, based on monolines (lines of one thickness, with no variation of thick and thin as in old-styles), perfect circles, and triangular shapes. Such typefaces are associated with Modernism in the early part of the 20th century, but continue to be popular.

Type classification

Before you examine the various factors involved in selecting type, it is worth considering the broad categories into which typefaces can be placed: type classification systems. Categorizing type is never an exact process, and there are many layers to the classification process, but a rough guide can help in distinguishing the characteristics of typefaces and learning the appropriate uses for the various type families. A clear initial division is sometimes made between text and display type, each of which has its own criteria for selection, but there are also faces that function well in both roles.

Text type: old style, transitional, and modern

Primarily, text types are meant to be read in continuous form or at least with few interruptions.

• **Old-style serif typefaces,** such as Bembo, Garamond, and Caslon, are ideal for this purpose. They are regarded as "classic" fonts because they have stood the test of time and still command respect. These Roman fonts have been in use since the origins of printing in the 15th century, and are considered humanist, because the original designs referenced the hand-drawn characteristics of manuscripts. Much later, during the 1930s, a number of new "Romans" were introduced to coincide with the new monotype hot-metal typesetting system and many of the classics were also recut for the same purpose. Times New Roman and Imprint are good examples of this group, known as 20th-century Romans. Later the German type designers Hermann Zapf and Jan Tschichold added, respectively, Palatino and Sabon to this group. Contemporary Romans, such as Minion, have now been designed using digital tools.

• **Transitional Roman fonts** have a vertical stress, sharp and bracketed serifs, and in most cases a medium to high contrast between thick and thin letterstrokes. Baskerville and Century Schoolbook are prime examples. The term captures a movement away from the old-style group, influenced by pen-drawn forms, toward modern faces rooted in geometry rather than the traditional pen stroke.

• **Modern serif faces** also have a vertical stress, but an abrupt contrast between the thick and thin letterstrokes, fine horizontal serifs, and a narrow set width (in most cases). Bodoni is one of the earliest and best-known examples; Walbaum is a slightly more contemporary version of a "modern" typeface.

There are many fonts in these three groups, which cover pretty much all kinds of book work. They can also be found in brochures and magazines, but other groups are more often used for this kind of publication.

Classifying differences Type classification charts are useful guides to the various characteristics (sometimes known as "earmarks") of different typefaces. They allow you to place typefaces within their historical contexts and to see how their basic visual attributes are shared across different, but related, fonts. For example, Romans always have serifs, while sans-serif humanist typefaces such as Gill Sans share properties associated with both old-style Roman and sans-serif typefaces.

Old-style serif faces

ABCabc
Bembo

ABCabc
Garamond

ABCabc
Caslon

ABCabc
Times new roman

ABCabc
Imprint

ABCabc
Palatino

ABCabc
Sabon

ABCabc
Minion

Traditional roman fonts

ABCabc
Baskerville

ABCabc
Century schoolbook

Modern serif faces

ABCabc
Walbaum

ABCabc
Bodoni

Correct fonts

Italic **Bold** SMALL CAPS Condensed Expanded

Pseudo fonts

Italic **Bold** SMALL CAPS Condensed Expanded

Unless you choose a real italic from the font menu, a computer will only slant Roman letterforms

Pseudo bold is simply thickened digitally rather than being the true, carefully crafted font

Small caps are used within lowercase text when smaller, non-dominant capital letters are required. They are used for emphasis within traditional typesetting

Artificially condensed or expanded letterforms should be avoided, since the computer distorts them by applying a percentage reduction or expansion. Always use a "true" condensed or expanded typeface

Display type

Major social changes in the 19th century brought about the need for display type. The Industrial Revolution brought the masses into the cities, increasing production and consumption of goods and services, which led to the need to communicate to a wider audience. Existing fonts were used primarily for books, then limited to an elite sector. Printers found the available typefaces inadequate for the new billboards, posters, and pamphlets produced, especially since there were many more messages being displayed in public spaces, all vying for attention. Bolder, stronger faces were needed to suit this new context, and to meet demand.

The sans-serif typeface was bolder and more "industrial" in its look, along with slab serifs and thickened modern letters known as fat faces. The Victorians were innovative; their typefaces are full of vigor and still fascinate today. John Lewis' book *Printed Ephemera* has excellent examples of Victorian display fonts used on posters and playbills.

Sans-serif and script typefaces

The 20th century saw the extensive development of the sans serif, notably by the Bauhaus school in the 1920s and 1930s. Their philosophy was to sweep away the traditional forms characterized by excessive ornament, employing the principle of "form equals function." Simple typographic structures called for clean, functional typefaces, hence the interest in the sans serif with its mono weight and functional forms. Futura was introduced in 1927, and two years later Gill Sans was unveiled. In the decades that followed, well-known fonts such as Helvetica and Optima in Europe, and Franklin Gothic and Avant Garde in the USA, kept the sans serif among the most popular of type styles.

A significant advantage of the sans serif is the large number of potential variants within one typeface. In 1957 Adrian Frutiger introduced a complete family of different weights and forms when he conceived the design of Univers, which comprises 21 variants ranging from light condensed to bold expanded.

⬆ **New again** This poster design uses Baskerville in a contemporary way, eliminating the formality of the original design and creating texture and depth using the descriptive words that define the Old Style font (see page 68).

Stone Sans Semibold
Stone Sans Medium

This intro type is set in Stone Serif Semibold, this intro type is set in Stone Serif Semibold

This body type is set in Stone Serif Medium. Designed in 1987, the Stone family consists of three types of font—a serif, a sans-serif, and an informal style—all designed to work together. The styles are legible, modern, and dynamic, combining the old with the new. The Stone fonts integrate perfectly with each other, giving the typeface a wide range of design applications.

⬅ **Perfect harmony** Type designers have recently produced serif and sans-serif versions of the same typeface—for example, Officina and Stone. The advantage is that you can use a serif for the text setting and a sans for the display, and they will harmonize perfectly because they have been specifically designed to work together.

⬆ **Elegant letterforms** In this example, beautifully formed mixed serif and sans-serif letters are centered on each page composition in this promotion for *U&lc* magazine.

Experimental type *Emigre* magazine was published between 1984 and 2005. Only 69 issues were produced, but the impact of the experimental design and innovative use of typography are still impacting contemporary design. *Emigre* was among the first to champion digital typography and was one of the first publications to recognize the impact of the personal computer on the discipline of graphic design.

Inspiration before and after Iconic graphic designer Paula Scher's Best of Jazz poster for CBS Records in 1979 shows the influence of constructivism and the beginnings of her own influence on the contemporary use of type as image. Recommended reading: *Make it Bigger* by Paula Scher (2002).

Custom typography Master typographer John Langdon styled this custom lettering for a heavy-metal band. The designer cited the influence of Century for its classic formality. Designing custom letterforms requires excellent knowledge of typefaces and letterform construction. Work your way up to it, and reference existing fonts when you begin.

Hand made Logo and type-design legend Gerard Huerta hand crafted custom letterforms that connect with elaborate swashes and cartouches, creating a beautifully decorative emblem for the *Cigar Collector's Guide & Journal*.

Selecting fonts

The content of the material and the purpose of the design are the main factors in deciding your choice of font. Design clarity is essential in information dissemination, and it is telling that sans-serif types such as Interstate, with their simple mono-weight structures, are designed to maximize readability for highway signage. Sans serif is also ideal for small notation in diagrams, captions, and maps. The font Arial is one of the most widely used for onscreen and web, and arrives pre-installed in most computers.

- Font choice can be influenced by subject matter, and knowledge of the font origins might help in the final decision; for example, Caslon and Baskerville are classical English, Garamond is French, Goudy American, Bodoni Italian, and so on.
- Publication design can be more adventurous, because magazine readers tend to jump in and out of the text rather than reading from cover to cover. With small segments of copy, unusual fonts can sometimes bring freshness to the overall feeling of the design. However, it's wise not to mix too many fonts together in one design.
- Display types offer much more variety than text types because their purpose is expression rather than readability, so you can engage in playful experimentation in your headline design.
- Sans-serif and slab-serif faces are seen as more authoritative and bolder than typefaces that are designed for reading over long periods. If you are reversing out type or printing tints in small sizes, sans serifs are a good bet. For elegance, serifs have the advantage of tradition.

⊕ **SEE ALSO:** THE ANATOMY OF TYPE, P64

➡ **Opposites attract**
Design Bridge used contrasting fonts to reflect the subject content in their self-promotion book *25 Stories*.

⬅ **Simplicity rules**
The development of the logo for New York's Public Theater, and the sophisticated simplicity of the sans-serif type on the theater's promotional materials, show the influence of old wood type in different weights. Designer Paula Scher developed a typographic style that defined the theater for years to come. For Sam Shepard's play *Simpatico*, 1994, a staircase of condensed letterforms easily brings the eye up and down through the composition.

Sans serif: Without serif. Typefaces such as Univers, Helvetica, Aksidenz Grotesque, and Futura, characterized by their lack of serifs. Predominantly associated with the 19th/20th centuries.

Serif: Structural details at the ends of some strokes in old-style capital and lowercase letters.

45 Light

45 Light italic

47 Condensed light

47 Condensed light italic

55 Regular

55 Regular italic

57 Condensed

57 Condensed italic

65 Bold

65 Bold italic

67 Condensed bold

67 Condensed bold italic

75 Black

75 Black italic

Extended

Extended italic

Ultra condensed

Bold extended

Bold extended italic

Extra black

Extra black extended

Extra black extended italic

Univers Designed by Adrian Frutiger in 1954, Univers is a modular system, with 44 numbered typefaces in various weights, widths, and oblique versions. This flexibility makes the font ideal for incorporating many differing levels of information within a design. It's interesting to compare the slight but important differences with other sans-serif typefaces such as Helvetica. You should learn to observe the fine distinctions when choosing between one sans serif and another.

INLAND EMPIRE

DAVID LYNCH
DOWN THE RABBIT HOLE...

Clarity Well-chosen fonts for the body text can support the message it delivers. Here, a rigid column of justified, sans-serif text offers descriptive support to the direct and unblinking works of Gilbert and George.

Fluid Serif type in long columns of uneven lengths seems to drift down the page in concert with hazy watercolor-hued images in an article about filmmaker David Lynch, titled *Down the Rabbit Hole*.

PART 1	PRINCIPLES
UNIT 3	FUNDAMENTALS OF TYPOGRAPHY
MODULE 4	**Spacing**

Understanding how to deal with space in typography is essential. Proper spacing affects legibility, and space is also an integral and powerful part of any composition, whether symmetrical or asymmetrical. Develop an eye for detail, and consider the role of space in both legibility and meaning as you progress at every stage of the design development.

In most cases, the designs you produce will consist of a mixture of images and copy in the form of either headings (display type) or main copy (text). Display type ranges in size from 14pt and upward, whereas the main text (also referred to as body copy or body text) generally falls between 8 and 14pt. As you design, important choices will need to be made regarding typefaces, sizes, and measure (width of line). You will also need to decide about spacing (letter, word, and line) and, later, adjustments will need to be made by eye, even if the tool is a computer. There is no automated function on any computer that can replace the keen eye of an experienced designer.

Letterspacing

When you keystroke or import text from a file, a computer sets the type at default space settings, both between individual letters (letterspace) and between lines of type (leading). The computer doesn't make the fine-tuning decisions that a designer must. If your type is too close together, with the letters almost touching, the letterspacing needs to be adjusted (called kerning). If they are too far apart, individual word shapes break down and legibility is compromised. One of the most common mistakes that new designers make is to set their text either too closely or too widely, or to accept the computer's spacing decisions. Designers need to learn as much as possible about the ways in which leading affects readability and impacts on the overall texture, sometimes called "tone," of the text on the page.

Extra or negative letterspace can be inserted to customize and reinforce a particular idea, but these are the exceptions and need to be carefully considered. Type designers for software programs are careful to produce settings for good visual spacing between letters at different sizes. However, never take this for granted. For instance, condensed typefaces should always be treated cautiously, as should those set in justified measures: in these cases, small additions or subtractions can improve the evenness of spacing, or allow a word to be taken into a line to avoid widows or orphans (single words from the end of a paragraph left at the end or beginning of a column of text).

Design objectives

The main aim in display and text type is to try to achieve visual evenness throughout a series of characters. Consistency is important, because readers interpret shapes of words rather than individual letters. If there is unevenness in letterspacing, the eye can be distracted by the space rather than seeing the words. You can test the importance of even letterspacing by

↑ Delicate balance
Dramatic display and body text keeps the correct visual balance in letterspacing, even when there are dramatic changes in scale. Note the carefully managed spacing within the display text where the point sizes change, and look closely for the beautiful h2a agency letterform logo.

⊕ SEE ALSO: THE ANATOMY OF TYPE, P64

READABILITY AND LEGIBILITY, P76

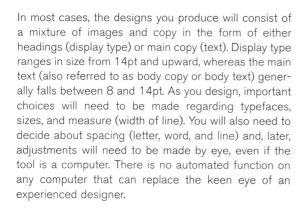

The lowercase i i is a good guide

Word spacing is traditionally based upon a space equivalent to the body width of a lowercase "i."

setting text with different spacing, including altering it within the same line. As type size increases the unevenness can worsen, requiring the designer to make optical adjustments. This problem is prevalent with capital letters, because they fit together in complicated ways because of their inherent forms. Characters with straight stems such as "I," "J," "E," and "F," when placed together, require more space between individual letters than those with rounded shapes, like "O" and "Q," or those with diagonal strokes, such as "A," "V," "Y," and "W." Letters in certain words may need adjusted spacing to compensate for the reduced space between characters, such as "A" and "V." This is because the letters occupy different amounts of space, having varied widths.

Kerning allows for individual reductions or incremental increases to the letterspacing, whereas tracking increases or reduces space between words. Always trust your eyes.

⊕ Type in motion Paula Scher's 1996 iconic poster design for New York City's Public Theater is a masterful example of text management that redefined designing with type for a generation of graphic designers. The movement of the dancer is embodied in the placement of the letterforms, creating enormous energy while managing a huge amount of information at the same time. Note the use of a controlled palette to assist the hierarchy.

⊕ Kern your caps Kerning is the process of optically adjusting the space between (mostly capital) letters, so that they appear evenly spaced.

These upright letters appear much tighter visually than the rounded letters below

Rounded shapes give the illusion of more space between each letterform

The word "AVID" has been set with InDesign metrics auto kerning; the same word below has been adjusted by eye to visually even out the letterspacing.

Word spacing

In display type, one way to gauge the amount of space to leave between words is the width of a lowercase "i," but it will depend on the design sensibility. In some fonts, more than an "i" space will exacerbate difficulties in reading.

Word spacing in text type also needs careful scrutiny, and typesetting style plays an important part. There are two basic setting styles for continuous reading: justified and ranged (or ragged) left. With justified setting, word spacing will vary because words are pushed out to fill the requirements of the measure. Space between words can become excessive, particularly if the chosen measure is too small or the typeface too large. Hyphenation (word breaks) can be adjusted to even out word spacing as far as possible, but justified setting is always tricky unless type size in relation to set measure is carefully considered. Setting justified text on a short measure with many long words is especially difficult, since fewer words end up on a line. This often occurs in newspapers.

With ranged-left setting, you have the advantage of being able to space words consistently. Many designers prefer this style for obvious reasons, although problems of legibility can still arise and ragging text (lines that jut out farther than others causing unevenness) becomes a major issue. Type style also plays an important part in

word spacing. Percentage adjustments can be made within the hyphenation and justification (H and J) settings of electronic page-layout programs, to accommodate closer or wider word spacing depending on the width of character of the typeface. In general, ranged-left setting should not be hyphenated, except sometimes for shorter column widths; otherwise you can end up with lines of uneven length.

⬇ **H and Js** Hyphenation and justification can be fine-tuned manually, giving an excellent level of control; here the dialog boxes from InDesign are shown.

Changes space between words

Changes space between letters

Applies horizontal scaling to characters

Enter values to control how words are hyphenated

Amount of white space at the end of a non-justified line

Controls a single word occupying a line

How many consecutive lines can be hyphenated

JUSTIFICATION OPTIONS

1. No H and J This justified setting has no word breaks. You can easily see the problem of excessive word spacing, which causes rivers of space to form.

2. Hyphenation Using hyphens can help to reduce the problem of excessive word spacing, but don't hyphenate too often in a block of text.

3. Unjustified Excessive word spacing can be made to disappear with the ranged-left style of setting. With no word breaks you can shorten lines, giving a ragged look.

1. With justified setting—that is, alignment on both the right and left of the measure—the word spacing will vary because words are pushed out to fulfill the requirements of the measure. Herein lies the problem. The space can become excessive, particularly if the chosen measure is too small or the typeface too large. The result is often bad word spacing, which can cause "rivers" of space to run down the page.

2. Hyphenation can be adjusted to even out the word spacing as far as possible and avoid ugly spacing. Hyphenation specifications are sets of automatic hyphenation rules that you can create and apply to paragraphs. You can specifiy the smallest number of characters that must precede an automatic hyphen (the default is 3), and the minimum number of characters that must follow an automatic hyphen (the default is 2). These controls do not affect manual hyphenation.

3. With ranged-left setting you have the decided advantage of being able to space words consistently—the inherent difficulties of justified text can be avoided. For this reason, many designers prefer this style, though problems of legibility can still arise. As mentioned earlier, style of type also plays an important part in the amount of word spacing to have. Percentage adjustments can be made within hyphenation and justification (H and J).

Leading

This term derives from "hot-metal" typesetting, where strips of lead were placed between lines of type, and it refers to the amount of horizontal spacing between lines of type. In display type, the designer will invariably have to adjust individual lines and not just rely on a constant setting. Each line of type is spaced differently, according to need. The role of leading becomes particularly important when setting large areas of text, notably in books. There are no clear rules regarding the adjustments of line spacing for display matter; it is a matter of skill in developing an even look and in letting your eye be your guide. Every time you use display type, analyze each case individually. For example, designers sometimes use negative leading (in which the leading has a lower numerical value than the type size). This can be effective in giving a dynamic visual appearance, but should be used with care.

All type settings are enhanced by the careful consideration of leading. Factors such as x-height, measure, and weight of typeface will all influence the amount of leading you should employ.

① Left versus right
Ranged-right text is considered harder to read than ranged-left text, because the eye travels to the end of the line and seeks a consistent location for the beginning of the next line. If the lines (on the left) are uneven, it's more difficult to do this.

➔ Artful rag The abstract patterns made by controlled ragged type are used as design elements in this experimental page design. The hierarchy remains clear, despite the activity of the page division.

RAGGING TEXT

Creating ragging text, which is ranged left, takes time, practice, and patience. The key is to create a "soft" right-hand edge to the type, by bringing words down onto the following lines, and avoiding making harsh, obvious shapes—such as sharp diagonals—at the right edge of the text that distract the eye. A tried-and-true rule of thumb is to alternate longer and shorter lines. Avoid putting in hyphenation to solve ragging issues; it is better to work with the natural flow of the words in the copy and only break where it's absolutely necessary.

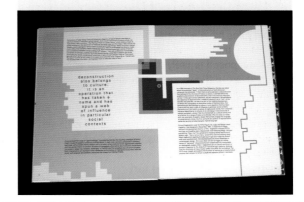

X-HEIGHTS AND READABILITY

Helvetica Medium, designed in 1957 by Max Miedinger, a Swiss type designer, is a sans-serif typeface that has a relatively large x-height in relation to its ascenders and descenders. This means that when setting text in this font you may need to add extra leading (space between the lines) to ensure maximum readability.

Set in 8pt, with 4 points of leading, or 8/12pt.

The same size of type in Futura Medium, designed in the mid-1920s by Paul Renner and based on simple geometric forms, has a relatively small x-height for a sans-serif typeface. However, its long ascenders and descenders (see the "l" and the "y") mean that when setting text in this font you may need to add extra leading to ensure maximum readability.

Set in 8pt, with 4 points of leading, or 8/12pt.

This text is set in the same size of type, in the transitional serif typeface Times New Roman, designed specifically for *The Times* newspaper in 1931, by Stanley Morison. It has a smaller x-height in relation to its ascenders and descenders, and therefore an overall smaller appearance on the page, needing less leading.

Set in 8pt, with 3 points of leading, or 8/11pt.

The same size of type in the old-style typeface Bembo, originally cut by Francesco Griffo in 1496, has an even smaller x-height, although it is in the same size as before. This means that when setting text in this font you may want to reduce the space between the lines to ensure maximum readability. This typeface also looks less visually dense when set as text on the page, because the weight of its strokes is less heavy.

Set in 8pt, with 2 points of leading, or 8/10pt.

PART 1	PRINCIPLES
UNIT 3	FUNDAMENTALS OF TYPOGRAPHY
MODULE 5	**Readability and legibility**

Debate continues between traditionalists and modernists as to whether sans-serif typefaces are more or less legible than serif faces. Traditionalists argue that serifs aid legibility by helping to differentiate letterforms, factors that keep the eye moving along the horizontal line. However, modernists argue that sans serifs do not really decrease legibility; it is just a question of readers becoming culturally acclimatized to the sans-serif face, historically a much more recent phenomenon aided by electronic devices.

Certain rules have evolved about setting type and using letterforms that still apply. One rule is that long passages composed entirely of either capital letters or very bold text are difficult to read. Multiple capitals can be difficult to read because the words have similar visual shapes or outlines and all are the same height. Ascenders and descenders in capital and lowercase settings aid in the differentiation between words.

Justified versus ranged left
Another perennially hot topic is the relative virtues of justified and ranged-left settings. Justified text may be no easier to follow than lines ranged left. Ranged-right settings force the reader to search for the beginning of each line, which can get very annoying over long passages

and should generally be avoided. If you are reversing type out of black or a color, then a sans-serif typeface might be a safer option than the alternative, with its finer lines and serifs. Of course, much will depend on the size of type, choice of color, and quality of paper or media.

Between 60 and 72 characters per line (on any given measure) is the best number for optimum readability. However, these parameters will change according to type size. When lines are too long, the eye loses its place; too short and the reader will become distracted by the constant returning to the start of a new line. The text throughout these paragraphs is set in Berthold Akzidenz Grotesk at 9 points, with a leading measure of 11 points.

➡ Contrast Serif and sans-serif fonts can be used successfully in the same system. Sans serif is used here to emphasize the difference between the call-out and the body text, and is used again to highlight and separate the captions. Note that all of the selected typefaces are well proportioned, with the weights relatively balanced to keep the system elegantly consistent.

Justified: Lines or paragraphs of type aligned to both margins simultaneously, creating different spacing in between words.

Measure: The length of a line of text on a page, based in inches, centimeters, points, or picas.

Ranged left: Paragraphs or lines of text aligned to the left-hand side margin.

Ranged right: Paragraphs or lines of text aligned to the right-hand side margin.

⬅ Systems A change in the typographic styling can be used as a navigation device that separates elements in the extended system: pagination, captions, body text, and in this case, evocative display type used as part of the photographic image, all have distinct styles that work together.

➕ SEE ALSO:
UNDERSTANDING AND SELECTING TYPEFACES, P66

SPACING, P72

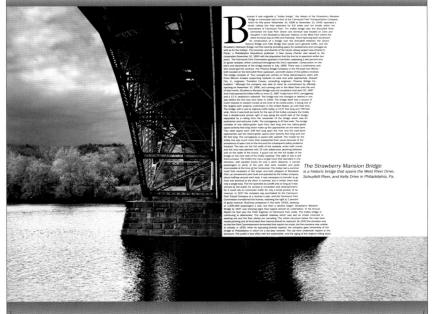

Structure and shape Justified type can be used decoratively, but the lines and the H & Js need to be managed line by line, as does the tracking and kerning on each word. When it's done correctly, the results can be a stunning integration of type and image. Choose a typeface that is easy to read, in this case a clean sans serif, and manage your paragraph breaks carefully to avoid widows.

KEY FEATURES: READABILITY

Measure (line length), type size, and leading (spacing between lines) work in concert and affect readability.

- We have established that the optimum number of characters per line is between 60 and 72. Any more and the eye has problems picking up the next line; fewer characters per line can interrupt reading flow. Of course, the needs of different design types will influence these decisions; in fact, context is everything. In magazines, measures tend to be shorter because readers dip into articles rather than reading from cover to cover. Novels, which have to satisfy a criterion of continuous reading, look very different to advertisements, where immediate impact is a primary concern. Indeed, it is a useful exercise to ask why certain publications—newspapers, timetables, cookbooks, etc.—differ in their standards of readability depending on their function.
- Choice of type size and measure also depends on the amount of copy. Readers can cope with small amounts if the setting is smaller or on a narrower measure than the recommended optimum.
- Leading is a major element in readability. If there is insufficient space between lines, the eye will be hampered from moving smoothly to the next line. Increased leading is also required if the typeface is condensed, or if a serif typeface with a heavy or bold characteristic is being used.
- Typefaces with large x-heights have reduced ascenders and descenders, resulting in less differentiation in word shapes. Therefore, these typefaces need to have more leading.

PART 1	PRINCIPLES
UNIT 3	FUNDAMENTALS OF TYPOGRAPHY
MODULE 6	**Typographic emphasis and hierarchy**

Knowing how to solve problems of emphasis using type is a critical skill. This involves considering the relationship between multiple elements—the size and weight of type, the position on the page, and the dynamic between elements—as well as developing an understanding of how these decisions call forth some contents while suppressing others. These kinds of typographic decisions relate to what are called hierarchies of information, since in any design, some things will need to be read first, with secondary information to follow.

Before starting any design, it is crucial to understand where the main points of emphasis fall in terms of headings, subheadings, intro copy, captions, quotes, and so on. These levels of importance are called hierarchies. Once established, hierarchies can be indicated in various ways: by space, weight, color, and form.

- **Adding vertical "white" space** in the form of a one-line or half-line space above or below a heading, separating it from the surrounding elements, creates emphasis.
- **The density of black ink** creates its own visual emphasis. Sans-serif typefaces, such as Univers, are good for this because they typically have various weight combinations you can use: light with bold, medium with extra bold, and so on. Bear in mind that a smaller size of bold type is visually "heavier" than a larger size of regular-weight type.
- **Changing the typestyle** is a third method—switching from roman to italics, for example. Italics add informality and movement to a design and are also effective for highlighting key phrases within text. Because of their more delicate form, you will probably need to increase the size proportionally for readability where needed.
- **Changing some lowercase to capitals** can add formality to a design. Capitals need more letterspacing, and so consume more space, though

you don't have the problem of ascenders clashing with descenders. Small capitals provide an even more subtle shift of emphasis.

The power of contrast
Other techniques involving the use of contrast can be applied to add emphasis effectively.

- **Contrasting condensed with extended type** can be effective, but use it sparingly with short, concise headlines. Remember that condensed type requires more leading, and that expanded type pushes out the length of the copy. Simple, effective paragraph styling adds emphasis, too, such as indents at the start of paragraphs or sections.
- **Color is a valuable tool** and type does not have to be black and white to create contrast. Make sure that you have tested ink color on the stock color if you are printing. Transparent inks can compromise readability, and colors too close together in value or hue will not work. Colors with complementary values, such as red and green, can cause type to vibrate. When adding delicate color to type, consider using a typeface with more weight, and provide a larger area of color. Experiment with reversing out type or adding rules to draw attention to parts of the text.
- **Changing type size or weight** is a popular option. Again, when using shifts of size for emphasis,

🔄 **Whispers and shouts**
The delicate serifs chosen for the brand's name complement the graceful illustration of a blackbird. The stacked and centered typography, the careful mixture of caps and lower case in serif and sans-serif fonts, and screened back color stand apart like a wine label on a bottle.

Contrast: The difference between elements, which allows for comparison and emphasis. Contrast is closely related to hierarchy, since it allows different levels of information to be identified.

Hierarchy: In this context, the name for differing levels of text in a document. A page title, for example, is at the top of the hierarchy, whereas paragraphs of text are below.

➕ **SEE ALSO:** SPACING, P72

ensure that there is a substantial difference between the main text and the heading. If the sizes are too close, then the point is not well made. The difference in size has to be great enough to make the point.

Less is more

Try not to have too many means of emphasis going on at once. Too many techniques in one place will confuse the eye and detract, rather than add, to the concept. "Less is more" is often a good principle when trying to work through problems of emphasis and hierarchy. Don't overstate your points by setting type in a large point size, bold, italics, underlined, and at an angle. With computers, it is easy to change things, and you need to be disciplined to avoid creating a mishmash of weights, sizes, forms, and indents. Resist the temptation to use all your techniques at once—and remember, you do not always have to shout to be heard.

⬆ Customize and complement
A slight parting in the negative space at the base of the logo's double letter "l" is just enough to express the root-to-tip promise of swell haircare products, designed by Aloof. Keeping the rest of the type clean and simple allows the subtlety of the logo to shine and stays true to the brand.

ANATOMY OF A PAGE

Work with your copywriter and your client to assign the page hierarchy before you begin your design work. If you have a system that repeats formats, as in book design, be sure to stay consistent in assigning fonts and weights to your style sheets.

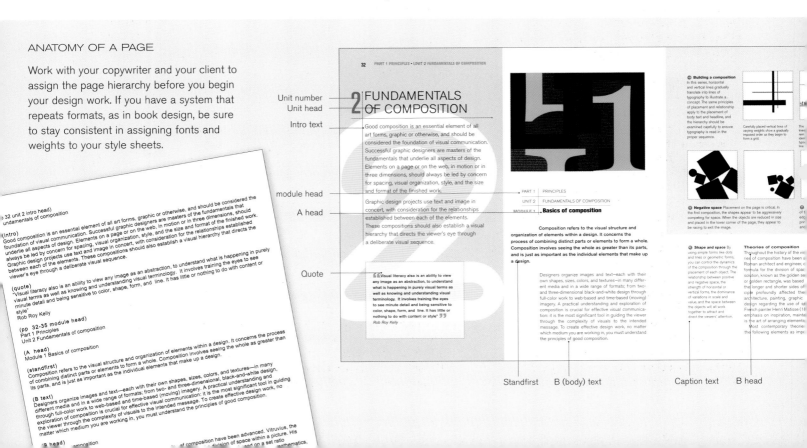

Type size

Your choice of font, weight of heading, or amount of leading all depend on other decisions you have made. The same is true of type size: point size is an absolute measure of how big type is, but remember the same-sized type can look very different depending on other factors—the amount of space around it, the relative size of the text copy, the weight of font used, and so on. The central point about increasing type size is that it works as a strong form of emphasis, providing a focal point that attracts the reader's attention.

Headings

Once agreement has been reached about the different levels of importance in the main text, they need to be translated into appropriate sizes and a format for the document should be designed. If headings are of varying levels of importance, try to make sure they are visually segregated.

There are numerous ways in which you can play with headings to improve the visual feel of a design.

- Breaking a line or word into different parts, or using alternating sizes with a heading, can look dynamic. For example, articles and conjunctions ("a," "the," "and," "or") could be made smaller to give important words more stress.
- The logotypes of magazines (known as mastheads), billboards, newspaper headlines, and posters are all working to catch people's attention in a short time span, so they often need to have large, well-differentiated typography to communicate effectively and quickly. Books, on the other hand, work on a slower timetable and their typographic presentation can be subtle.

⊙ **Size variations** A sidebar accommodates a pull quote set in oversize text. The hierarchy is tightly controlled by the use of black text on a nearly black background, effectively making the quote function as background information, but preserving the readability because of the size and weight.

⊙ **Titling components** Assigning importance to the components of the titling in this article adds interest. It also allowed the designer to keep the height of the word cluster equal to the height of the short columns, creating a "sight line" to the image of the eye.

⊙ **Sizing**

If you think it should be 10pt, make it 9. It's often the case that when we try to differentiate and create hierarchies through type, we overemphasize the importance of size. Try to use space and position before enlarging the size of your type. Depending on your client, market, and product, keep the type slightly smaller than you think it should be until you have become really familiar with the details of your favorite fonts.

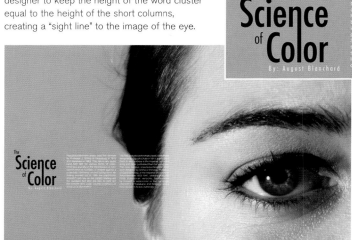

Title 46pt
Subtitle 28pt
Subhead 18pt

Text   10pt

caption   8pt

Title, sans serif, all caps, condensed

Navigation bar, lower case, serif

Subject headlines, caps, sans-serif condensed

Body text, serif

Subject headlines, caps, sans serif, color change

Body text in two columns

⬆ Number series Some typographers determine a hierarchy of sizes by using a Fibonacci series, in which each number is the sum of the preceding two. This may result in a sequence such as 8, 10, 18, 28, 46 or 8, 12, 20, 32, 52. Do the math if you like, but trust your sense of proportion and be true to the content.

➡ Establish a hierarchy Choose a font family that gives you plenty of options such as light, book, medium, bold, and Xtrabold weights, and good italics and numerals. Keep your choices limited to one to three fonts per layout.

⬇ Call-outs and pull quotes Both are used effectively to add emphasis to highlighted sections of the content in this architecturally styled page design. On the right-hand page, the emphasized phrase forms a bridge across the gutter, linking the two columns inventively, but maintaining the separation from the body text.

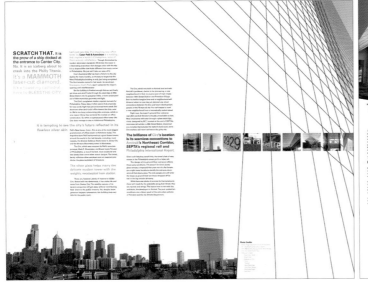

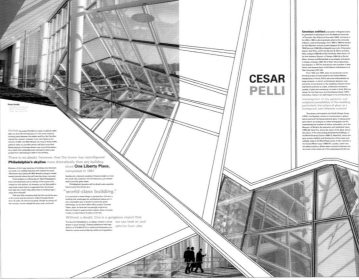

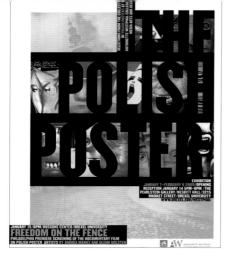

Typographic rules (lines) and ornaments have been inherited from the letterpress tradition of setting and arranging type matter. They are still invaluable to the designer today because they serve both functional and aesthetic roles.

Poetica

◀ **Confine** Heavy dividing bars bleeding into the headline letters create a strong sense of confinement. The message is reinforced by hints of the posters in the actual exhibition, effectively behind the bars of type, in this evocative poster.

Rules draw attention to specific parts of copy and break it into sections. Vertical rules can be used to separate blocks of text when other means of division are neither possible nor sufficient.

Generally, the weight (thickness) of the rules should match the tonal value of the text to which they relate. Horizontal rules work well for organizing information and aiding readability. Examples can be found in tabular matter, such as timetables and contents pages, and sometimes between columns of text in newspapers and/ or in books, where they can be used between each entry and to help direct the eye from item to page number.

Highlighting text—rules and panels

Rules have gained in popularity since computer commands can underline a word or words. Some designers argue that there are more subtle means available if you want to emphasize typographic elements. Nevertheless, rules can be effectively used to highlight a piece of copy by placing them in the margin alongside the text, or as a dynamic component in the composition of a design. Widths available range from a ½-pt (hairline) rule upward, and are often measured in points, so that we might use a 1pt or 2pt rule.

Tinted, outlined, or solid-colored panels are popular in magazines for their ability to provide in-depth focus on a particular editorial theme, while relieving the eye from the potential strain caused by reading column after

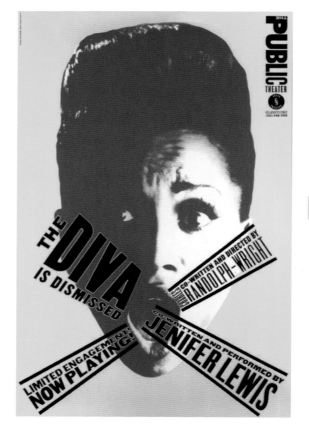

◀ **Exclaim** Paula Scher used matched weights of rules above and below each copy point to house each one in radiating shapes of near equal size. Note the control of the hierarchy through the point sizes and weights.

⊕ **SEE ALSO:** TYPOGRAPHIC EMPHASIS AND HIERARCHY, P78

zapf dingbats

Construct Powerful words in tightly fitted boxes add sharp diagonals to this composition, and build an interlocked urban landscape of image and text.

Poetica

column of main text type in a single size. These "side-bars" are most effective when they contain supplementary information and are used to distinguish separate content. However, rules and boxes can easily overtake a design, particularly when they are used "decoratively" rather than functionally.

Rules in display type

In display setting, rules can create emphasis by drawing attention. The Constructivist art movement in early 20th-century Russia pioneered the use of rules in this way. Very heavy rules were used, running alongside, or at angles to, the copy. The popularity of the rule is still evident in today's designs.

Ornaments

Ornaments have been in use since the origin of printing. They give a decorative feel to a layout and invoke a sense of tradition. They can also separate information, as in the title pages of traditional books. Zapf Dingbats is a well-known digital font made up of ornaments, as is Whirligig, by Zuzana Licko. However, as with rules and boxes or sidebars, overuse of ornaments should generally be avoided. If your content is unique, invent your own ornaments, icons, or embellishments to enhance your type design and stay constant with your concept.

Decorate Printer's flowers and dingbats can be incorporated into a design system with great effect. The exuberance of these pages owes much to the enlarged ornaments that separate sections of information.

Punctuate The classic forms that serve as punctuation and ornament are celebrated as design elements in their own right. Given dimension and scale, they become the beautiful subjects of this article.

Wingdings

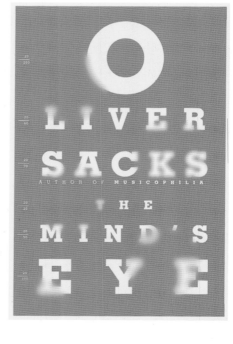

PART 1	PRINCIPLES
UNIT 3	FUNDAMENTALS OF TYPOGRAPHY
MODULE 8	**Text as image**

Contemporary designers know that type not only communicates specific meaning, but also possesses aesthetically powerful characteristics in its own right. If you think about how many expressive fonts are now available, and the way in which one can apply color, weight, form, and spacing to customize and achieve specific effects, it is possible to see type functioning as an image in its own right.

Illustrative, photographic, calligraphic, and shaped text are further variations that add excitement to a design and effectively convey the mood and concept. Working with text as image requires an understanding of both the communicative and aesthetic properties of typography, and beautiful, illustrative typographic artworks are considered a collectable art form as well as a form of visual communication.

Display type
Display type is chosen, in part, for mood, and each face has its own characteristics. Just as an artist can create mood through illustration, so can a typographer subtly illustrate meaning by choice of font, type size, and weight. This effect of typography is normally seen at its fullest potential when type is used for display (above a certain size, for example 14pt), since smaller type is meant for reading. Display type exploits the specific characteristics of a given typeface.

Symbolization
Designers can exploit the familiarity of type by carefully manipulating suggestive letterforms so that they become images in their own right. This means that type can actually stand in for objects. Conversely, objects that resemble images can replace letters.

Form matching content
Techniques for using type as illustration are numerous and transcend type as simple objects and vice versa. Certain words, such as verbs indicating action, particularly lend themselves to typography reflecting meaning. There can be word repetition; overlapping of characters; distorting characters to break them up, blur, or roughen them; outlining or shadowing type; setting type along a curved path or in a circle; adjusting color, weight, or form; and so on. To be effective, however, positions and forms in type arrangement must reflect meaning and, as always, try to avoid clichés.

To be used effectively, our Latin alphabet, composed basically of straight lines, circles, and part circles, has to be resourcefully manipulated. The decorative nature of shaped text transforms reading into a visual experience, and advertising and logotype design frequently use these techniques to give text enhanced visual impact to convey a specific message.

⊙ Intelligent design
This design concept by book designer Chip Kidd uses a recognizable typographic arrangement with a twist to illustrate points made by the author, Dr. Oliver Sacks. The book examines how the visual cortex processes visual information. The title was designed to evoke an eye-chart, then key areas were blurred in Photoshop.

GLOSSARY

Onomatopoeia: In typography, the use of type to suggest the sounds of a spoken language, such as adding a large "o" to the word "open." Marinetti and the Futurists were effective in employing onomatopoeia, in the design of books such as *Zang Tumb Tumb.*

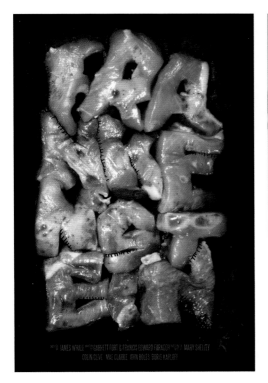

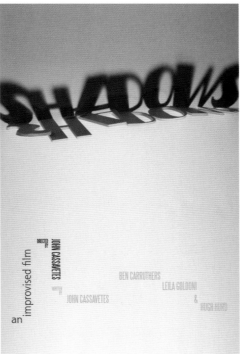

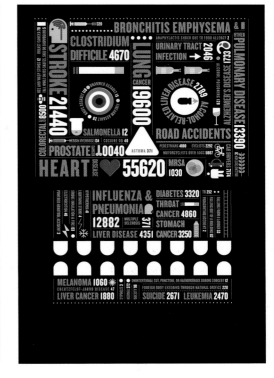

⬆ **Interpretive typography** In repackaging a classic tale of horror, the designer used raw chicken meat stitched together with thick twine and photographed the title for *Frankenstein*, bringing content into the concept and, in this case, to the process. Support text was added to the final image. A black-and-white half-tone minimizes the gore and sets the image in an earlier time period.

⬆ **Media as message** Paper letters are edge lit and photographed to express the title word of the film: *Shadows*. Letters can be constructed out of different media, reconstructed from found objects, or hand painted to become illustrations.

⬆ **Information is beautiful** Peter Grundy's witty commentary on the statistics of death for *Men's Health* magazine arranges lines of type into a grinning and winking skull. Masterful scale management and excellent spatial relationships keep the illustration balanced and evenly colored, and establish the headline hierarchy by the highest numbers.

⬅ **Found object design** With a bit of imagination, letterform shapes can be found in everyday objects and pressed into service. In "Beauty," the objects that help us define the standard spell out the word. They can be photographed, solar-printed, or hand drawn.

DESIGN HISTORY

Having a good knowledge of design history enables you to pursue type-as-image concepts in a more informed way. Look at the work of Josef Müller-Brockmann, H. N. Werkman, and Philippe Apeloig. Also, see examples of calligraphy and shaped text throughout history, and you will see how typographers, artists, and designers have exploited type as image to enhance meaning.

UNIT 3: ASSIGNMENTS

⊙ THE ANATOMY OF TYPE

1 Select two typefaces, one serif and one sans serif.

2 On a single 11- x 14-in (28- x 35.5-cm) page, in landscape format, set the uppercase and lowercase of the letters 'Aa' and 'Gg' on the same baseline, using the same point size and leaving space between each grouping. Diagram and identify as many parts of the letterform as you can, taking your time to design the page nicely. Note any differences in x-height and proportion.

3 On a separate 11- x 14-in (28- x 35.5-cm) page, in landscape format, create a poster using a complete word of your own choosing. Using a maximum of four colors, overlap the word three times using letterforms from three distinctly different typefaces, serif or sans serif. You may not vary the baseline and you must use the same point size for all three typefaces, but you may use uppercase or lowercase, in any combination.

4 Distinguish the differences made by the overlaps, and add any three of the following terms into your composition in a way you find meaningful:
• x-height
• baseline
• ascender
• descender
• cap height

⊙ TYPOGRAPHY AND MEANING

You will want to do this exercise on a computer, and Adobe Illustrator software is strongly recommended. Working on a computer will allow you to create many variations, or electronic thumbnails, more rapidly than drawing the typeface accurately each time. This will keep your creative process moving and reveal a great number of options before you commit to a final selection.

Select two words from the list below:

> Transition
> Disruption
> Relaxation
> Migration
> Expansion
> Evolution
> Compression
> Exhilaration
> Repression
> Elimination

Take the time to consider their meanings carefully and think about how the meanings can be expressed typographically.

Create two distinct designs, one for each word, that best express the meaning of each word. Each type poster should be 11 x 17in (28 x 43cm) in a tabloid format, and only black and white or grayscale may be used. As you generate your thumbnails, consider all of your design decisions, including the placement on the page and the proportion and orientation of the word. Be aware of the interaction of white space and your design elements as you compose the page. You may elect any means of visual communication at your disposal—contrast and scale, cropping and proportion, letterspacing and repetition with (or without) variation—but you must work from a single principal typeface. You can mix the variations in a single font—bold, light, condensed, italic, and so on—and you may also overlap, omit, slice, crop, or tint the letters. You may not distort the type in any way, or use drop shadows behind the letterforms. The end result should be an engaging and well-designed page. It should also be legible, and the principal typeface easily identified.

⊙ ADJUSTING LETTERSPACING

1 In 60-point, sans-serif type, set the headline:

RAILROADS IN CRISIS

2 Print out your page, and look closely at the spaces between each of the letters. With a red pen, mark any spaces that seem uneven within the words, and return to your computer to kern the type. Print your second version, and compare the differences made by your adjustments.

3 Reset the headline in 60-point, serif type. Repeat the exercise, making special note of any differences encountered in kerning serif and sans-serif type.

○ HISTORY OF TYPE DESIGN/ PARAGRAPH DESIGN AND HIERARCHY

1 Research the work of one of the following type designers:
John Baskerville
Giambattista Bodoni
William Caslon
Claude Garamond
Eric Gill
Frederic W. Goudy
Adrian Frutiger
Paul Renner

2 From your research material, select and save a sizable paragraph, or two shorter ones, about the designer or about a typeface they designed. Using the typeface you have researched, consider the following elements:
• Headline: the name of your subject.
• Body text: the paragraph you have selected.
• A complete alphabet of the typeface, with all numerals and select punctuation.

3 In tabloid format, create a dynamic page design that uses all three of the above elements. Your headline may be placed anywhere on the page, but you must use some element of contrast or scale to call it out as the headline. You may elect justified or ragged type for the body copy, and you may incorporate the alphabet in any way that

is aesthetically pleasing, as long as the hierarchy is clear and the reader is able to clearly find each element in the proper order. As always, be aware of the placement on the page, the integration and sequencing of the visual hierarchy, and the legibility of the point size and leading. Remember to produce several versions before you finalize your finished artwork, and be true to the nature of the type designer's work: is the face old style or modern, formal or informal?

Note: Always print your work
Type sizes can be very misleading on the screen. Always view your work in whatever format it is intended, so that you can see it as the audience will.

4 Show your exercises to a designer or to another design student and have a candid discussion about your intention with this work. As the projects and practices become more complex, it's easy to get caught up in designing to please yourself, and to forget about the necessary function of visual communication. Always make sure your intentions are clear, and keep an open mind as you exchange ideas.

Further Reading:
Robert Bringhurst, *The Elements of Typographic Style*, Hartley and Marks Publishers, 2004
Robert Bringhurst and Warren Chappell, *A Short History of the Printed Word*, Marboro Books, 1989
Rob Carter, Philip Meggs, and Ben Day, *Typographic Design: Form and Communication*, Wiley, 2011
Ellen Lupton, *Thinking with Type*, Princeton Architectural Press, 2010
Emil Ruder, *Typography: A Manual of Design*, Verlag Niggli AG, 2001
Erik Spiekermann and E. M. Ginger, *Stop Stealing Sheep and Find Out How Type Works*, Adobe Press, 2002
Herbert Spencer and Rick Poynor, *Pioneers of Modern Typography*, The MIT Press, 2004
Paula Scher, *Make It Bigger*, Chronicle, 2005
Andreu Balius, *Type at Work: The Use of Type in Editorial Design*, BIS, 2003

○ TYPE AS IMAGE

Select one of the following titles, or substitute one of your own favorite film or book titles. Be sure to select one that inspires visuals.

Pride and Prejudice
The Bell Jar
The Alchemist
On the Road
Black Hawk Down
The Hobbit
Moby Dick
The Scarlet Letter
Dr. Jekyll and Mr Hyde

Using only the letterforms provided, create a typographic illustration that communicates the meaning of the title. You may use any media you find appropriate, such as traditional media, three-dimensional construction, photography, or photomontage. Your finished work should be 9 x 12in (23 x 30cm).

Develop your concepts first, then collect the materials you need to create your imagery, but work with recognizable typefaces before you substitute your artwork for the conventional letterforms. This will help you to control the composition and to create your final artwork in the correct proportion.

Remember to look for inspiration in nature and the environment, as well as design history and museums. Letterforms can be "seen" wherever geometry and spatial relationships exist—you just have to remember to look for them.

4 FUNDAMENTALS OF COLOR

A thorough understanding of color is essential to expert design, and is one of the most important tools in graphic design. There are infinite variations of colors at the designer's disposal, and endless ways of combining them across many media, from printed inks to screen-based colors, each with their own characteristics.

Color has a unique, complex language, and the ability to change its meaning when partnered with other colors. When choosing colors to incorporate into your design, you will need to consider issues of contrast and harmony, and how these might affect legibility in typography. You can also set the mood of a design by using the psychology of color, but you must be sure your selected colors convey the correct message at an unconscious level, and that they are suitable for the audience your project is intended to reach.

PART 1	PRINCIPLES
UNIT 4	FUNDAMENTALS OF COLOR
MODULE 1	**Color terminology**

To understand how to choose or assign color for a specific purpose, designers must first develop knowledge of how color works, how colors are classified, and the terms used to describe them.

Color is differentiated in three main ways: hue, tone, and saturation. "Hue" refers to the color's generic name—for example, red, yellow, or blue. A single hue will have many variations ranging from light (tint) to dark (shade). This is called tone or value. A single hue will also vary according to its saturation or chroma (also known as intensity). Saturation ranges from full intensity to low intensity, or from brightness to grayness. Color can also be described by its temperature and movement. Hues in the red spectrum appear warmer and closer to the viewer than hues in the blue spectrum, which appear colder and farther away.

Complementary colors, such as red and green, lie opposite each other on the color wheel, whereas analogous colors, such as green and blue, lie adjacent to each other. The former are associated with contrast; the latter are linked to harmony. Certain colors have a profound affect on each other when combined. They can vibrate or blend, appear vibrant when partnered with one color and muted when placed with another. The more you experiment with color, the more you will understand how to select and group various hues for meaning.

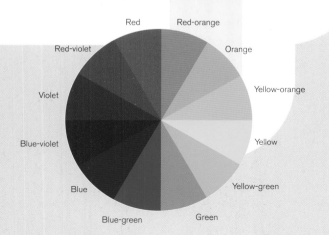

Red · Red-orange · Orange · Yellow-orange · Yellow · Yellow-green · Green · Blue-green · Blue · Blue-violet · Violet · Red-violet

Color wheel Primary, secondary, and tertiary colors of pigment are shown on the wheel. The primary colors are red, yellow, and blue. Secondary colors are made by mixing any two primary colors together, producing orange, green, and violet. A tertiary color is produced by mixing a primary color with the secondary color nearest to it on the wheel. The tertiary colors here are red-orange, yellow-orange, yellow-green, blue-green, blue-violet, and red-violet.

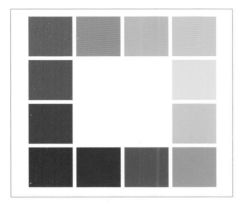

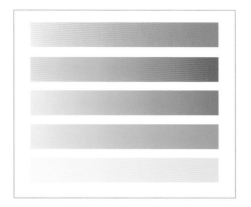

⬆ **Hue** distinguishes one color from another. It is the generic name of the color—red, say, as opposed to blue.

⬆ **Tone** (or value) is the relative lightness or darkness of a color. A color with added white is called a tint; a color with added black is called a shade.

⬆ **Saturation** (or chroma) is roughly equivalent to brightness. A line of high intensity is a bright color, whereas one of low intensity is a dull color. Two colors can be of the same line but have different intensities.

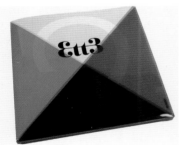

⬆ **Subtractive color** An acetate envelope printed with transparent primary colors transforms the cover of a publication and creates multiple triangles in varying hues and tones as it is removed. This same effect can be viewed digitally by working with transparencies and adding layers to your file. Experimenting with color will help you learn to control the hierarchy in page design, create readability in typography, and set the mood and pace.

GLOSSARY

Additive color: System used on monitors and televisions, based on RGB (red, green, blue). When combined, these form white light.

Analogous color: Colors that lie adjacent to each other on the color wheel—for example, blue and green.

CMYK: Cyan, magenta, yellow, key (black): the four colors that make up the full-color printing process.

Complementary color: Colors that lie opposite each other on the color wheel—for example, red and green.

Gamut: The complete range of colors available within one system of reproduction—for example, CMYK or RGB gamut.

Primary color: Red, yellow, or blue.

Secondary color: A mix of any two primaries: orange, green, or violet.

Spot color: Any flat color, like Pantone or Toyo colors, printed as a solid, and not made up of CMYK.

Subtractive color: System used in printing, based on CMYK colors.

Tertiary color: A mix of any two secondaries.

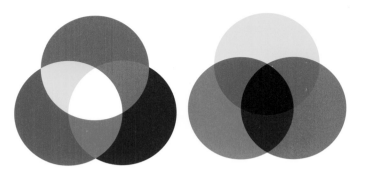

◀ **On-screen color** Additive primaries and RGB light are used to create colors on computers, televisions, and monitors. Combined, the additive primaries result in white light.

◀ **Printing primaries** Subtractive primaries and CMYK—cyan, magenta, yellow, and key (black)—are the primaries used in printing. When combined, subtractive colors make black.

Additive and subtractive primaries

To understand how color works, the most important point to know is that colored light (additive colors or the RGB system) and colored pigment (subtractive colors or the CMYK system) do not work in the same way. To put this differently, if you are working with your computer, the color on your monitor (RGB system) will not be the same as the color that is printed (CMYK system). This phenomenon creates problems for printed projects, since colors on screen appear brighter than in print.

With printed matter you will be working with subtractive color. Here, each color printed onto a paper stock subtracts from white, and if the three primaries overlap, black results. The color wheel shows primary colors; the subtractive primaries are red, yellow, and blue. Secondaries are a mix of any two primaries, resulting in orange, green, and violet, and tertiaries are a mix of any two secondaries. The term "full color" refers to four-color printing and to achieve a full range of colors, printers use cyan, yellow, magenta, and black (known as CMYK; K = black = key color).

Pantone

An additional color used in a design project is called a flat color or sometimes a spot color. When selecting colors for this, you should use a universal matching system known as Pantone Matching System (PMS). Pantone color is mixed from 15 pigments (including black and white) and is primarily used for print color matching. This system is different from the CMYK system and few colors can be matched between them. For more information, see pages 132–133.

Process charts and modes

When printing in full color (CMYK), you will find it useful to identify and specify the exact color that you want to see printed by using a printer's process color guide. This will show you all of the colors that you can make by specifying and combining different tints of cyan, magenta, yellow, and black. When designing for print on a screen, be sure you are working in CMYK mode, not RGB. Once you have chosen your color, you can make a new swatch on your document, specifying the different tints. This is the only accurate way to specify the printed color that you will achieve when ink goes onto paper.

⊕ **SEE ALSO:** PRINTED COLOR, PAGE 132

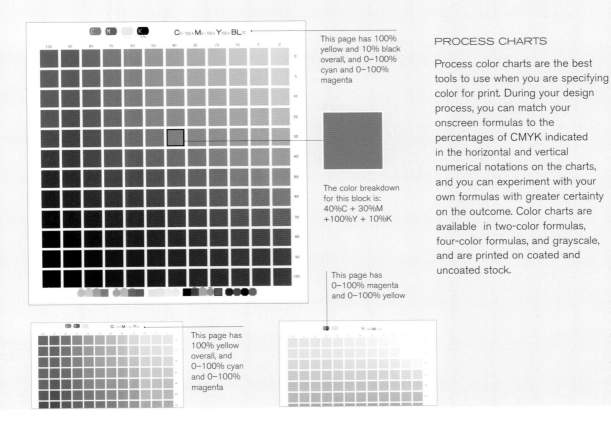

C 0–100 + M 0–100 + Y 100 + BL 10

This page has 100% yellow and 10% black overall, and 0–100% cyan and 0–100% magenta

The color breakdown for this block is:
40%C + 30%M +100%Y + 10%K

This page has 0–100% magenta and 0–100% yellow

This page has 100% yellow overall, and 0–100% cyan and 0–100% magenta

PROCESS CHARTS

Process color charts are the best tools to use when you are specifying color for print. During your design process, you can match your onscreen formulas to the percentages of CMYK indicated in the horizontal and vertical numerical notations on the charts, and you can experiment with your own formulas with greater certainty on the outcome. Color charts are available in two-color formulas, four-color formulas, and grayscale, and are printed on coated and uncoated stock.

Gray scale Squares in tones of black and white create halftones and can define light and shadow in both an abstract and a representational way. Subtle variations in the value of each square will create gradients that blend seamlessly.

Movement and contrast Reds, yellows, and orange values come to the foreground of the composition, and blues and greens seem to be farther away. This example adds scale change to color theory to complete the effect of motion.

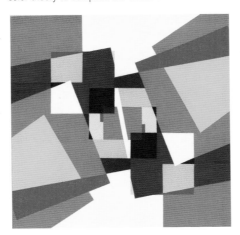

Vibrating edge When complements in red and green are adjacent, the eye perceives a faint white line along the edge. Vibrating edge is used to stunning effect in this design, but the same technique can render typography unreadable.

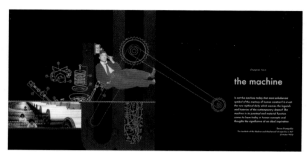

◀ Monochromes and brights Monochrome tones in large areas of flat color provide a perfect field for a bright pop of color in delicate line art. The same sensibility is repeated in the headline and text, both reversed out of black for high contrast. The purple and yellow are complements, but the hue of both colors has been desaturated.

PART 1	PRINCIPLES
UNIT 4	FUNDAMENTALS OF COLOR
MODULE 2	**Color legibility, contrast, and harmony**

Knowledge of the context in which finished work will be viewed is fundamental to the use of color in graphic design. How that color is perceived, and how legible it is, will vary greatly depending on whether it is viewed on a screen or in a print-based medium. Color has a dramatic effect on legibility and needs to be considered very carefully. Contrast and harmony are ways in which a design can be further enhanced.

⬆ Depth and dimension
Letterforms leap from the page in this carefully controlled typographic design. The styles of the letterforms were chosen to evoke roadside signage, and each added color treatment surrounding the letters provides an active field that sets the letterform apart without compromising its readability. The dark, textural background pushes the typography into the foreground.

⊕ SEE ALSO: READABILITY AND LEGIBILITY, P76
COLOR TERMINOLOGY, P88

If you are designing a website or an onscreen project such as film credits, you'll be working with additive colors in the RGB mode. These are somewhat reliable monitor to monitor and have the lumens associated with onscreen colors. Very subtle variations may go unnoticed on screen, and care should be taken to avoid additional vibration when combining colors. If you are designing for print, be sure you are working in CMYK mode. This will enable you to come reasonably close to your intended selections, but test printing is the only reliable way to be sure your colors are correct. As explained in Module 1, problems can occur on translation to print in subtractive colors. Both clients and designers can be misled into expecting printed colors to have the same saturation and tonal range as those approved on screen. Don't rely on your monitor unless the finished design work is intended for the screen. View your work in the same context as your intended audience whenever you can.

Color legibility
Legibility refers to how clearly something can be read. Many factors can influence color perception and legibility; for example:

• lighting and viewing conditions in the reading environment will have a clear effect on the legibility of both print- and screen-based work—compare viewing a monitor in a darkened room and under direct sunlight;
• selection of colors;
• background colors and textures on which colors are printed; and
• size and shape of type or image used.

Good color legibility is achieved when ground and color have contrast—for example, deep violet (the color nearest to black) on a white ground. The legibility decreases by moving the image color toward yellow, however, because violet and yellow are complementary and may cause a vibrating edge. Changing the contrast is key to legibility, and this means using your knowledge of the color wheel.

Contrast and harmony

Color should both contribute to and support the content of a design, and it should reinforce the ideas you are giving visual form to. Therefore, it is important to understand how color can work in contrast and in harmony. Both are related to legibility and color associations, and affect design function and perception.

Allocating color proportion is a critical decision. For example, a small amount of bright red in a complementary scheme can have a stronger impact than equal proportions of red and green. Equal amounts of a saturated red and green can actually result in unpleasant visual discord, and may bisect your composition in undesirable ways. You can avoid this by varying the saturation levels of the hues. By using a greater proportion of green with less saturation and a red with good saturation, the red is given extra emphasis. You can reduce the vibrancy of a hue by adding a bit of its complement to it, graying the color effectively enough to change the relationship between your selections. With analogous schemes, the hues tend to have less vibrancy and therefore similar proportions can be used to pleasing effect.

Designers who develop an understanding of the complex and subtle ways in which colors interact will be able to explore new ways to express graphic ideas. Practical needs, such as legibility and the requirements of the work, should always be considered as a fundamental part of the design process. Experimentation will further your color expertise; try a design project without using black or white, and use the values, tints, and hues of color to solve your design challenges.

← **Texture and contrast** Layered values of neutral and vibrant colors can create interesting textures. Varied intensity in the letterforms that create the textural field in this design are created with transparent tones and sophisticated hues that suggest a complementary relationship. The title is set apart in white, to contrast with the active background, and retains a hint of the texture below to incorporate it in the composition.

↑ **Hierarchy and order** Complementary colors and grayscale are used to direct the eye toward blocks of text that form complete packets of information, and to separate them from each other. This constructivist-inspired design neatly integrates a transition from red text to green text by using a CMYK mix to create a deeper green that has a dose of its complement to neutralize it.

PART 1	PRINCIPLES
UNIT 4	FUNDAMENTALS OF COLOR
MODULE 3	**Color associations**

Why are certain colors preferred, or seen to be more effective? It is because colors have, throughout history, come to hold particular associations that most likely derive from nature, and have, over time, become rooted in human psychology. They have come to possess cultural, symbolic, and often personal associations. To use it well, you need to understand how color works both as a language and as a system of signs, and how it creates an emotional response.

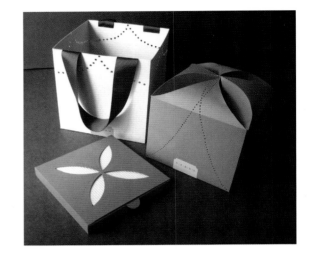

Intelligence, memory, experience, history, and culture all play a part in color perception. Although individuals may perceive colors with slight variation, color perceptions have different meanings depending on psychology and cultural background. Colors have symbolic associations in all societies, depending on context, and different cultures assign different meanings.

• Black is the color of mourning and death in the industrialized West, whereas in China and India the color of mourning is white.
• Red does not have the instant conventional association with "stop" in those countries where automobiles are less pervasive, and is associated with good luck in China.
• Green was associated with poison in the 19th century through its links with arsenic, whereas today it is seen as the color of spring and environmental awareness.
• Blue is associated with postage in the US, where the mailboxes are blue, whereas in Sweden or Britain you would look for the color red.
• Yellow is the color of courage in Japan.

The meaning of color can change over time and across different cultures. If you are designing for international markets, you need to be particularly aware of such differences.

⬆ **Seeing red** The color red is associated with caution in most Western cultures, but with good fortune and luck in China. This bilingual logo type uses the brilliance of a nearly primary red to evoke the imprint made by a traditional Chinese ink seal and to announce an American exhibition of contemporary Chinese artists. The strength of the color also allows the viewer to see the letter "I" in ink, even though it is bleeding off the edge.

⬆ **Muted elegance** Sophisticated, muted values are often associated with a higher price point in retail packaging. Soft color values and repeated forms combine with a sudden pop of vibrant green in these retail packages to add an edgy element to an elegant treatment.

Color in emotion and language

While color associations are highly subjective, despite local differences, colors and hues may have some universal characteristics. Reds, oranges, and yellows stimulate the senses and tend to be perceived as warm, capable of exciting feelings of cheeriness, good health, or aggression. Opposite on the color wheel, blues and greens are seen as cool, with connotations of calmness, peace, safety, and/or depression.

Other dimensions also influence perception. Compositions close in value may seem hazy, vague, or introspective, whereas dark combinations might evoke night, fear, or mystery. High color intensities are dynamic and create a feeling of movement. Clearly, color perceptions are rooted in psychology. They are even used figuratively to describe feelings. "Seeing red" or "singing the blues" are common descriptions of states of mind.

COLOR THEORISTS

Josef Albers (1888–1976) proposed that colors are never stationary; that is, they are constantly changing in relation to the colors surrounding them.

Johannes Itten (1888–1967) created color experiments based on contrasts such as temperature or hue, and associations based on seasons.

Wassily Kandinsky (1866–1944) developed his color usage in terms of spiritual moods and relations to musical instruments and sounds. His paintings are a synthetic color expression of sound.

Wilhelm Ostwald (1853–1932) set up an order of colors based around the concepts of harmony and disharmony.

Associations: Connections between colors and emotions, culture, experience, and memory.

Connotations: A color's broader associations, for example: green—jealousy, naivety, illness, environment, nature.

Denotations: What the color literally means, or is; for example, a red rose is a green stem with red petals.

⊕ **SEE ALSO:** COLOR TERMINOLOGY, P88

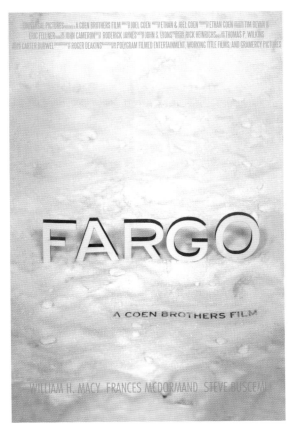

Hot palette The right palette can associate the viewer with the message or the product immediately. This colorful display of gestural forms has a palette inspired by the actual ingredients of the hot sauce in the package. The concept image is resonating the heat of the peppers and is even suggestive of smoke. Text set in an acid green color has placement as lively as the illustration, with both offset by a deep background.

Chilling palette The juxtaposition of the coldest and warmest of colors evokes a chilling message in this poster for the Coen brothers' story of murder in the great white north. The uninterrupted use of white space nearly obscures the typography, much as snow hides things in the landscape, adding a sense of the unknown to the mood of the image, and a touch of red predicts a hint of violence.

Sweet palette Natural hues and soft contrasts produce a quiet, relaxed sensibility. The quiet of a garden is reflected in tones of moss greens and earthy browns, mixed with a dappled texture of cream and taupe in the background. Typography and illustrations are sized and placed to simulate the perspective one might see in a landscape, and no high-contrast images or type spoil the pastoral mood.

PART 1	PRINCIPLES
UNIT 4	FUNDAMENTALS OF COLOR
MODULE 4	**Color as information**

Color is a powerful tool, especially in information design, where it is used to help the designer organize data into various structures, and to aid the experience of "reading" a design. Psychologists have proved that the color of an object is seen before its shape and details. Because color works at this basic level, it is very good at keeping things defined, reinforcing informational hierarchies, guiding the eye through complex systems and data, and aiding navigation through physical spaces.

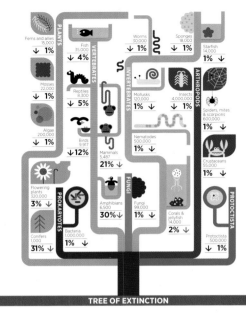

TREE OF EXTINCTION

Systems are anything that contains a flow of complex information—maps, signage, sections, structures, web pages. Color helps to categorize that information. Environmental graphic designers specialize in designing wayfinding systems, architectural signage, exhibition design, and data mapping, and rely on color as an important organizational tool.

- Complex buildings, such as hospitals and airports, need excellent signage systems to help people navigate through large, complicated architectural spaces. Color is an obvious means to correct paths. Many shopping malls are so large that parking zones are now color coded—a memorable way to help you remember where you left your vehicle.
- The London Underground map, developed by engineer Harry Beck, is one of the most famous maps in city transport. Beck used color to differentiate lines, so that people could readily identify the right route. The map is schematic: it is a simplified diagram that uses abstract graphic elements (lines) to represent a complex real-world situation. This most original of designs is a model copied in various forms throughout the world, including on maps for the Paris and New York City metro systems.

- In finance, color has traditionally been used in many ways. Debits in balance sheets would be in red to denote arrears, hence the phrase "in the red." This custom is still in use to separate trading figures from year to year.
- Charts apply color to quantitative and statistical information, where differing quantities of data need to be reinforced.
- Catalogs and books often have different color-coded sections to aid navigation through pages. Penguin Books introduced the first paperbacks in Britain in the 1930s using a bright orange background. This color quickly became fused with the books' identity. Later, the same publisher introduced another imprint, called Pelican, whose books were given a blue background. Customers quickly came to recognize the differences through the use of color. Such visual associations can also help to delineate sections within a body of text and highlight a number of different levels of importance. The designer can set crucial parts in a bold typeface and use a different color from the rest of the text. The eye picks up this difference very quickly.
- Web designers use color to help people navigate through the structure of a site.

Charting info Beautifully organized, well-designed information gets attention, and it is likely to be examined thoroughly. Here, a whimsical style is used in the infographic Tree of Extinction. The chart follows a six-column modular grid system and is color coded for easy navigation.

GLOSSARY

Data: Facts or pieces of information of any kind.

Diagram: Drawing or plan that explains the parts of something, or how something works.

Quantitative: Related to quantities of things, or measurements (numerical).

Schematic: Simplified diagram or plan related to a larger scheme or structure.

Statistical: Related to the collection, classification, and organization of (often numerical) information.

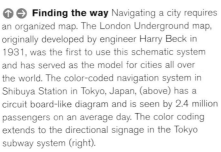

Finding the way Navigating a city requires an organized map. The London Underground map, originally developed by engineer Harry Beck in 1931, was the first to use this schematic system and has served as the model for cities all over the world. The color-coded navigation system in Shibuya Station in Tokyo, Japan, (above) has a circuit board-like diagram and is seen by 2.4 million passengers on an average day. The color coding extends to the directional signage in the Tokyo subway system (right).

Menus A well-designed extended system can create opportunities for the designer to encode navigation and still stay true to the coloration of the brand identity. Simple divisions on a restaurant menu will make it easier for consumers to select their meal.

Universal language Color is a universal way to communicate. In an setting where many languages are spoken, such as an airport or a hospital, color-coding pictograms (see page 21) and information systems can be easily understood.

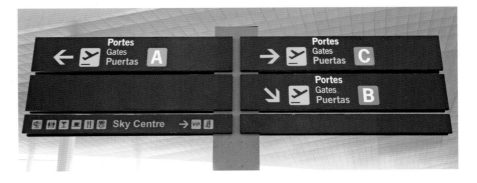

UNIT 4: ASSIGNMENTS

○ DEFINING COLORS

This exercise can be done in Photoshop, Illustrator, or InDesign. If you work in Photoshop, please be sure you are working in CMYK mode: that way, the colors should be the same if you export your files to Illustrator or InDesign later.

In landscape format, set up a document to 11 x 17in (28 x 43cm). Create five squares in one aligned row, sized to occupy at least two-thirds of the width of your page. Make multiple pages, with your squares in the same position, to do the following experiments with color.

• **Advancing color** Select two different hues, one for the squares and one for the background, that will make the squares advance. Alter the tone on four of the five squares to see how it affects the advancement of the image.

• **Receding color** Repeat the previous exercise with receding color in the foreground squares.

• **Tints** Choosing tints of the same hue, fill the background with one and the foreground squares with the other. Create two variations, one that shows contrast and one that makes the squares barely visible. Add a small amount of the complementary color to either the foreground squares or the background to see how it is affected.

• **Simultaneous contrast** Use the same hue for all five squares and the background. Then, alter the background hue two different ways and note how the squares appear. Select one variation and alter four of the five squares to give them more and less contrast.

• **Complementary colors** Select two hues to demonstrate the term "complementary colors." Use them at full intensity on the foreground and background until you can see a vibrating edge. Change the complements to a different pair and see which combination is more vibrant.

○ CONTROLLING TINTS AND VALUES

1 Using Illustrator, set up a document that is 14in (35.5cm) square. Along the top of the page, create a row of ten 1-in (2.5-cm) squares evenly spaced. Do not add any color to the background.

2 Beginning on the top left and working right, fill each square with tints of cyan, dropping by 10% each time, working from 100% on the top left to 0% on the top right. Select and copy the entire row and paste it nine times below the original. You should have ten rows of ten squares ranging from 0% to 100% cyan. Do not use layers in your file, since they will make the file much too big.

3 Beginning on the top right and working down to the bottom, fill the first row with increasing percentages of yellow, beginning with 0% on the top right and ending with 100% at the bottom right.

4 Now, working from left to right, begin adding the corresponding amount of yellow to each cyan square on the row, until all the squares on the second row across have 20% yellow added to them, the third row has 30% added, and so on.

5 When you have completed the chart, change the background to black to see how the tints are affected.

6 You can repeat the exercise with cyan and magenta, and magenta and yellow. If you do, save the charts, since they will make a handy reference tool for you moving forward.

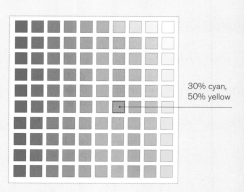

30% cyan,
50% yellow

○ COLOR AND LEGIBILITY

1 Type the word "legibility" in a landscape format on a white background in a color that has great contrast, such as violet. Change the color of the word gradually, working backward through the color wheel from violet to blue, green, red, orange to yellow, and note the legibility of the word.

2 Show the word "legibility" against a background of contrasting colors from opposite ends of the color wheel. Reverse them until all legibility disappears, as with red on an orange background. Note which cause vibration, which become readable but subtle, and which ones just cannot be read at all.

3 Repeat the exercise with a paragraph of 10-point type.

Further Reading:
Josef Albers and Nicholas Fox Weber, *Interaction of Color*, Yale, 2013
Leatrice Eisman and Keith Recker, *Pantone: The Twentieth Century in Color*, Chronicle Books, 2011
Adams Morioka, *Color Design Workbook: A Real World Guide to Using Color in Graphic Design*, Rockport, 2008
Pantone Formula Guide Books

○ COLOR AND MEANING

1 Explore your associations with each of the colors on the color wheel. Make notes on which emotions you associate with each of them, and how you think most people perceive them. Research and record how these same colors are perceived in different cultures.

2 Find examples of everyday things that are defined by their color and photograph them in their surroundings as they are seen normally. They might be road signs, transit vehicles, street numbers, food, or holiday items.

3 If you are familiar enough with Photoshop to work in color, upload images to your computer and alter the feeling of each by changing the color of one object, leaving the surrounding area alone. Note how your perception of the object has changed. Does a glass of milk still look appetizing when it has a pale green-gray cast? Is the emergency vehicle still obvious in traffic when the color changes? Can you change a clear sky to threatening or peaceful? If your proficiency in Photoshop is still developing, you can work in Illustrator using tints and transparencies on your placed image, or you can simply print your photos and paint on them.

○ WAYFINDING

1 Using only black and white and tints of black, design a simple map, diagramming your journey from home to the nearest grocery store and back again. Develop simple icons and/or labels to represent as many different landmarks as you need—street names, parking garages, retail stores, banks, ATM machines, parking lots, bus stops, and so on—and place them on your map. Include lines of typography along your route that describe your state of mind as you travel to and from your destination, and as you pass various notable points.

2 Repeat the exercise using color to differentiate the labels and icons, with the most important ones in the most contrasting colors. Add a background color to the design. Assign a legible color to your dialogue that does not disturb the readability of the landmarks. You may use any tints or colors you find appropriate. Note how important it is for information design to be clear, and immediately readable as you work.

Practice

In this part, you will be introduced to the tools and techniques of design, which form a key group of skills for professional practice in any field. No designer can ignore the requirements of technology, and while you may use powerful digital tools regularly in the production of work, it is essential that you familiarize yourself with the industry-standard technologies that designers utilize. However, these tools cannot generate the idea, nor can they execute the design for you, and the kinds of conceptual, intellectual, and formal skills you bring are what will differentiate you from other designers. In short, you need both an excellent understanding of principles alongside outstanding technical skills. Being able to design formally and/or conceptually eloquent and innovative work is only half the story, since

you then need to get the work into print, on screen, in three dimensions, or across multiple platforms, and so on. "Design is the battle, but printing is the war," used to be the designer's battle cry, describing the problems designers face when getting a design from the sketch stage to a final, printed piece of work. Those problems still exist but designers now need to be able to deliver graphics that will be viewed in multimedia applications, the screen being preeminent. Unit 5 introduces basic image making and sourcing, followed by an overview of the key technical and software skills used in design today, including Photoshop and InDesign. In Unit 6, various production issues, including color for print, PDFs, paper stocks, and press checks are introduced. Unit 7 is dedicated to design for web and

MANNER

EXPERIMENTATION

PART 2

mobile applications, and summarizes the specific technical skills, tools, and languages these platforms require. Here, you'll find design considerations for different styles of website, key software tools, and how to bring creativity to an "off-the-peg" CMS (and the acronyms are explained, too!). There is even a tick list of questions to ask a client during the website planning stages. Unit 8 overviews seven of the key areas of design, including editorial design, web design, and motion graphics. These "tasters" aim to give a sense of the key skills and aptitudes needed to work in each field, and of the highs and lows of each profession, and to provide pointers to additional resources, including "Best in the business," which highlights some of the most influential practitioners in that area of design.

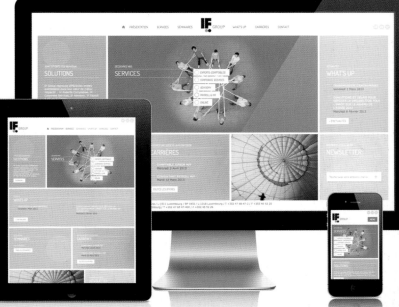

5 TOOLS AND TECHNOLOGIES

Graphic design production and practice is almost completely digital, and dependent on changing technologies. Previously, typographers would set type, pre-press production would be crafted by specialists at a printing company, and designers would commission a photographer. Now, one person can do all of these jobs on a computer, under the gamut of desktop publishing (DTP).

This unit introduces you to the software applications and tools that are most commonly used in the graphic design industry today. Each module focuses on a specific medium, such as photography, or a specific software application, such as Photoshop, grounding you in its unique tools, history, and terminology and giving you the opportunity to explore further. New applications, and updated versions of the ones in use now, will continue to be adopted into the practice of graphic design. The best way to prepare for a constant learning curve is to recognize the commonalities in the way they function, and gain your proficiency through practice.

➡ **Golden ratio** Think about composition as you frame your images, and remember the rule of thirds (see page 37). Dramatic spirals evoke the Fibonacci spiral, and create drama and tension.

PART 2	PRACTICE
UNIT 5	TOOLS AND TECHNOLOGIES
MODULE 1	**Photography basics and sourcing images**

Photography and image-making/sourcing are key skills for graphic designers. Not all designers are good photographers, but an understanding of the skills needed to compose and shoot images is essential. Your photograph may only serve as a placeholder, but having the image on hand will help you work out rough proportions, assign and design a composition, and can serve as research for drawing and/or digital illustration.

Fortunately, the rules of good design—composition, contrast, hierarchy, rule of thirds, and color theory—don't change much for different design disciplines. Frame your photos the way you would approach any design assignment, and compose each shot with purpose.

Types of photography
There are many broad categories of photography and image production that are relevant to designers. For our purposes, we'll focus on the most common, which are:

• objects and products
• portraits and images of people
• landscapes and buildings
• ephemera and texture
• reference and research

⬇ **Depth** Strong perspective lines connect foreground and background for the viewer, and enhance the feeling of depth.

⬇ **Contrast** Intense light and shadow work in concert to form a compelling composition.

⬇ **Symmetry** Centered and still, a symmetrical composition can evoke peaceful, relaxed feelings. Drama is added by the pop of bright green in an otherwise monochromatic setting.

Consider the purpose of your design challenge and what your needs might be before you shoot. Make sure the resulting images fit the purpose, and that you have considered all aspects of your image as it relates to your design work. For example, product images are generally brightly lit, sharp, and clear, whereas landscapes and portraits may have a variety of styles and convey a specific mood.

Your designs will be more powerful if you learn how to spot an effective, well-composed picture and can recognize a good tonal range. Think about how the image can combine effectively with typography, color treatments, and other illustrations.

There are many reasons why one image will make you stop and stare and another will make you turn the page without stopping to look at all. It certainly helps if a picture is in focus, correctly exposed, placed where it is shown off at its best, and has some interesting content, but images can be a powerful form of expression within a design. Try to capture images that reflect the design sensibility you need to communicate your message, and note that there are limits to how much you can alter them electronically.

⬅ **Chiaroscuro** High contrast in darks and lights adds depth and drama to images, and can be used with a vivid range of highly saturated color.

⬆ **Asymmetry** Positioning the focal point off-center can add dynamism.

⬆ Format and composition Repetition of bold triangular shapes and variation in color are dramatically elongated in a landscape composition. Examine the potential of your subject through the lens, and take several versions for your files.

➡ Orientation Some landscape photos have a greater impact when cropped to portrait format, a technique that can also be used to get rid of unwanted background

Which camera?

With improvements in digital cameras, high-quality, high-resolution images are easy to create instantly, and fewer people are using traditional film cameras. Digital cameras are immediate, versatile, and capable of taking reasonable-quality images in less-than-ideal lighting conditions. Most have great storage space, and you can select and delete unwanted images immediately. Many smartphones have great internal cameras that offer instant availability and the option to email the photo as soon as you have taken it, but the quality may not have the tonal range you need for a final image.

To take a good picture you will need a decent camera. If possible, beginners should use at least an 8 megapixel digital SLR (single lens reflex) with a 22–80mm zoom range, a viewfinder or viewing screen, and a macro setting option. A macro setting will allow easy focusing for close up and detail. Good SLR cameras allow you to shoot what you see, and choose where to focus the image and exactly how to compose it. Automatic digital cameras calculate lighting, focal distance, and aperture settings with no input from the photographer, setting up a point-and-shoot attitude with reasonable results. For manual digital photography, knowledge and understanding of how the camera works is necessary to give the photographer far greater control. Practice and study will allow you to create unorthodox and striking images.

Light and color, composition, and cropping

If you are creating photographs for illustration work, you want the initial photograph to feature as much detail and clarity, and balanced lighting, as possible. Further effects can be added electronically or manipulated in Photoshop, if desired. You can always blur a clear image, then return to a clear image, but a blurred photo will be of limited use. Consider what you need from the photo before you shoot. You might be thinking in terms of high-saturated color, black and white, or sepia tone, but always shoot in color first to give yourself the option to experiment with all types of color manipulations in post-production. Also consider the lighting: direct bright sunlight may bleach out the image, whereas overcast conditions will flatten the contrast. Most cameras have a built-in light meter. When composing your shot, make sure that it is as close to the center of the contrast range as possible.

To crop an image is to select only a part of the final shot. Often, cropping is used to take out an unwanted part of the picture. It is a useful tool that can help improve composition and eliminate superfluous information to strengthen the image.

WHICH LENS?

Different lenses extend the capabilities of the camera.

- A normal lens on a digital or film SLR is 35mm, considered to be near enough to human vision.
- A macro lens captures sharp, extreme close-ups of objects.
- A wide-angle lens captures a wider vision, but with perspective distortion.
- A telephoto lens captures objects at a distance.

Archiving your images

The storage of digital images needs care. It is not enough to have them saved only on a computer; they also need to be backed up on portable external hard drives or a cloud-based (virtual) system of digital storage, such as Dropbox, iCloud, or Carbonite. If a negative is scratched, it can still be printed and retouched, but the failure of a hard drive will result in complete loss of all your images.

Sourcing images

When making decisions regarding what images to use, the principal point to consider is whether the brief, timetable, and fee allow or justify producing an image from scratch, or if it might be necessary to source, or purchase, a ready-made image from elsewhere. The Internet provides the quickest way to source stock images, from websites such as iStockphoto, Corbis, or Dreamstime. These images can be purchased and downloaded from a website on a royalty-free basis using a credit system, and are usually priced by usage. For example, on some sites a picture of a dog can be purchased for one credit for a 72dpi image, acceptable for a web-based illustration, or for five credits as a 300dpi image, for a print-based illustration.

Images can be bought either for specific time periods or outright. A drawback to purchasing a temporary license is that there is no guarantee that other designers will not use the same picture in their designs. Your client may prefer that you purchase the picture outright, which will undoubtedly cost more. Customizing the image is always the best creative option. You can select the elements you need and create your own image through collage, retouching, or simply reimagining the existing image to suit your project.

⊕ **SEE ALSO:**
FUNDAMENTALS OF
COMPOSITION, P32
FUNDAMENTALS OF
COLOR, P88
PHOTOSHOP, P110
PHOTOMONTAGE AND
COLLAGE, P113

TIPS AND TERMS

Take time to check and adjust your settings, and always bracket your shots—adjust your f-stop up and down as you take multiple versions.

- **Depth of field:** Distance between the object of focus and where the focus starts to blur. For example, a photographer may want a product to be in sharp, clear focus but the background to be blurred, so would choose a smaller aperture (f22), a slower film speed (ISO 100) for higher resolution, and have extra lighting and external flashes set up.
- **F-stop/Focal length and aperture:** Size of aperture or "iris" inside a camera, which controls the amount of light that hits the film or pixel sensor; the range on a general camera is f4 (large aperture) to f22 (small aperture). A large aperture (f2, for example) brings more light into the camera and results in a softer image; a small aperture (f16, for example) allows less light into the camera but gives a sharper image.
- **Filter:** Plates of glass or plastic attached to the front of the lens in order to accentuate different qualities. For example, a polarizing filter cuts down light glare; a color filter enhances different colors.
- **SLR:** Single lens reflex. These types of camera use a viewfinder and mirrors so that the photographer's sightline goes through the main lens and results in a what-you-see-is-what-you-get image.

→ **Soft focus** Delicate use of soft focus can evoke a wistful, lyrical image and can lead the viewer to a different perception of the subject.

GLOSSARY

ISO: International Organization for Standardization. This sets a standard range for virtual film speeds in digital cameras: ISO 100, for example, works best in good lighting conditions for stationary objects; ISO 1600 works best in poor lighting conditions and for mobile objects.

Placeholder or FPO (For Position Only): A temporary or low-resolution image in place of the high-quality counterpart during the design process.

Resolution: The resulting output from a digital camera. Digital cameras and some top-of-the-range camera phones have up to ten megapixel sensors and can produce less pixelated, sharper, and higher-quality images.

PART 2	PRACTICE
UNIT 5	TOOLS AND TECHNOLOGIES
MODULE 2	**Page-assembly programs**

Page-assembly applications bring all your lessons in composition, page layout, contrast, and typography into play. In these applications the elements you create in vector software, or the imagery you edit in raster-based applications, merge with your content. Using this WYSIWYG (what-you-see-is-what-you-get) layout-generating word processor, you can combine text and image to create brochures, magazines, posters, or multi-volume novels or publications.

Although Adobe InDesign may be the industry standard, at some point somebody may email you a .qxd file. Whereas QuarkXPress is similar to InDesign, just a bit less agile and less featured, it's the differences in how they handle file types from image-making programs that may cause problems. As native products, Adobe files work between programs without filtering, but an Adobe Illustrator or Photoshop image brought to Quark will always need to be exported to an EPS or TIFF. Each file type has its own characteristics, but none has the same full-on editability that Illustrator/Photoshop-to-InDesign provides.

Crop mark: Vertical and horizontal lines at the corners of an image or page to indicate to a vendor where to trim off the bleed area.

Gutter: The inside margins or blank space between two facing pages in a publication. Used to accommodate binding, the amount of gutter needed changes depending on how the project will be bound.

Handle: An anchor point in a design program connected to the main vector path by tangential lines that can be manipulated to change the shape of the curve.

Margin: The usually blank space to the top, bottom, and sides of a page between the trim and the live printing area. Headers, footers, and page numbers are traditionally placed within this area.

Work area
The main toolbar sits to the left of the screen, the canvas in the center, and the secondary toolbars to the right.

◉ Main toolbar
InDesign localizes its main tools into one long toolbox. Mirroring many of the functions found in Illustrator, Photoshop, and Quark, the tools in this panel can be accessed by clicking the icons or utilizing the keystrokes assigned to each item, such as "V" for the Selection Tool, "P" for the Pen Tool, and "G" for the Gradient Tool. Note that some of the items with a small arrow also reveal other fly-out tools such as Rounded Frames, the Fill Tool, and the Measure Tool.

USEFUL TOOLS AND FEATURES

InDesign has many tools full of features and functions to help create compositions. Here are some of the more basic yet powerful tools that are the mainstays of any InDesign user. The keyboard commands for each tool are shown in brackets.

1 Selection Tool (V)
Selects the entire shape or line, which can then be stretched, rotated, or moved anywhere on the page.

2 Direct Selection Tool (A)
Selects and manipulates specific lines, path points, or handle ends distinctly to change the position of individual lines, points, or curves of a shape.

3 Pen Tool (P) Enables you to create straight or curved lines by selecting two points on the page and "bending" to your desired shape. By clicking the Pen Tool, you can reveal the Add Anchor Point, Delete Anchor Point, and Convert Direction Point Tools to manipulate the points that make up curves and lines.

The Control Panel can be docked at the top or bottom of the screen, as well as float freely, like all of the panels

Master pages are the page templates upon which you can program elements such as grids, header and footer elements, and automatic page numbering

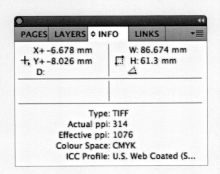

Swatches Panel This is where all the colors used in a document are located.

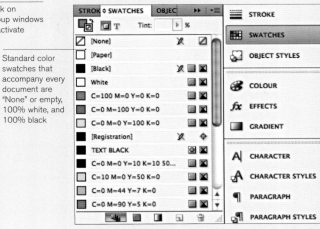

Click on Popup windows to activate

Standard color swatches that accompany every document are "None" or empty, 100% white, and 100% black

To modify a color's mix—either by typing in its numerical values or PMS number—click a swatch twice to reveal the Color Mixer

Popup windows Window organization is important, because the amount of panels and tools necessary to do a job can easily fill up your screen. The Adobe CS3 and CS4 applications help reclaim screen real-estate by allowing users to "dock" and minimize panels as they see fit. With a variety of options available under Window > Workspace, you can select one of the pre-organized panel arrangements or create your own.

X+ -6.678 mm	W: 86.674 mm
Y+ -8.026 mm	H: 61.3 mm
D:	

Type: TIFF
Actual ppi: 314
Effective ppi: 1076
Colour Space: CMYK
ICC Profile: U.S. Web Coated (S...

Info panel Displays layout information for the document or selected objects, including values for position, color, size, text, and rotation. For viewing only—you cannot enter or edit the information in the panel, but you can ascertain many qualities of an on-page object by hovering over it with your cursor.

4 Type Tool (T) Used in the creation of text boxes and edits the type within them. By working in conjunction with the Control Panel and Type Panels, this tool will allow you to select and modify text to create headlines, paragraph blocks, and captions.

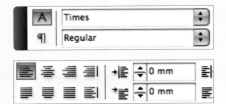

5 The Control Panel Provides a customizable array of functions for the Type Tool in relation to choosing font, leading, tracking, text weight and style, paragraph alignment, column count, and margin spacing.

6 Rectangle Frame Tool (F) and Rectangle Tool (M) Both create rectangular, polygon, and rounded forms: the Rectangle Frame Tool creates frames to insert graphics and imagery; the Rectangle Tool is for drawing shapes to fill or outline with color. Precise adjustments can be made to size and position with the Transform Panel.

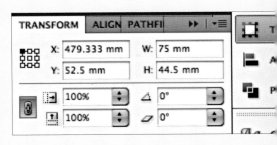

Page layout

Creative layout design utilizes different on-page items such as text boxes and image boxes to help place imagery and content, and assign color in compositions on a generated pasteboard. These compositions can be sorted into a virtual pagination structure, comfortably up to hundreds of pages. The program also manages issues such as page size, orientation, and output. The following tools are standard.

❯ **Guides** Imaginary rules are pulled over the page and viewed upon request. They do not print, but help in creating layouts and grids and lining up items. Usually gutters and margins are set with guidelines in the Master Pages.

❶ **Bleed**

When preparing imagery, remember to compensate for the bleed. If any of your pictures go to the edge of the page, remember to add about ⅛in (0.3175cm) to that side of the image to be clipped off at press-time. This goes for background colors and lines as well.

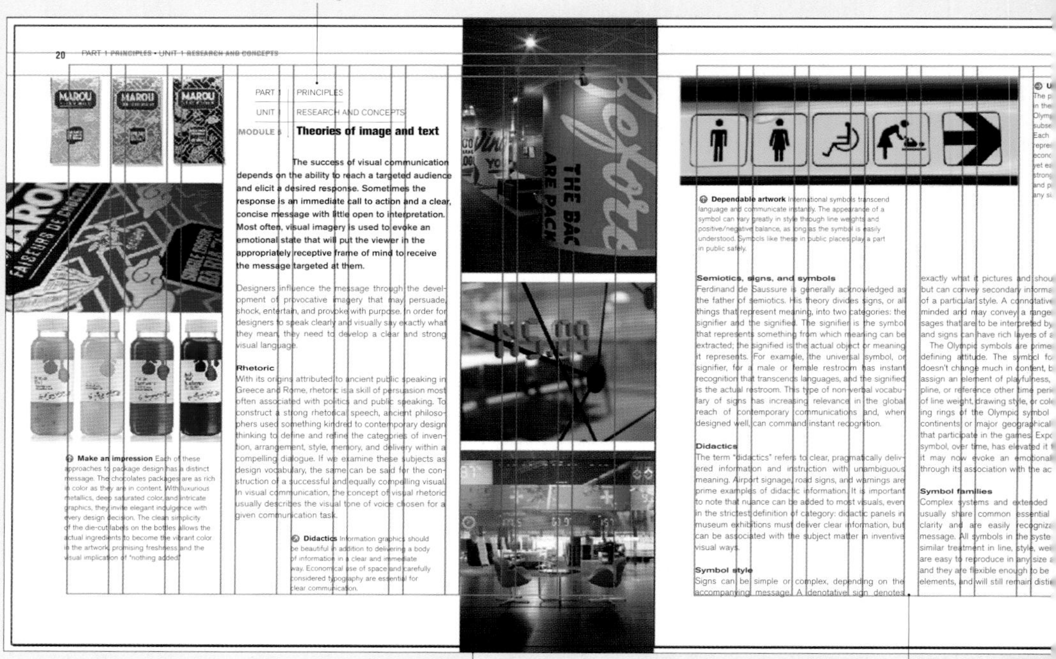

Reoccurring graphics can be set up in the Master Pages

Image bleed

Grid lines can be switched on or off

Page layout concepts

Beyond placing and sizing imagery, the designer can use page-assembly programs to express content meaning with extensive control of typography. Through automatic flowing of text from multiple columns to multiple pages, hierarchy and information organization is easily controlled and experimentation and changes are easily handled. Creative composition and invention in text layout require manipulation of the page items, and will cause countless ragging and adjusting. Make it part of your process to address this and leave time to fine-tune your typography when the document is completed.

Magazines and newspapers around the world use page-assembly programs to get as many words as is comfortably legible and aesthetically pleasing on a page, with grids, layouts, templates, and columns to make it happen.

Master Pages and Style Sheets will help you to create almost any composition and project. In Master Pages, you can create formats to be repeated throughout a multi-page document—for example, headers, page numbers, and call-outs. In the Style Sheet palette window, you can select your typographic hierarchy and set it to be constant throughout the document.

⊙ **Master Pages** These template pages, upon which pre-defined pages mimic grid elements and on-page template elements such as text block items, header and footer elements, and automatic page numbering, are usually found at the top of the Pages or Page Layout panel. These pre-styled layouts help in creating uniform changes throughout a large document, but can be specifically changed on a per-page basis when necessary.

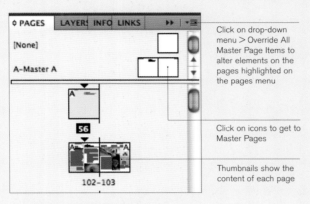

Page numbers and running heads are set in the Master Pages

Click on drop-down menu > Override All Master Page Items to alter elements on the pages highlighted on the pages menu

Click on icons to get to Master Pages

Thumbnails show the content of each page

⊙ **Page numbering**
On a Master Page, create a text box and go to Type>Insert Special Character>Markers—Current Page Number. Now, that same text block on each page will reflect the appropriate page number.

Style Sheets Design and typographic styles such as color, size, leading, position, and decoration may be applied to text automatically with Style Sheets. Selections of text may be tagged with certain pre-defined meta-information at the click of a button. By naming a series of elements Headline, you can globally affect the styles and attributes of each selection.

Object styles can be assigned to objects, groups, and frames to modify the stroke, color, fill, drop shadows, transparency, text wrap, and more

In paragraph styles, character and paragraph formatting attributes can be applied to a paragraph or series of paragraphs to adjust overall spacing, leading, and style

Character styles are formatting attributes that can be applied to selected items of text, such as size, weight, tracking, and italics

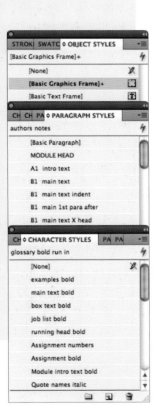

Packaging
Exporting documents for proofing—most commonly with PDFs—and file preparation for publishing with an outside printing vendor are important details usually handled well by page-assembly programs, but you should know what vendors are looking for. Proper packaging for an exported package to a service bureau should include the updated document file, PDF for proofing, and all the assets and links to the file, including a folder of imagery and a folder of all fonts in use.

⊕ **SEE ALSO:** PHOTOSHOP, P110

ILLUSTRATOR, P114

PREPARING FILES FOR PRINT, P124

PART 2	PRACTICE
UNIT 5	TOOLS AND TECHNOLOGIES
MODULE 3	**Photoshop**

Photoshop is the industry-standard software package for raster-graphics editing and manipulation and is frequently used for collecting images and to select elements for montage or photo retouching. Text can be incorporated into designs, allowing for the seamless integration of text and image within a single digital environment. It's a wonderful tool if you are using type as image, but it should not be substituted for a program that allows document formatting if there's a significant amount of copy.

Photoshop replaces and enhances darkroom techniques such as retouching and editing brightness and contrast, and allows for ease of cropping while providing a cleaner, "dry," chemical-free environment for editing. The most common tools used in Photoshop for photo editing are the Spot Healing Brush, the Clone/Stamp Tool, and the Patch Tool. These allow the editor to remove imperfections and unwanted objects.

Photoshop's major advantage is that imported images can be moved, edited, and layered over a potentially infinite canvas without loss of information, quality, or resolution. Photoshop documents with multiple layers can get quite large and may compromise the memory allocated on your computer. Be sure you save and archive

↑ **A tablet** with stylus pen is the preferred tool of many Photoshop artists. The pen gives the designer free range of hand movement and pinpoint precision by emulating the feel of using a brush or a pencil. The most common brand of tablet is made by Wacom.

Work area

This section shows the general layout of Photoshop. Additional pullouts can be accessed through the "Window" menu on the header bar.

➲ **Main toolbar**
This bar has easy icon access to all of the main tools, some of which also have keyboard shortcuts.

Foreground/background color selection. Clicking on the squares selects the color, whereas the "X" key swaps them over.

USEFUL TOOLS AND FEATURES

There are five main tools that enable you to edit an isolated area of pixels without altering the rest of the image. Each of these can be accessed through the main toolbar, and many have additional options to customize the tool, located at the top of your screen in the header bar. The keyboard commands for each tool are shown in brackets.

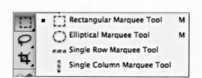

1 Marquee Tool (M) Selects an area or sets up a boundary within the layer that is being worked on. Different Marquee Tools can select rectangles and ovals, and, when holding down the Shift key, geometric circles and squares can be selected. This tool also allows you to select a one-pixel-width line down or across the entire layer. This is useful when making a striped page pattern or creating a boundary line.

2 Magic Wand Tool (M) Selects pixels of the same color with the Tolerance option set to 1, but within a range of color with Tolerance set to more than 1. If the Contiguous box is unchecked, the tool will select all the pixels in the entire document that are of the same color value, regardless of whether they are joined together or not. Use the Shift key to add pixels to the selection and the Alt key to subtract.

Main toolbar

Filters can be accessed through the header bar

The canvas

Secondary toolbars

The canvas navigator is useful when you are zoomed in to work on a detail, as you can find where you are

The History pullout gives you a list of the actions that you have carried out

The Layers pullout details each canvas layer and which filters or additions are on each layer

◀ Color editor The Photoshop Color editor, currently set to the CMYK (cyan, magenta, yellow, key/black) range that is used for print color. The RGB (red, green, blue) color editor is used when designing for the web/television. Each range has different effects on the color usage.

◀ Preset color swatches The swatches are used as a standard range of colors, for example black, white, 10%, 20%, and 50% grays. If you have mixed your own standard swatch, or have been set a range in a brief, you can save and keep it to select when working on a design.

3 Pen Tool (P) Creates vector-based lines and curves with control points (see Illustrator, p114). These points can be dragged over the layer for a better fit, converting them from fixed points. An area enclosed by the Pen Tool boundary can be affected by various fill functions or made transparent to add texture and depth.

4 Lasso Tool (L) Draws and selects freehand shapes. Use the Shift key to add a new selection or the Alt key to subtract. The Polygonal Lasso draws straight-line sections. Use the Alt key to toggle between the Lasso and the Polygonal Lasso Tool, and the Shift key to draw perpendicular or 45° angles. The Magnetic Lasso is the fastest way to outline and isolate a shape. The Magnetic Lasso will attach to the pixels that describe the outer edges of any photographic subject, making it a simple matter to eliminate a background or copy and paste the object into a different layer or file.

5 Brush Tool (B) The size, shape, and color of the Brush Tool can be changed, as can its hardness and scatter range. Alter the brush's flow rate or opacity to achieve different effects for use in retouching, adding texture, or digital painting. The Brush Tool options can be found under the header bar.

the original PSD version, and flatten and save the document correctly. All Photoshop artists must have knowledge of all the selection tools available and an understanding of layering and saving options.

Pixels

The best way to describe a pixel is as a tiny square in a grid of squares on the monitor screen. Each square is lit by different intensities of red, green, or blue light (RGB) to form the entire gamut of colors. These pixels can be modified either on their own or as a group. If these pixels are tiny enough, they merge together to form a smooth picture. Another name for this is a raster image.

⊕ **SEE ALSO:** PAGE-ASSEMBLY PROGRAMS, P106

① Scanning

One way to import images into Photoshop for modification and incorporation into a design is to scan them. Most scanners will provide their own software, designed to work seamlessly with Photoshop. Options can range from the most simplistic image capture to a full range of customizable color settings, and resolution options for photos, line art, documents, or pre-screened printed material. Scanning is an essential skill, and many scanners will allow the capture of actual objects if the depth of field is not too great. For example, if you need an image of a key, you can actually place a key on the scanner bed and capture the image. The image can then be altered like any other photographic subject.

GLOSSARY

Canvas: The virtual "ground" that images are placed onto in Photoshop.

Collage: Derived from the French word for "to glue," involving the assemblage of elements of texture, found materials, and newspapers

DPI: Dots per (square) inch; the common form of resolution measurement. Designers typically use 72dpi-sized images for web images and 300dpi-sized images for photo-realistic prints.

Ephemera: Objects such as newspapers, bus and train tickets, and other found textures and typography.

Juxtaposition: The process of putting two or more unrelated or opposite elements or objects together to create different effects.

Montage: Derived from the French word for "assemble"; a picture made from pieces of other pictures.

Photomontage: The assemblage of various fragments of photographs.

Pixel: The smallest element of a computer screen or printed image. The word "pixel" is an amalgamation of picture (pix-) and element (-el).

PPI: Pixels per inch.

Raster: Assemblages of pixels on a 2D grid system that can be viewed on computer screens or print media.

Resolution: The clarity of a digital image. A low-resolution image (30dpi, for example) will have clearly visible pixels; a high-resolution image (300dpi, for example) will not.

Resolution

Image resolution is a key area of knowledge for a graphic designer. The most common measurement of resolution is dots per inch, or DPI. At 25dpi an image is heavily pixelated; at 72dpi (used for all web-based imagery) it is clearer but not a high-enough quality for print. The standard resolution for photo quality and print images is 300dpi, or for large posters, 600dpi. Be sure your image is at 100% scale, and at the right DPI. If you enlarge a small 300dpi image by 200%, it becomes 150dpi, and will not print at a high quality.

Image resolution is altered here

Shows image/document proportions will remain the same

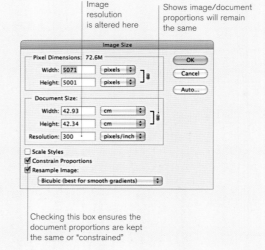

Checking this box ensures the document proportions are kept the same or "constrained"

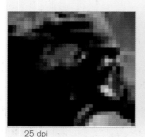

25 dpi

72 dpi

300 dpi

Layering

Photoshop can layer different images and elements so that each can be worked on separately without altering the rest of the image:

Opacity Changes how translucent each layer is.

Presets Adds color styles and textures to the layer.

Layer styles Adds effects such as shadows, strokes, glowing edges, and textures to the layer.

Blending options Changes the properties of the layer.

Layer>Merge/Flatten Merges all or some of the layers together.

Filter Applies effects such as blur, sharpen, lighting, and textures.

Use these to adjust the size, resolution, color values, and white balance of each layer:
Image>Adjustments>Hue/ Saturation
Brightness/Contrast
Image Size/Resolution
Canvas Size

Click and hold on a layer to drag it to different positions, bringing it to the front or moving it behind other layers.

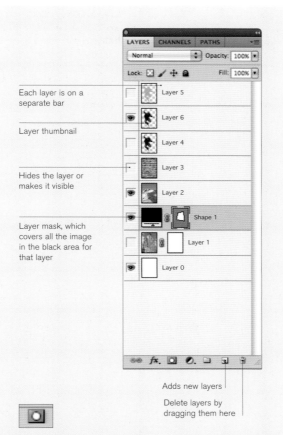

Each layer is on a separate bar

Layer thumbnail

Hides the layer or makes it visible

Layer mask, which covers all the image in the black area for that layer

Adds new layers

Delete layers by dragging them here

MASKS

Quick Mask selects and masks out an area that needs to be protected from editing. Using a selection tool, outline the area you want to edit, then select the Quick Mask option from the main toolbar. To add to the selection, paint in black; to subtract, paint in white. When you select the Standard Editing mode, the selection will reflect the edits made in the Quick Mask mode. Layer Mask creates an isolated section of the existing image to which more effects can be added. When you select the Layer Mask it will tell you that you are in "layer mask edit mode" in your filename. Remember to check the status of your layer before you alter the image, otherwise you may be working outside the masked area.

PHOTOMONTAGE AND COLLAGE

Photomontage and collage are historical artistic methods, in which fragments of photographs, images, elements, textures, and typography are brought together to create new meanings and new images. Photoshop extends this process by making it possible to hide the methods of assembly, creating a seamless picture. Photomontage is a process concerned with manipulation of photographs and is historically associated with graphic artists such as Hannah Höch and John Heartfield, as well as contemporary illustrators such as Dave McKean. The process pulls in and reassembles fragments to construct images that appear seamless, or that leave the edges exposed for a handmade look. Collage is a process more concerned with the assemblage of ephemera, textures, and typography, and can be seen in the work of artists Kurt Schwitters and Romare Bearden. Many of these images are based on found objects or materials, and result in abstract assemblages and patterns that are rich with texture and aesthetic qualities but do not, necessarily, convey any particular meaning.

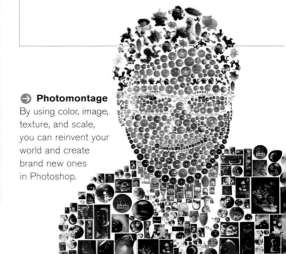

→ Photomontage
By using color, image, texture, and scale, you can reinvent your world and create brand new ones in Photoshop.

Adobe Illustrator is a vector-based package used for illustrative, logo, and page-layout design, because of its shape-rendering and text-editing capabilities. Its linear handling complements Photoshop's pixel-based format, and most designers have knowledge of both programs.

Illustrator's main advantage is the resizing of vector-based illustration without loss of detail, from its "point and line" function. For example, at billboard size a raster image becomes pixelated and blurry, whereas a vector image retains design by angle geometry and proportion, and remains sharp.

For the graphic designer, Illustrator offers a clean, crisp edge to the produced objects and brushes, and mapped along "paths" can be moved, edited, and recolored easily. As in Photoshop, you can build layers of illustration using textures, transparencies, and typography, and create finished artworks to import into a page-assembly program.

 Agile editing
Illustrator's vector-based format allows for exclusive editing on objects and custom typography, making it an excellent format for many illustrative techniques.

USEFUL TOOLS AND FEATURES

Many of the tools found in Photoshop are duplicated across the Adobe range, such as the Selection Tools, Lassos, and Pen Tools. Here are five of the most commonly used tools in Illustrator. The keyboard commands for each tool are shown in brackets.

 1 Pen Tool (P) Creates vector-based lines and editable points.

2 Type Tool (T) The most useful tool in the best program for creating crisp logos and typographic solutions.

 3 Rectangle Tool (M) Creates customized shapes.

4 Warp Tools (Shift + R) These tools change the geometry of vector objects. The Warp Tool drags a specific area of an object. The Twirl Tool changes the local geometry/color into a spiral. The Crystallize Tool changes the local geometry/color to splines.

5 Mesh Tool (U) Creates color graduations within a 2D vector object. For example, making a star with the Star Tool and clicking within the shape with the Mesh Tool sets up a gradient, which can then be edited.

Work area

The main toolbar sits to the left of the screen, the canvas in the center, and the secondary toolbars to the right.

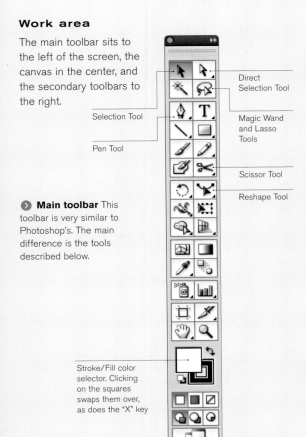

Selection Tool

Pen Tool

Direct Selection Tool

Magic Wand and Lasso Tools

Scissor Tool

Reshape Tool

Main toolbar This toolbar is very similar to Photoshop's. The main difference is the tools described below.

Stroke/Fill color selector. Clicking on the squares swaps them over, as does the "X" key

Main toolbar

Header bar

Palettes, including Swatches and Layers

Pathfinder Use these boxes to transform simple shapes into more complex ones, through merging, overlapping, and subtracting parts.

Align Clicking on these options will realign selected objects into the formations shown or add space evenly between objects as desired.

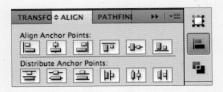

PRINCIPLES AND COMPONENTS

- Curves are never fixed with the finished image. A composite image/shape can be manipulated in size, color, stroke, gradient, and layer without affecting nearby shapes. More complex shapes and images can be built up by layering lines and the many standard shape tools such as the rectangle, circle, and pentagon.
- Superior text-editing abilities, such as kerning, leading, stroke, font size, and typeface options, are on the secondary toolbars to the right of the work page.

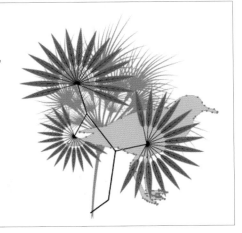

File types
There are three main file types: PDF (Portable Document Format); EPS (Encapsulated PostScript); and AI (Adobe Illustrator Artwork). Generally, PDF format is used for final images sent for print or submission, whereas EPS and AI are file formats kept in-house.

CMYK
Illustrator documents need initially to be set to CMYK in preparation for the output to be delivered to print.

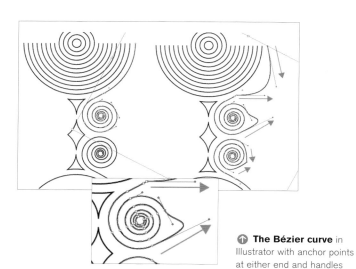

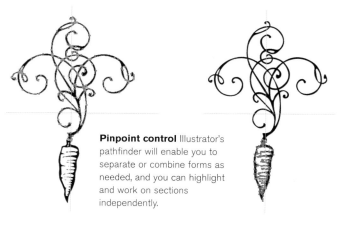

Pinpoint control Illustrator's pathfinder will enable you to separate or combine forms as needed, and you can highlight and work on sections independently.

⬆ **The Bézier curve** in Illustrator with anchor points at either end and handles (straight blue lines) that control the curve.

Vectors

Bézier curves are mathematically determined paths or vectors created between two points, which can be manipulated by handles at either end. These curves, popularized by Pierre Bézier in 1962 from Paul de Casteljau's algorithms, provide the backbone of objects produced in Illustrator, and are found in the Adobe range as paths created by the Pen Tool, lines, objects, and type guides in InDesign. They are also the basis for digital type used in "what-you-see-is-what-you-get" (WYSIWYG) publishing, text-editing software, and 3D software programs.

Clean control

Precise adjustments and easy scaling are perfect for logo design work, whether the logo is pictorial or typographic. Vector.eps images are used because they can be enlarged to fit a billboard or scaled down to a business card without loss of detail. Customized typography should always be done in Illustrator; because the resolution does not change with size, typography will always be crisp.

➡ **Brand of choice**
Extended brand details can be easily and perfectly replicated, and customized changes to placement and color are relatively simple. On the Habitat Design logo, elements have been extracted from the logo and used to create a retail hang-tag.

Anchor point: A point on or at the end of a curve or line that can be "grabbed" by the cursor and moved around the canvas, either to change the curve shape or to move the entire curve.

Artboard: Like Photoshop, the virtual "ground" into which images are placed.

Handle: An anchor point connected to the main vector path by tangential lines that can be manipulated to change the shape of a curve.

Path: A drawn line, mathematically determined; also called a vector.

⊕ **SEE ALSO:** COLOR TERMINOLOGY, P 88
PAGE-ASSEMBLY PROGRAMS, P106
PHOTOSHOP, P110
PREPARING FILES FOR PRINT, P124

Application of Illustrator This example shows how fundamental and versatile Illustrator can be in establishing a corporate identity. The Illustrator logo at right is displayed on the shop frontage and the company website.

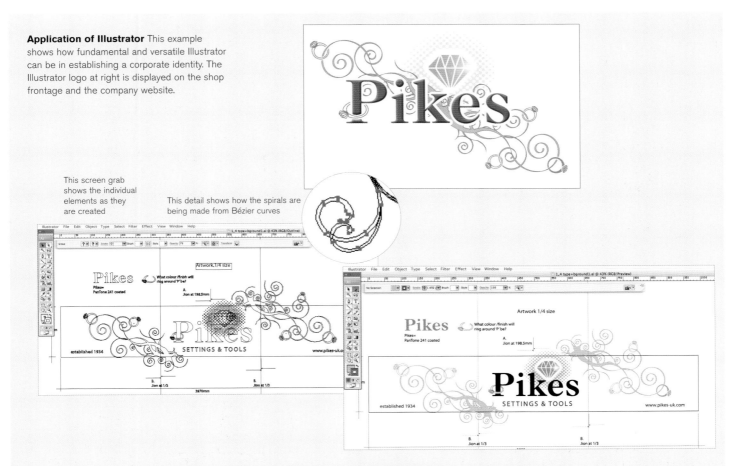

This screen grab shows the individual elements as they are created

This detail shows how the spirals are being made from Bézier curves

The design is now uploaded to the company website

Here, the spirals have been printed on frosted-glass panels for the business frontage, keeping the pattern running throughout

PART 2	PRACTICE
UNIT 5	TOOLS AND TECHNOLOGIES
MODULE 5	**Flash and After Effects**

Adobe Flash and Adobe After Effects are two of the main software packages for creation of time-based presentation. Both compose "moving imagery" for screen or web, use timelines and keyframes to order workspace, and incorporate both pixel and vector graphics. They differ in how material is rendered in the program and how it is delivered to the audience.

Flash

Flash excels with vector graphics, and is used for interactive web-based applications and animation, with a range of features.

- Illustrator images can be imported then animated, or created in the design stage.
- Complex animations, such as an acorn growing into a shoot, require each seminal stage of the animation to be drawn, called a keyframe. "Tweening" then creates transitions between two keyframes. A higher number of frames per minute (frame rate) creates a smoother transition. Unlike After Effects, transitions between different scenes or forms need to be built in by hand.
- Animations within the main animation can be set up—for instance, a leaf circling as it drops.
- Flash supports ActionScript, a scripting language that creates computer-generated geometry and timing for complex animations.

- There are open-source community libraries of script for assembling into the desired forms, and Flash is prevalent on the Internet, in the form of animations, navigation, and video, due to its discreet file size.

After Effects

After Effects excels with raster graphics, from either stills or video clips imported from Photoshop, video cameras, or animation packages, and is used primarily as a post-production effects and compositing tool. As a stand-alone product for viewing (.mpeg or .qt [Quicktime] file formats), clips and stills are organized on tracks similar to audio-editing programs. Transitions and fades can be drag-and-dropped between tracks that will then automatically render. After Effects also has many filters and effects, such as film scratches or blurring, to create a mood or tone to your project.

USEFUL TOOLS
AND FEATURES

The Flash interface is set up in a similar way to most of the Adobe software. The After Effects interface is less similar to the Adobe range, which reflects its use as a film compositor. Here are some tools and resources that stand out from both programs.

1 Flash: Bone Tool One of the developments in Flash, the Bone Tool can be used for inverse kinematics (IK)—in other words, to link several elements on the canvas with armatures, so that movement of one element will translate back through the link and respond as if the elements are connected by bones.

2 Flash: online tools and applications Visit www. swftools.com for tools to convert Powerpoint to Flash, 3D tools, and animated map tools. Check whether the license on the tool or application that you want to use is freeware, open source, or commercial. ActionScript at www.actionscript.org has tutorials, libraries of scripts, and forums.

3 After Effects: Cartoon Effect Create a cartoon aesthetic similar to *A Scanner Darkly* and other rotoscoped films. Simply import the live footage into the work environment, go to the Effects and Presets menu, and select Cartoon. Tweaking the presets and using the Blur options flattens the colors, removes some of the detail, and creates a cartoon effect.

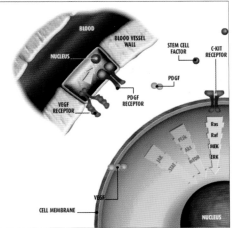
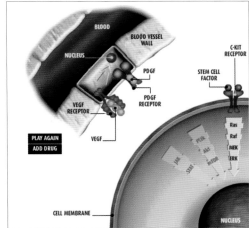

INTRODUCTION
BEVACIZUMAB
SORAFENIB
IMATINIB
TAMOXIFEN
BORTEZOMIB
EVEROLIMUS
GEFITINIB
TRASTUZUMAB
RITUXIMAB
TOSITUMOMAB

SORAFENIB
Brand name: Nexavar
Type: Small molecule
Target: Multiple receptors and enzymes
Cancer: Kidney; liver

HOW IT WORKS: Sorafenib attaches to two proteins on the surface of cells lining blood vessels: vascular endothelial growth factor receptor (VEGFR) and platelet-derived growth factor receptor (PDGFR). By binding to these receptors, sorafenib turns off signals that cause new blood vessels to grow towards cancer cells – a process called angiogenesis. Sorafenib also attaches to the c-kit receptors at the surface of the cancer cell and to enzymes called protein kinases, such as Raf, which carry the signals from these receptors to the nucleus, causing the cell to grow and divide. Sorafenib blocks these signals, preventing the cancer from growing

LESSON: Sorafenib demonstrates that a targeted therapy can have more than one target

LINKS:
US National Cancer Institute drug information
Cancerbackup treatment information
Clinical trials

⬆ ↗ **Interactive presentation** This interactive graphic uses Flash and AS3 commands to demonstrate how new cancer drugs target affected cells only, sparing healthy cells and avoiding side effects. In the first instance, the graphic shows how the disease attacks cells (above). Upon user interaction the drug is added, showing how collateral damage is averted (above right).

➔ **Seamless transitions** After Effects provides drag-and-drop features for simple animations that will render the in-between frames. Here, a combination of Illustrator and Photoshop montage images imported into After Effects create vivid illustrations in a beautifully fluid motion graphic. This storyboard illustrates a few of the transitions in the animation.

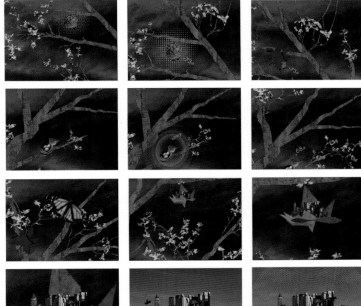

4 After Effects: Mocha Enables you to motion-track objects within a film so that words, images, or symbols can be spliced into the film, even if the film tracks fast or is blurred. For example, you could track a different billboard image onto a billboard as a car passes and the camera pans to follow the car.

❶ **Less is more** Keep banner advertisements simple; a few well-judged movements and transitions in text and image will be more effective than trying to be complex. With both After Effects and Flash, the same theories of composition apply: keep it legible and make it striking.

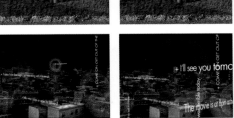

UNIT 5: ASSIGNMENTS

○ CHOOSING PHOTOGRAPHS

For this assignment, you'll need to produce about 25 photographic images that define your life. They can be images of friends and family, objects, textures, places, or situations. Try to incorporate as much variety as you can, but be sure each image is well framed and in focus. These will be used for exercises in Photoshop, and for a photomontage, so be sure to include as much information in the shot as you can. Cropping will be done at a later time.

1 Take photographs at home and in your neighborhood or city, shooting more images than you think you will need. Be sure to include images with a range of color, contrast, and texture, as well as interesting subjects. You can edit them later.

2 When you have finished your shoot, group the images by category, including portraits, landscapes, textures, and objects, and save them to your computer in a file titled "Photo Images" on your hard drive or on an external device. Put each category into its own folder. If you need more of any particular type, go out with your camera again.

○ SOURCING STOCK IMAGES

Sometimes you just can't take a custom shot or make it to a distant location. In this instance, Internet stock photo services can come in handy, but remember to use the images you choose as source material to be customized for your own purpose, and make them distinctive.

1 Choose a stock photo service such as Corbis, iStockphoto, or Dreamstime and explore their websites. All of them have search engines that allow you to find images on any subject, and most will provide a download option for comping purposes.

2 Use the search engine to research images you could not find during your photo shoot. Need an airplane? An exotic location? A racehorse? Stock has everything, but you need to be specific. Try describing your desired image in three to four words, such as "Jewel Diamond Necklace" or "Cat Tabby Outdoors."

3 If your quest is successful, add these images to a folder marked "Stock," but be sure to save the image numbers and the subjects, and label them in case you want to purchase them later.

Note: Your clients would want to see images before you purchase them. Never use an image for commercial purposes without purchasing it!

○ ELIMINATING A PHOTOGRAPHIC BACKGROUND IN PHOTOSHOP

This assignment will demonstrate how to cut out a subject and remove it from the background through the use of a clipping path

1 Select one of the photographs from the previous assignments that has a background you would like to remove. Make sure your foreground is focused and distinct from the background for your first try.

2 Open the image in Photoshop and select the Pen Tool.

3 Under the Path tab, select New Path. Double click on your path and name it.

4 Using the Pen Tool, begin to draw a line around the subject. Set as many points as you need to describe the detail, especially in areas with complex curves. Points can be edited or eliminated later.

5 Once the entire outline is complete, zoom in on the object and, using the Selection Tool, edit the points for better accuracy around the object by moving points or lengthening or shortening the handles of each curve point to adjust it. It's good practice to keep your outline slightly within the subject by a pixel, but be careful not to edit the subject accidentally.

6 To remove your image and paste it into a new Photoshop background, first highlight your selection. At the top right of your path palette, select the drop-down window and chose Make Selection. You can now cut and paste the image into another Photoshop file.

7 To remove your image and paste it into a page-assembly program file background, at the top right of your path palette select the drop-down window and chose Clipping Path. From the drop-down menu within this window, select the path you just named. Click OK. Save the file as a .tiff file and import it into in any page layout program.

Further Reading:
Peter Lourekas, Elain Weinmann, *Illustrator 6: Visual Quickstart Guide*, Peachpit Press, 2012
Corey Barker, *Photoshop Down & Dirty Tricks for Designers*, Peachpit Press, 2011
Barbara Brundage, *Photoshop Elements 10: the Missing Manual*, Pogue Press, 2011
Adobe Creative Team, *Adobe InDesign: Classroom in a Book*, Adobe Press, 2011
Nigel French, *InDesign Type*, Adobe Press, 2010

O PHOTOMONTAGE IN PHOTOSHOP

Now that you understand how to remove an object or a subject from a background, you can create new images by combining elements in new situations using backgrounds or textures.

1 Select three to five images from your objects folder or your stock images. Select three to five backgrounds and textures from your folders.

2 Open a new Photoshop document. Under the File tab, select New and create an 8½ x 11-in (21.5 x 28-cm) document. Make the resolution 300dpi, so you can print it, and name the file "Photomontage 1."

3 Under the Layers tab, select Background and change it to Layer 0. Import one of your backgrounds or textures.

4 Create paths on your objects or subjects and copy and paste them onto a new background. Each one will come in on its own layer. Using the Move Tool, you can reposition or scale any of your imported objects. Hold down the Shift button to scale your images without distorting them.

5 Create three photomontages, placing objects or subjects into new situations. Experiment with filters to affect your color, and make your subjects look as realistic as you can in their new setting. Pay attention to the

lighting in the foreground and background, and see if you can adjust them to work well together.

6 When you have a file you like, save it with all of the layers intact. Then, flatten the image, crop it to suit your liking, and, using the Save As selection, rename your file and save the compressed version with a different name. It will be smaller and easier to import, but always save the original, layered version, in case you want to make a change.

O PAGE ASSEMBLY IN INDESIGN

In this assignment, you'll be learning to create a page design electronically and to toggle between programs, as necessary, to import your assets into the page design.

1 Find an article on the Web about something that interests you. It should be at least 250 words long and have a subject you can easily find visuals for. Collect the text from the article or retype it into a Word document. Save it in a WORD.doc format, name it "Article Text," and put it in a folder on your computer titled "InDesign Assignment."

2 Select a photograph from your collection that might be appropriate and put it in the same folder. If you don't have a suitable photo, go to one of the stock photo services and do a search, or take an image of your own and upload it.

3 In InDesign, create a new document using command+n. In the pop-up window, set your number of pages, the size of the document,

your columns, gutter size, and bleed. Select OK.

4 In the Tool Bar, select the T (Type Tool) and draw a text box to fit one of your columns. Import your text using File > Place and locate the Word document. Your text will appear in the box, but it may not all fit. If there is more text, you'll see a small red plus symbol (+) in the lower right corner of the box. With the Selection Tool, click on the symbol and draw another text box on your page. The text will flow from one box to another and will indicate the connection with a thin blue line that connects each box.

5 You can now edit your type for size, font, and location. Change it at least once, just to see the differences in the type flow and word count per line. Add a headline and subheads if you need them.

6 Select the Picture Tool and draw a picture box in your layout. Import your photograph using File > Place. The image may not fit the

box. To size your image go to: Object (in the main menu), choose Fitting, and choose Fit content to frame. To resize your image easily, press the "e" key once, hold in the Shift button, and drag a corner of the image to the desired size.

7 Now you have a headline, body text, and a photographic subject. Experiment with changes in the composition and use color to convey the mood of the subject. If you need to alter the color in your photo, go back into Photoshop and change it, then replace it in your InDesign file.

○ CREATING A LEAF IN ILLUSTRATOR

1 Select the Arc Tool and make four lines as shown. Make sure that the two outside lines, the inside lines that create the "stem," and the other end of the leaf all end at the same point. You will need to use the White Selection arrow to move the anchor points into place as well as move the handles on each of the lines.

2 Select the two inner lines by holding down the Shift key and clicking on each of them with the Black Selection tool. Then give the lines a mid-green color or C80 M15 Y100 K5. Next, select the topmost line and give it a yellow color or C5 M0 Y100 K0. Finally, select the bottommost line and give it a rust color or C40 M70 Y85 K35.

3 Select the bottom two lines with the Black Selection arrow. Go to Object > Blend > Blend Options, choose the Smooth Color option, and press OK. Next, press Alt + B and either (Mac) or ctrl (PC). The bottom half of the leaf should now be filled.

4 Select the top two lines and repeat stage 3. The whole leaf should now be filled. Finally, select both sides of the leaf and go to Object > Group. The leaf is now one object.

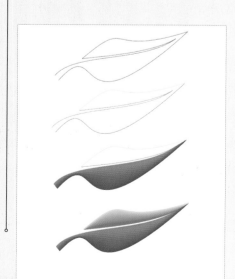

○ FLASH TUTORIAL

1 Open a new Flash file, in which you should see a single Layer called "Layer 1" in the timeline at the top of the page.

2 Select the first frame. Import the leaf image you created in the previous assignment onto the stage. You can easily do this by going to File > Import > Import to Stage. If you have not completed the Adobe Illustrator leaf assignment, you can import another image or even make your own using the drawing tools.

3 Now select your object on the stage and go to Modify > Convert To Symbol in the menu (or press F8) to convert this image to a Symbol. When the Convert to Symbol window opens, name your symbol whatever you like. Select Graphic behavior and press OK.

4 At this point, your symbol is in Frame 1 of Layer 1. Select Frame 30 and go to Insert >

Timeline > Keyframe in the menu (or press F6) to insert a new keyframe.

5 While still keeping playhead (the red vertical line) on Frame 30, move your image to any other position on the page other than where it's at now.

6 Select any frame between 2 to 29 and select Motion from the tween pop-up menu in the Property Inspector, usually found at the bottom of the screen (if you don't have the Property Inspector activated, go to Window > Properties > Properties).

7 Go to File > Publish Preview to preview the results. You can also modify the easing, rotation, and sound effects of the object by adjusting the settings found in the Property Inspector.

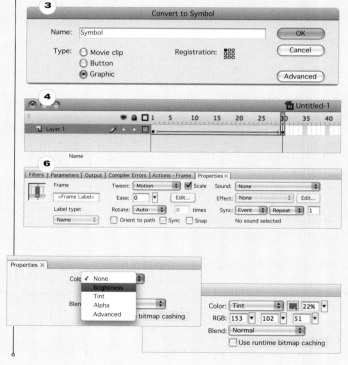

ⓘ Making changes

By selecting Frame 30 and clicking directly on the image, you can see that the Property Inspector will allow you to modify the end result's brightness, opacity, and tint using the Color drop-down. After adjusting these settings, previewing again will show the animation change color and opacity from start to finish, depending on the parameters you set.

○ CREATING A RED BALL IN FLASH

1 Open a new flash file. You will see one layer in your timeline labeled "Layer 1." Double click the layer name and rename it "red ball."

2 Select the Oval Tool, either via the tool bar or by pressing "o" on the keyboard. Before you draw the circle, you need to change the color to red. Double click on the Fill Color box at the bottom of the tool bar. Select a red color with the eye dropper.

3 While holding the shift key down, draw a circle toward the left side of your stage. Once you have a circle shape you are happy with, select the Selection Tool or press "v" on the keyboard.

4 Next, you have to convert this shape into a movie clip. Select the red circle. Then go to the top of the screen and choose Modify >

Convert to Symbol. This will bring up a new window where you can give your new symbol a name. Let's call this symbol "redBall_mc." For the type, make sure MovieClip is selected. The rest of the settings can stay the same. Click OK to create the redBall movie clip.

5 The last step is to give your redBall movie clip an instance name, so that you can target that movie clip in your action script code. Select the redBall movie clip on the stage. Open up the properties panel by going to the top menu and selecting Window > Properties. At the top of the properties window there is an input bar with the default name of <Instance Name>. Select the bar to remove the name and you can type in your own name: redBall. By doing this you now have a reference to your red ball movie clip on the

stage. Next, we will set up the actions script window to move this red ball.

6 Save the file and called it red_ball_animation. Remember where you saved this file, as we will be adding a folder to this location in the next assignment.

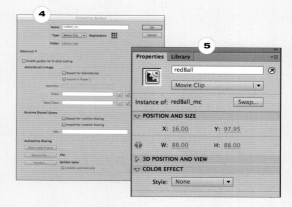

○ SET UP YOUR ACTIONS WINDOW IN FLASH

1 Create a new layer above your red ball layer by selecting Insert > Timeline > Layer on the tool bar. This will create a new layer above your red ball layer, and by default the layer is named Layer 2. Change the name of this layer as well by double clicking the name of the layer, and typing in "actions." You are now ready to write some code in your project to make your ball move. But first you need to download the action script library you will use to do so.

2 Download the Greensock code library by opening up your web browser and navigating to http://www.greensock.com. Once there, click on the "get GSAP" button on the left side of the screen. This will open up a new window that will ask you to "pick your flavor." For this project, we need the Actionscript 3 version of the library, so click on that and download the zip. Once the download is complete, unzip the file and you will be left with a folder labeled "greensock-v12-as3".

Open up that folder, and inside you will see a few files and folders. We are interested in the folder labeled "com". Move that "com" folder to the same location as your red_ball_animation file. Now you should have two files: the "red_ball_animation.fla" file and the "com" folder.

3 Now that you have the Greensock library download, you need to import it into Flash. Open up the Actions Window by going to Window > Actions. The first thing you need to type is your import statement.
Type the following:
import com.greensock.*;
Now that you have imported the Greensock library, you can animate your red ball. Under your import statement, type the following:
TweenLite.to(redBall,3,{x:stage.stageWidth - redBall.width});
This line is telling us that it will animate the red ball to a specific location on the screen. For that location, you are using the stage width minus the redBall width to give you a

number that will animate the redBall to the right side of your screen, no matter where you start the red Ball.

4 Test out your work by pressing Command + Return on a mac.

6 PRINT PRODUCTION AND PRESENTATIONS

When working in the realm of printed media, print production is the last stage in the design process, but it can be the first to be overlooked by the junior designer focusing intently on "design." It is really the final oversight of the creative decision-making process, and there are still options to be considered, even with the most detailed planning. If you have considered the project carefully and chosen colors, paper stocks, and processes to suit, this final phase becomes a shared creative experience between designer and vendor.

Familiarity with print-production techniques and issues is vital to ensure the final printed job looks and feels the way it was intended. Planning for the use of a special-effect ink, stock, or particular finish will only be achievable if you have a thorough (and up-to-date) understanding of the print-production process. Make it a habit to enlist your production representative early in the process. They can provide dummy booklets on various stock samples, help to adjust packaging templates, solve bindery and fastening challenges, and provide ink-on-paper samples (ink draw-downs) so you can see how a Pantone ink color might behave on colored stock.

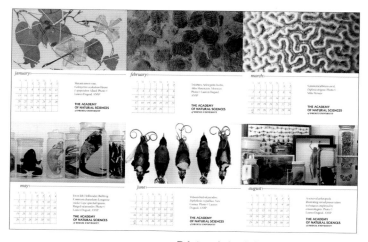

Print and check Be the first one to spot mistakes. Print your PDF files and check them for typos and color fidelity, especially with four-color subjects and tints.

PART 2	PRACTICE
UNIT 6	PRINT PRODUCTION AND PRESENTATIONS
MODULE 1	**Preparing files for print**

Keeping your digital work habits pristine will restrict to an absolute minimum the need to tidy up files just before sending them. By this stage your bleeds should be set, your colors checked against samples and swatches, all photography should have been purchased/prepared, page items should be aligned, ragging adjusted, and the spell check complete. Creating a positive workflow, from design stage to finished product, will help ensure a successful outcome every time. A true measure of a designer is not only apparent in your conceptual design and typographic skills, but also in your handling of the process from start to finish, including preparing and sending out files to service bureaus and print vendors.

After a final proof is signed off by the client, many issues often remain before work can be printed. Remind yourself that because every piece of design work is unique, it creates a unique set of problems: this stage is your last chance to check your work before handing it over to a printer.

PDF ADVANTAGES

- Highly compressed files can be generated—with optimized imagery and fonts embedded—to create a very close copy to the original working document. This condensed and mobile format can be easily emailed *en masse* to clients and co-workers for feedback, with edits and mistakes more easily caught during the production process.
- To print, the recipient needs only the free Adobe Acrobat Reader download. Many systems have this pre-installed, but it is always best to get the latest version.
- Newspaper and magazine publishers often receive ads as high-resolution PDFs only, with properly embedded fonts and images at the correct resolution and profile. Advanced tools in Adobe Acrobat Professional, such as Preflight, optimizer, and fix-ups, can be key to achieving a successful run.
- Email and Internet creators can link files to web pages for online viewing or attach files to emails.

Note: Keep in mind that you cannot easily edit a PDF document. Any changes that might be needed after a PDF leaves your computer will require the original document for editing. That means edits can only be done by the designer, in the original format, unless you decide to provide the native file to your vendor.

PDF OPTIONS

When Preflighting, you can bring your PDF to PDF/X and PDF/A standards. These file types, defined by the International Organization for Standardization (ISO), adhere to standards that facilitate reliable PDF transmission. They apply the wills and will-nots of a file. Using a PDF-X1, a file generated from Acrobat Preflight (a recognizable pre-set option in the Pre-Flight menu) is considered the best way to ensure that your file is correct and secure, and is an option in InDesign.

- Be meticulous. It is your responsibility to check everything from tint specifications and image color spaces to tidying up unused colors in your palette menu, style sheets, unintentional indents on justified edges, extra spaces, and missing fonts. Programs such as InDesign have spell check and Preflight capabilities.
- Printers are often sent postscript or PDF files—locked documents including all fonts and images—thereby reducing the potential for error. PDFs play an important role these days in near-instant proofing, and are the primary format used for sending files.

The role of PDFs

The Portable Document Format (PDF) has come a long way from the aim of the "paperless office," and is now a means to instantaneously review in-progress drafts and final sign-offs (or soft proofs) with clients, vendors, and colleagues. PDF has become the standard for version editing, as well as submitting ads and media to newspaper and periodical publishers; the final output for the printer is itself a high-resolution PDF.

Many programs create reliable PDFs automatically, ensuring correct color profiles and linking to final images and fonts. In creating PDFs using Acrobat, InDesign, or Illustrator, you should start the press optimization process using predefined settings. In InDesign you can go to Adobe PDF Presets>Press Quality. To customize the PDF settings, first go to File>Export and choose your format for print from the drop-down window. When you select Save, another option window will allow you to select Compression > Do Not Downsample; then select Marks and Bleeds to set your crops, bleeds, and printer's registration marks. Always

GLOSSARY

AAs: Author's alterations are edits made to the content of a file by the client. Usually handled before sent to press, if the client makes edits while the job is at the printer—usually in the proofing stage—AAs can prove very costly.

Adobe Acrobat: The family of Adobe programs that create and manage PDFs.

Downsampling: A form of compression that lowers the resolution of images by eliminating unnecessary pixel data.

Embedding: A PDF removes the need for multiple requisite files by including fonts and compressed imagery in one file.

Lossy: A compression format that removes or "loses" certain areas to achieve a smaller file size, yet reopening the file causes the program to "guess" at the missing data, possibly creating a lower-quality version.

PEs: Printer's errors are mistakes and omissions found at the proofing stage by the designer or client that did not, for whatever reason, make it from the supplied file to the press. The cost of these errors is usually absorbed by the vendor as a matter of customer service.

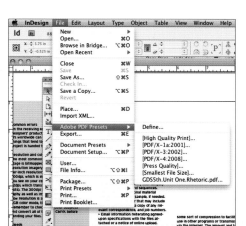

PDF presets Select the correct PDF Preset setting for your file. Choose low-resolution, 72-dpi formats for sending files for email review, and high-resolution files for production.

double check the PDF in Acrobat to make sure everything is correct.

Font embedding When a font is not embedded, it is usually because it is missing from the document folder or has vendor restrictions; when opened or printed, a generic typeface might be substituted. Nothing is worse than opening a publication with your client's advertisement—a masterpiece in Gill Sans, say—and being greeted with a horror dripping in Courier. Proper embedding during your process prevents font substitution at the viewing stage, and ensures that vendors reprint the text in its intended font. Preflight tools in InDesign and Illustrator usually help you steer clear of errors before reaching PDFs, and you can always check Properties when viewing PDFs to check that fonts are embedded.

PDF/X When Preflighting, you can bring your PDF to PDF/X and PDF/A standards. These file types, defined by the International Organization for Standardization (ISO), adhere to standards that facilitate reliable PDF transmission. They apply the wills and will-nots of a file. Using a PDF-X1a file generated from Acrobat Preflight (a recognizable pre-set option in the Pre-Flight menu) is considered the best way to ensure that your file is correct and secure, and is an option in InDesign.

What to send

When collecting a project for output, essentially you are mirroring requisite elements that make up the design: fonts, images, and page layouts. However, you are also augmenting these with as many items as possible to help translate to your vendor what you are trying to achieve in production. You can do this by including a satisfactory comp (comprehensive) printout to be used as a guide.

Traditionally, elements such as images and fonts were strung together in page-layout programs such as InDesign and Quark; naturally, these included a suite of Preflight and Packaging capabilities to check and collect everything for output.

File types and compression

Different applications store and compress data in various ways. Misunderstand or misuse these formats and you are heading for trouble. For example, you might

---

PRINT CHECKLIST

To send a file electronically, be sure to include all of the following.

› **Your final approved document** (InDesign: .indd; Quark: .qxd and pdf).

› **A folder of all linked images** (.eps, .tif, .pdf), entitled either "links" or "images." You should also include original files in .psd or .ai, in case your printer needs to make an adjustment.

› **A folder of all fonts** (PostScript, TrueType, OpenType).

› **Printer instructions and profiles** (included in the Preflight and Packaging options).

› **Output or a low-resolution PDF** for the printer to use as a guide, clearly labeled as such to avoid confusion.

› **A detailed comp dummy** that tangibly demonstrates folds and sequences.

› **Ink swatches**, additional material samples, and a paper sample, if needed.

› **A note to the vendor** that may include specific instructions, a copy of any relevant correspondence, and job numbers.

› **Email information** reiterating agreed-upon specifications with the files attached or a notice of online upload.

---

spend hours scanning-in files and creating artwork for a magazine, only to save your hard work in the wrong format. At best, this will cost you hours; at worst, the job. A working knowledge of file formats and the process of compression could go a long way in preventing this scenario.

Electronic files appear to travel many distances around the city or around the globe, when in fact one computer is just copying from another. During this process, corruption can occur, especially to page layout and font files. Compressing files before sending via email or FTP (File Transfer Protocol) is an effective way of preventing this. Most files that are not native application formats can include some sort of compression to facilitate use in other programs or transmission via the Internet. The amount and type of compression, especially with imagery, video, and audio projects, can affect the quality and performance of your final file.

.ZIP and .SIT compression file types reduce the number of bytes by removing the redundant areas of

---

FILE NAMING

• Do not put any spaces in the name or extension; if you need to separate words, use an underscore: "my_file.jpg."

• Use lowercase, not uppercase, characters.

• Use only alpha (abc) or numeric (123) characters. Avoid characters such as @%^&*(), and use a period (.) to separate name and extension.

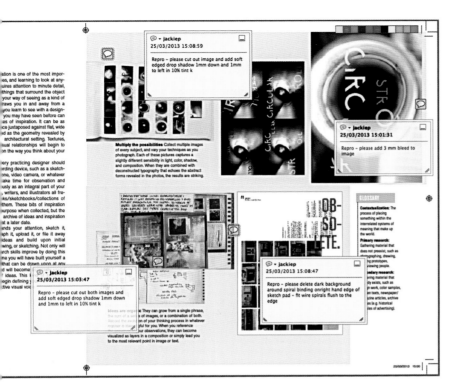

underlying code that make up every file. These repeated and replaceable areas are put back into the file using a program such as WinZip or Stuffit to "unzip" or "unstuff" the file back to its original format. The final, expanded file is identical to the original before it was compressed. Macs and PCs natively create and open ZIP files, whereas Stuffit file creation and expansion needs a separate program.

Sometimes called archives, these compression formats are in all walks of design and production because they speed up and simplify data transmission across the Internet. Used primarily to send large files within emails, many studios and companies utilize an FTP set-up on their web server to easily transfer files online.

PDF Tools PDFs are commonly sent as email attachments for approval and opinion during the design process. The Tools function in Adobe Acrobat Pro allows you to edit PDF file content or to attach your notes and comments to your replies.

Key graphic file formats

  PSD and **AI** are the file formats for Adobe Photoshop and Adobe Illustrator used for image creation.

Compatible with: Photoshop, Illustrator, and InDesign with minor restrictions.

Tip: Make sure to always save an unflattened master version of your Photoshop files to fall back on, and save Illustrator files with unoutlined text.

 EPS used to be the most widely used file format in artwork preparation for print. It can contain either vector or bitmap information and is best used when dealing with logos and illustrations as well as vinyl printing and one- and two-color jobs.

Compatible with: Adobe Illustrator for edits; InDesign and QuarkXpress for layout.

Tip: EPSes themselves can contain font data that may need to be backed up with a font file at the collection stage, or font outlines can be created.

 TIFF creates one of the largest files because it saves an alpha channel in the file, which allows for transparency at the art's edge, not at the pasteboard's edge. Best when dealing with monotone, grayscale, or watermarks for color toning, TIFF is the highest-quality image format for full-color photography as well.

Compatible with: Photoshop for editing; InDesign and QuarkXpress for layout.

Tip: Make sure to check with your printer as to whether they accept files with LZW compression, which is an option while saving.

 JPEG is a format that uses lossy compression— meaning that a certain amount of the image quality is lost during the saving process. With a complex photographic image this would usually remain unnoticed (unless the image is over-compressed).

Compatible with: Photoshop for editing; InDesign and QuarkXpress for layout.

Tip: Nowadays, most digital cameras save as large JPEGs, which can be resaved as high-quality images for print due to advances in image resampling and printing. For large, high-quality reproduction, you should be using .tif files.

PART 2	PRACTICE
UNIT 6	PRINT PRODUCTION AND PRESENTATIONS
MODULE 2	**Creating a convincing presentation**

↑ **Presentation** Packaging prototypes for retail, food, and beverages should represent how they will look and function at the point of purchase. There are software packages that will render images onto a digital object, but your client may want to simulate the consumer experience to help them decide.

➜ **Form and function** Work out the logistics of assembly, in simple and in complex constructions, as best you can. If it helps, consult a print vendor during the design process and determine the best way to commercially assemble your concept, then create your prototype.

It is critical that your client approve the final version of the electronic file, usually a PDF document, but presenting the idea clearly at the concept approval stage can influence the client's choice on which concept to produce. A comp, or comprehensive, is the designer's finished concept shown in the closest possible approximation to the produced product as is possible. Good craft skills are essential and, although a bad concept can't be saved by good craft, a great concept can sometimes suffer if it is poorly crafted.

Color

Electronic output from a high-quality desktop printer can come very close to matching the four-color process intended in production. Matching Pantone colors can be trickier. Colors on screen can be misleading, and will only come close if your monitor is perfectly calibrated. A Pantone number encoded in your document will ensure the color ink that prints, but to show that exact color to your client in comp form you may need to depend on a custom blend that adjusts the color for comping only. Make a separate file named "Comp" and adjust your colors there. That way you won't send the wrong document to the supplier.

Format

With your color perfected, you need to assemble the document into whatever form the product will take,

such as booklet, poster, or package design. Output papers come in various weights, and some color printers will accept the stock you intend to use in production. If you can, print on stock samples, which will give you and your client the best representation of the final product and will show you how duotones and tritones will be affected by the stock color.

Unfortunately, it's nearly impossible to register output on both sides of the paper, so you'll need to use a dry mastic sheet, like 3M mounting material, to glue—or dry mount—the sides together. Always leave some bleed and printer's registration marks, and trim your pages after you have assembled them. Cut and score the paper for folding after the assembly is completed in a clean, dry studio space.

Craft

Some techniques can't be imitated digitally and need to be done by hand. Die cutting will require careful handwork with a thin utility knife, and practicing your cutting and comping skills will lead to cleaner presentations. Metallic stamps will need to be hand cut and applied, also. In some cases, a poster, or board, of your intended materials and colors can help in the presentation, but there's no substitute for a clean comp.

◀ **Present appropriately**
Determine where you will be presenting, and how many clients will be attending. At a small meeting you can use a tabletop presentation, but with a larger group, you may need to post images or project them. Be prepared, and bring your tablet or laptop to the meeting.

⬇ **Match color and paper stock** Simulate the look of your recommended print process, as well as your format. You can come very close to simulating four-color process with a good laser or ink-jet printer. Assemble the product, even if you are showing it on screen.

⬇ **Craft is art** Die cutting, scoring, and folding by hand takes practice and patience. Laser cutters have simplified the process, but if you don't have access to one you'll need great craft skills. Be true to the product line and be sure to carefully create each element in the design system.

➕ **SEE ALSO:** PRINTED COLOR, P132

Paper is absolutely part of the picture, and it can enhance or diminish the vibrancy of your imagery. Paper stock is manufactured in a large assortment of weights, colors, textures, and finishes, and selecting the correct one can really add to the success of the finished product. Sampling is the ideal way to determine whether or not a particular stock will work for you. You should also be aware of the common terms used to describe paper, including the various attributes and how they apply to a particular job.

Matte finish Uncoated stock can have a variety of finishes, from silky smooth to rough linen texture. Choose appropriately for your concept and print process. A creamy, matte finish on cotton fiber reinforces the image in this booklet and feels environmentally friendly.

Paper is produced from pressed pulped wood, cotton, or recycled paper. Seven standard attributes describe different characteristics.

- Weight describes the density of the fibers that make up the sheet, and is measured in pounds (lb) or grams per square meter (gsm or g/m2). Letter weights vary from 24 lb or gsm to 140 lb cover weight. Specialty stocks can be even heavier.
- Thickness is measured in caliper (inches) or millimeters; however, greater thickness does not mean better quality.
- Texture depends on the size or quality of wood fibers and the method of construction. Tightly pressed, fine fibers result in a smoother paper normally used for writing or printing; less pressed, bigger fibers form board and fibrous card.
- Strength (tension and resilience) is affected by texture, density, weight, and thickness; for example, tissue paper and paperboard are both used for packaging, but in different contexts.
- Opacity depends on density and thickness, and refers to how much text or image on the overleaf page can be masked. Vellum paper is highly translucent and is made by immersing good-quality paper in acid, which alters the fibers.

- Brightness depends on how much the paper has been bleached before it is pressed. Brighter stock reflects more light and results in a fresher look to a page. Environmental concerns have resulted in a return to unbleached paper in recent years.
- Color is produced by dyeing the fiber pulp before it is pressed. Colored stocks can be more expensive than white stock.

Matte, satin, and gloss surfaces
Different paper qualities affect the intensity of printed ink—there is a stark difference between printed matte and gloss surfaces. When ink adheres to matte paper, it is absorbed and has no shine. Matte finish is used for printed-word texts such as newspapers and books, and tends to be easy to read. However, ink printed onto gloss paper stays on the surface, so more light hits the paper below and bounces off, giving a deeper, more intense color. This quality is used for book covers, magazines, brochures, and packaging. Satin paper (or dull coat) comes somewhere between the two, giving a slightly less intense color than gloss but without the shiny surface.

Add flavor Deeply textured cover stock in cocoa brown is a tantalizing entrée to the individually packaged chocolates on the inside of this package design. Beautiful typography and delicate matte colors partner to establish the brand as a luxury item.

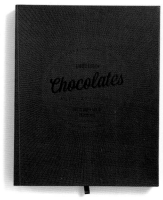

Going green
Concerns about sustainability in recent years mean that many designers now use recycled papers, or sheets made from cotton, not wood pulp. This is not the only concern for sustainable design, but an important consideration when choosing paper.

Finishes and coatings

Finishes and coatings are added either to protect printed ink, or in patches to emphasize an area of ink. There are four main kinds.

- Varnishes are coatings applied "on press," either with other inks or as a separate run, and can be matte, satin, or gloss, and tinted with added pigment.
- UV coatings are spread on as a liquid, then hardened with ultraviolet light. They can be matte or gloss, and applied accurately in spot form or as complete coverage.
- Aqueous coatings—matte, satin, and gloss—are relatively expensive and are laid at the end of a run. As such they cannot be controlled to be put in specific areas, only as a complete coat.
- Laminates are layers of sheet plastic or clear liquids that bind into the paper to protect it.
- Paper can also be embossed to emphasize lettering or an image, and it can be stamped with metallic foil or glossy, flat, or shiny color, a beautiful effect on matte paper. It can also be laser cut or die cut to expose pages underneath. These are beautiful but expensive techniques, so be sure your budget allows for the technique you choose.

Texture and light Die cuts add surprising pops of color and use light and shadow to add detail to an extended system. Consult your print vendor or paper merchant to choose the right stock for your project.

Surface texture Business cards are personal items. Adding a tactile element, such as a raised embossing, adds memorability and delicate light and shadow to the surface of the design.

Impression Add texture and tactility to your composition by embossing or debossing the surface of your stock. Uncoated, textured stocks work well, with or without ink coverage.

Samples Paper sample books will give you a much better idea of the print and finish possibilities for your projects. Each booklet has samples of the available colors, weights, and surface finishes on each sheet. This book of translucent stock is from Curious Papers, and also comes in metallics.

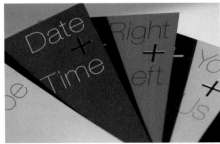
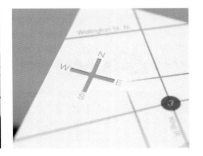
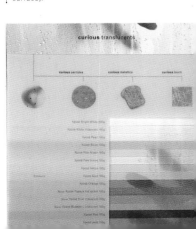

Various factors determine how many colors you use to produce a job. Aspects such as aesthetics, budget, and branding come into play when you make your selections, and you want to be sure the colors you choose are the ones that appear accurately on the finished product.

⬆ Pantone Color Bridge This not only shows you what a particular solid PMS color will look like, but also its full-color printed counterpart, while giving the CMYK, RGB, and hexidecimal formulas for typing it in.

⬇ PMS book Keep one of these books on hand when designing, attending client meetings, and going on press check as a guide to help choose and validate color.

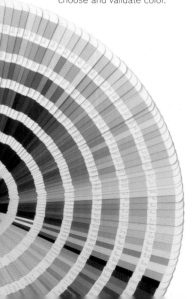

Any printed image we see is an illusion of light, paper, and patterns of ink that rely on the visual cortex "blending" the information our retinas perceive into a logical image. Many different kinds of printing types have been created in order to mass-produce this "illusion" over the decades.

Single-color (monotone or monochome) printing can be used when there are budget constraints or when there is a particular color that must be used. For instance, many companies specify a particular Pantone ink for consistency across all their printed work to ensure brand recognition.

Two- and three-color printing allows for interesting mixtures of Pantones: overprinting two translucent inks can generate a third color, and printing black-and-white images in two colors (duotone) and three colors (tritone) can enhance their effect.

Four-color process printing uses cyan (C), magenta (M), yellow (Y), and black (K) inks specified in percentage tints to create a huge variety of other colors. This more popular method is used for reproducing full-color imagery, photographs, or flat colors.

PMS

The Pantone Matching System consists of color reference manuals, or books, used for selection and input, either by PMS number or by precise CMYK formulas. Printers have these books and the corresponding matching inks.

Pantone colors, or spot colors, have different ink options, since color reacts differently with different printing processes and surfaces. To help approximate this, PMS swatch books come in many versions, made for different papers such as coated and matte, and in solid or process colors.

Workspace, monitor, and calibration

The key to consistent color is to work in a well-lit room with a properly calibrated monitor. Using color conventions such as PMS and composing colors using CMYK breaks help you achieve correct color from screen to press. When in doubt, do it by the numbers.

With color you can mix cyan, magenta, yellow, and black in any image-making program or by selecting colors from an image. This approach mimics the pioneer press person's experimentation with inks that forged the path for printing today. However, PMS is a more reliable way to ensure you are going to get the color you choose.

Calibrating your monitor The best place to begin a successful color workflow is with the monitor. Correct calibration and profile usage ensure that what you see on screen is what turns out in print. Reliable translation of material from scanner or camera to monitor and printer means proper communication from one device to the next. Many modern monitors come with presets and programs to help you get basic values, but in recent years colorimeters have become readily available to ensure every color point and setting is consistently and dependably adjusted to standard. Colorimeters cycle through a series of modes to read the current state of display and adjust the video card correctly, creating a new profile, called an ICC profile, for the monitor to create color from.

! Global standard
GRACOL is currently the standard color profile, but ask your service bureau which profile they prefer you to work with—they may even have created their own.

← Tints and opacities
Screen color doesn't always translate exactly in print. Proofing your design on the actual stock will give the best indication of the final outcome.

Every device has its own set of ICC profiles. Set up by the International Color Consortium, these standards facilitate the translation of color information of an image from one device to the next. When a screen, scanner, or camera is recalibrated, each is given a new profile and the image produced picks up that profile. Images opened in Photoshop can be reviewed; if a profile setting is different or missing, then the working profile of the monitor is used.

! RGB to CMYK
Printers often insist that you give final image files converted to a CMYK format. Generally, it's best to keep images in RGB format until you are ready to send the file to the printer, since image-manipulation programs such as Adobe Photoshop work best with RGB files for correction and effects. Printers recommend the Image>Mode>CMYK function to change an image from RGB to CMYK. They may also prefer to do their own pre-press production check to ensure that all electronic files are prepared to their satisfaction.

PMS AND PANTONE BOOK PAPER CHOICES

PMS
- **Solid** Over 1,000 PMS spot colors are contained in either the fan guide or the chip book, with specialty versions for metallic colors, pastels, neons, and tints.
- **Process** Over 3,000 Pantone Process Colors with their CMYK percentages are contained in these books.
- **Color Bridge** Formerly known as the Solid to Process Guide, this book provides a larger color swatch and tint comparison showing how solid colors will look in CMYK, and gives print and web formulas.

Pantone
- **Coated** This book contains PMS numbers followed by a "C," indicating that a color can only be matched by printing on a coated (glossy) surface.
- **Uncoated** This book contains PMS numbers followed by a "U," indicating an uncoated (matte) surface.

↑ Calibration
Many factors such as time, usage, and heat cause a monitor to go out of calibration—many colorimeters, such as the Spyder, are available to recalibrate.

DPI: Dots per inch is a measurement of printer resolution revealing how many colored dots are available to create a square inch of an image. The higher the DPI, the more refined the text or image will appear.

LPI: When printing halftones, such as in one-color newspapers and reproductions, the lines per inch is the number of lines that compose the resolution of a halftone screen.

PPI: Pixels per inch or pixel density is interchangeable with DPI, but usually refers to the resolution of an unprinted image displayed on screen or captured by a scanner or digital camera.

⊕ **SEE ALSO:** FUNDAMENTALS OF COLOR, P88

← Surface and ink
Coated paper allows the ink to sit on the paper surface so the shine of the stock is evident. On uncoated stock, the ink sinks into the paper fibers and dries to a matte finish. PMS coated and uncoated swatch books show you the differences on each PMS numbered ink.

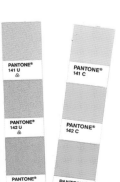

← ↖ Limited color
The two-color booklet has a friendly, environmentally conscious, and no-fuss appearance. Radiant colors in transparent inks create gorgeous value and hues when overlapped on the package design. Limited color can be used for its appearance as well as for value.

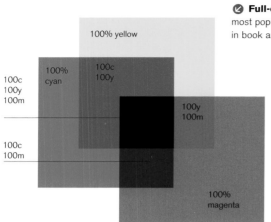

100% yellow

100c
100y
100m

100%
cyan

100c
100y

100y
100m

100c
100m

100%
magenta

Full-color printing CMYK is the most popular form of print used daily in book and magazine production.

PART 2	PRACTICE
UNIT 6	PRINT PRODUCTION AND PRESENTATIONS
MODULE 5	**Print media**

In all traditional printing methods (that is, everything except digital printing), your digital artwork needs to be separated into the constituent colors in which it will be printed.

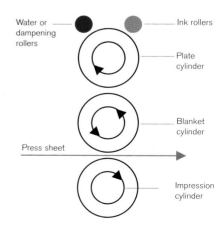

Printing on plastic Different printing methods are provided for different materials, so consult your vendor and research your options. Consider how many colors you will be printing and how many impressions you need. Most surfaces can be offset printed or screen printed, but new digital technologies are rapidly adding options.

To accomplish this in traditional lithography the printer will make plates, a separate one for each of the four process ink colors or an individual plate for each Pantone, or spot, color. Most large presses have room for at least six inks and can accommodate varnish as part of the process. Requesting too many spot colors may cause the job to run through the press more than once, and can really affect your printing costs.

The offset printing principle
This printing process is based on the principle that

water and oil do not mix. The digitally produced printing plate is treated chemically so that the image will accept ink and reject water. The simplified diagram below shows an exposed plate wrapped around the rotating plate cylinder, where the image is dampened and inked. The inked image on the plate is then transferred onto the blanket cylinder. The rubber blanket transfers the image onto the stock, which has been carried around the impression cylinder (adjusted depending on the stock used). This planographic process is rapid, and the plate is inked on each rotation.

The principle in action
This press diagram shows an exposed plate wrapped around the rotating plate cylinder, where the image is dampened and inked before being transferred onto the blanket cylinder.

On a roll Most presses feed one sheet of paper through at a time, but larger web presses, which are used for long runs, draw paper from a roll.

Water or dampening rollers

Ink rollers

Plate cylinder

Blanket cylinder

Press sheet

Impression cylinder

OFFSET ADVANTAGES

- High-quality images can be achieved by providing a higher-resolution print.
- Works on a wide range of print media such as paper, fabric, plastic, wood, metal, leather, and glass.
- Cost per printed piece decreases as the quantity increases.
- Quality, cost effectiveness, and bindery finishing are fully controllable in large-run jobs.
- Modern offset presses use computer-to-plate technology, increasing economy and quality.

🛇 Black

Many designers and printers prefer the "mega-black" or "super-black" formula for large areas of black. This formula, at 60C, 40M, 40Y, 100K, should be used in imagery, not text, and provides a much richer interpretation over 100K alone to create black.

⬆ Full black

Choose this process when your halftone photographic subjects have significant expanses of black and a full grayscale range to add richness to the subject. Printed body text and fine lines should be printed in as few color separations as possible to avoid registration issues. Use 100K or choose a Pantone black.

⊕ **SEE ALSO:**

FUNDAMENTALS OF COLOR P88

Styles of printed color and shade

75 dpi at actual printed size   300 dpi at actual printed size

⬆ **CMYK and resolution** When a full-color image is needed for print, it must be generated as a CMYK file. For full-color, duotone, and grayscale images, image size is reproduced and digital file resolution should be twice the lines per inch (lpi). The standard for high-resolution print is 300 dpi.

⬆ **Halftone** Many periodicals and screen printers use a halftone pattern to mimic the detail and gradients in a one-color printed image.

⬆ **Sketch** Used when you wish to reproduce an image in black and white and retain some of the detail, for effect or low-resolution photocopying. At reproduction size, digital file resolution should be eight times the lpi.

PART 2	PRACTICE
UNIT 6	PRINT PRODUCTION AND PRESENTATIONS
MODULE 6	**Digital printing**

With conventional offset lithography almost a century old, digital presses—emerging in the early 1990s with the ability to create print directly from a digital file—have opened up new frontiers. Forward-thinking printers have embraced any technology that enables them to provide more options for their customers. Different than traditional offset, from speed to price to flexibility, digital printing has worked its way into the workflow of many designers and print houses as clients' needs, wants, and timeframes accelerate with the changing times.

Stock options Paper finishes and surface textures affect digital and offset printing processes. Paper swatch books like this one, featuring stock samples for digital printing, will show you the wide range of effects that are possible.

Digital presses reproduce documents through a process of toner-based electro-photography—a technology inherent in the common desktop laser printer. This not only speeds up the process but also removes a variety of margins for error.

Generally used for print runs of fewer than 1,000 pieces, for economy, digital printing also opens up per-piece customization for direct mailing, variable data jobs, and frequently updated publications such as newsletters and timetables. Personalized printing and printing on demand are therefore growth industries, allowing for print-on-demand books and other items of varying printed details, page quantities, and binding techniques.

Vendors include online-and-on-demand service bureaus, traditional sheet-fed and web-offset printers, screen printers, sign manufacturers, and point-of-purchase display producers. Allow yourself and these agencies a margin for error in production stages as you prepare and oversee your digitally printed project. Always check a digital proof and discuss the options with your printer.

Ink versus toner

With digital printing the toner does not permeate the paper like conventional ink, but instead forms a thin layer on the surface. Some designers and printers believe that digitally printed color can appear more saturated. This happens due to lack of light absorption by the paper when ink "sinks in," as in traditionally printed items. It is not necessarily a bad thing, because "more saturated" to a printer can also mean "more vibrant" to a client. Make sure to discuss project adjustments to match your intended output more closely, since some newer presses use a combination of toner and ink to achieve more exact color values.

Some digital presses that use toner may produce large areas of solid color with banding and blending problems. Ask your printer to run samples, so you can review for yourself what may or may not work.

Timeframe

Digital printing cannot be beaten for production timing, since there is no set-up and clean-up of the press for each job. Some offset print houses are now offering shorter print-timing by utilizing such techniques as gang-run printing or shift-scheduling.

Personalization

Database-driven variable data printing allows digital printing to offer the most economical way to customize marketing materials, direct mail pieces, newsletters, and other items with different information or designs on each individual printed piece. Finally, all that information that companies have been collecting for years can be easily used in print!

DIGITAL OR OFFSET OPTIONS

- **Quantity** Short-run jobs can prove more cost effective with digital printing; larger quantities are likely to have a lower per-unit cost with offset printing. The rule of thumb is: over 1,000 pieces—go to offset.

- **Color** Digital presses are like large four-color process (CMYK) desktop printers. With monotone or duotone printing, offset printing may offer a more cost-effective solution. If Pantone colors are needed, traditional offset is the only way to go. However, digital printing may offer economical and scheduling advantages when it comes to full-color pieces.

- **Paper and finishing** Special paper, finishes, surfaces, and unique size options are increasing every year for digital, but offset printing still offers more flexibility because of the variety of print surfaces available. Also, most digital presses can only handle 14 x 20-in (35.5 x 50-cm) press sheets, whereas offset goes up to 40 x 28in (100 x 70cm), increasing the number of impressions you can group on a sheet.

- **Proofs** Digital offers more accurate proofs, since you receive a sample of the final printed piece using the exact process and paper that will be used for the intended final run. In offset printing, the proofs are generally being produced by digital printers.

⊼ **Multiple formats** Digital printing can be used for all types of projects as long as you are working with digital files in CMYK mode. Printing can be done in many formats, including large-format printers that accommodate much bigger surface areas for packaging, posters, and banners.

⬇ **Complete systems** Desktop digital printers are essential for printing comprehensives for client approval. A good-quality inkjet or laser printer will also help you to check your work in progress and simulate your intended printing effects.

⬆ **Complete systems** Color matching a complete identity system can be tricky. Digital color works wonderfully well on photographic subjects and is less expensive for shorter press runs.

GLOSSARY

Banding: Series of lighter or darker bands running across an area of solid color.

Digital presses: Automate direct image transfer from digital file to paper without the creation of plates.

Digital printing: Method of printing that uses a plateless, computer-controlled press.

Gang-run printing: Printing many different jobs on one large sheet.

Shift-scheduling: Allowing presses to run all day and night.

PART 2	PRACTICE
UNIT 6	PRINT PRODUCTION AND PRESENTATIONS
MODULE 7	**Correcting color proofs and press checks**

The arrival of color proofs from the printer is second only to the arrival of a finished printed piece of work you have created. However, at color proof stage, it is still possible to correct some flaws in photographic reproduction, both digital and conventional.

Your proof should be carefully examined for density, color, registration, and dots or spots that may appear on the surface, in addition to any potential text errors you or your client may have missed. It's better to catch them at the proofing stage, when they can still be corrected fairly inexpensively, than during the press check. Keep your comp with you and check the proof to be sure the trim, fold, and assembly have been detailed properly. Whenever possible, ask for a proof on the actual stock you will be imprinting, so you can check the color accurately. Circle anything that worries you, and ask your printer about it.

Press check

Printers are usually very receptive to clients overseeing their jobs at the beginning of the press run, and this almost always turns into a learning experience. It is especially helpful when aesthetic judgment is needed. The press person will pull a sheet off the press for you to review, approve, and sign off on. At this point you should take your time, pay attention, ask questions, and have a checklist to keep you focused.

Remember that at a press check time is expensive—egregious errors such as misspelled words and unaligned edges should have been handled at the proof stages. This will help to avoid any extra correction costs, set-up charges, and rescheduling for you and your client. When you are "on the floor" in the press room, you should focus on overall aesthetic considerations, although a keen eye is always on the hunt for an errant inch-mark instead of an apostrophe, or a random double space.

Grayscale density patches are printed in steps from no tint through to black. They are used to check black-and-white photography and black text in a similar way to that of a color control strip

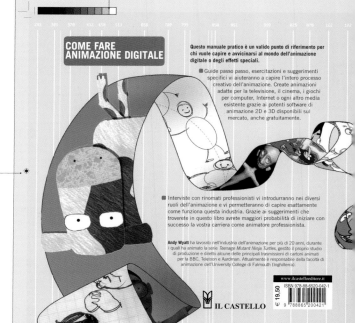

Check registration marks to see if the job has been proofed in register. If it is correct, all you will see is black. If it is out of register, one or more colors will show next to the black

Check trim marks for position and that the bleed allowance is correct

Linen tester (loupe) A magnifier called a linen tester, or a loupe, is used to check color separations, transparencies, and proofs. It will clearly show the dot screen of your half-tone images and will allow you to check the sharpness and dot registration easily. The built-in folding stand keeps the lens at the exact right distance from the sheet surface and leaves your hands free, so no fingerprints are confused with potential flaws.

⚠ Fit or registration
If the register marks fit but you can see colors sticking out from the edge of the picture, the job has been planned out of fit, or is "out of register."

PRESS CHECK CHECKLIST

Be prepared; bring these with you.
- An extra copy of electronic files or, even better, a laptop you can work directly from (with requisite fonts and imagery installed).
- The Pantone book (coated/uncoated, or spot or process). See page 133.
- The color proof that you signed. Although many vendors may want this back, be sure to ask for it again at press time.
- A linen tester or loupe to check for such things as registration, dot bleed, dot gain, and font clarity. It usually has a folding stand to hold the lens at the correct distance from the page.
- Patience. A press check on a multi-page document can be lengthy, especially on large print runs. Be prepared for down time, and settle in for the long run.

GLOSSARY

Dot gain: A printed dot that becomes bigger than intended due to spreading, causing a darkening of screened images, mid-tones, and textures. This varies with different paper stocks.

Quality control strip: Usually incorporated in printed sheets outside the grid to monitor the quality of plate-making, inking, and registration. Checking black sections helps point out color casting.

Registration marks: Hairline marks at the corners of a printed page to help ensure plates are lined up correctly, and that designate what will be cropped off at finishing time.

⊕ **SEE ALSO:** PREPARING FILES FOR PRINT, P124

PRINTED COLOR, P132

The color control strip tells the designer whether the proof is faithful to the film being proofed. For example, if the proofreader has used too much yellow ink, so that the proof looks too yellow when the film is correct, the color bar will help to show this

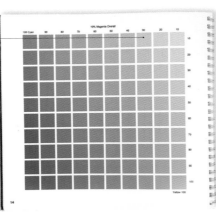

◀ **InDesign** Check the swatch colors in your native files if they need adjusting. In the InDesign main menu under Window>Color>Swatches, you can see the four-color breakdown of your tint.

On first specifying a tint, always give percentages of the process colors, obtainable from a tint chart, rather than a Pantone color swatch or reference number to match, because many special colors cannot be achieved from the four-color process. The tint on the proof can then be checked against the tint chart. Watch out for mottled tints, which can be caused by the film or plate being exposed out of contact

BACKGROUNDS

If a common special color or tint background is required for several pages in a publication, the designer should be aware of problems the printer might have in maintaining consistency between pages. For example, if a taupe background is used, consisting of a percentage tint of process yellow, and there are some pages that require a heavy weight of yellow to be run for the pictures, the tints on those pages may be heavier than on the other pages. The use of a special fifth Pantone color for the backgrounds only should prevent this problem—but remember that it is more expensive to run five colors than four.

UNIT 6: ASSIGNMENTS

○ PACKAGING A FILE FOR THE PRINTER

1 In InDesign, create a new layout that features: a solid-color background; a halftone image, either color or duotone—you can customize it in Photoshop; and body text and a headline. Use your design skills to create an interesting page, but bear in mind that this exercise is centered on packaging the file for reproduction.

2 Check for the following:

• **Resolution and color mode** The most common problem at the printing stage is bitmapped pictures due to low-resolution imagery. The standard dots-per-inch resolution for printed imagery is 300dpi, which is much higher than you see on your computer screens (a mere 72dpi, which translates to 72 rows of 72 dots). The 300dpi rule goes for photography as well as images and illustrations. Low resolution is also associated with the RGB color mode, the web-based resolution. Check your color subjects and convert all of them to CMYK mode before continuing.

• **Bleeds** With imagery and color reaching the end of the paper, an actual section of that color "bleeds" into the outer margin of the larger print sheet. Printers ask for at least ⅛in (0.3175cm) around the page. Be sure your photographic subjects are sized accordingly and that you have enough material for the bleed areas. When positioning photo imagery, remember to compensate for the bleed by placing the image to be trimmed in the full proper space. It may appear slightly off-center in the electronic file, but when printed and trimmed, it will equalize.

• **Fonts** In Illustrator-rendered pieces, you can change your type to artwork by selecting the Type> Create Outlines function to retain consistency. You will not need to send a font if the type has been converted. Do not assume that printers have the same fonts that you do. Fonts of the same name come in different versions and from different foundries, and so can have minor characteristic changes.

3 When you have completely checked your file, go to File>Package and follow the steps to create a new folder for the work. When you have electronically packaged the file, you'll see that InDesign has collected all of your assets and automatically placed them in titled folders. Open each folder and check the contents. If you make a change to the design work after this point, remember to package it again, or to save changes in images to the individual folders that house your assets.

○ CREATE PDF FILES

Preflight tools in InDesign, Photoshop, and Illustrator will allow you to save in PDF format. Each one offers preset options that allow you to optimize the PDF and customize it according to use.

1 Open a file in each program and explore the Adobe Preset options available, then create PDF files in low resolution for electronic approvals. Check them for errors, correct any you find, and try again.

2 Email them to yourself as attachments, and make sure they are traveling well electronically.

3 Using the same native files in InDesign and Illustrator, create high-resolution files intended for reproduction. Remember to add your bleeds and printers' marks. Save the files and check them on screen, then print them to see how accurate they look.

◉ CREATE AN EIGHT-PAGE ROLL-FOLD DOCUMENT

1 Start to prepare an eight-page roll-fold document by measuring it carefully. Each page will measure 4in wide by 8½in tall (10 x 21cm). Each of the end panels will fold in, so they will need to be slightly shorter than 4in (10cm) to clear the center fold.

2 Set up the file electronically if you have paper large enough to print on—13 x 19in (33 x 48.4cm)—or draw it out by hand using a T-square, metal ruler, and triangle. You will need a sheet of paper approximately 9 x 18in (23 x 45.5 cm) to complete it by hand.

3 Using an exacto knife with number 11 blade, carefully cut out the whole form, scoring the folds lightly with your knife. Your first try may be less than perfect. Make the adjustments and try again. Be sure the blade is sharp, and change it if it begins to drag on the surface.

Further Reading:

Raven Smith, *Paper: Tear, Fold, Rip, Cut*, Black Dog Publishing, 2009

Trish Witkowski, *Fold: The Professional's Guide to Folding*, Finishing Experts Group, 2002

Taka Nakanishi, *Special Effects: A Book About Special Print Effects*, All Rights Reserved Publishing, 2007

David Bann, *The All New Print Production Handbook*, Watson-Guptill, 2007

Gavin Ambrose, Paul Harris, *Basic Design 06: Print & Finish*, AVA, 2006

◉ COLOR COMPS

1 Create a small multi-page document in InDesign, either a simple four-page document with front and back cover and inside spread, or a trifold.

2 Create a PDF when you have finished, and print the document. If the document is double sided, you'll need to adhere the sides together. Do not trim it yet. Use a dry mounting sheet, such as 3M mounting material, burnish down the material and then attach the back. You can also use rubber cement, but be sure you let it dry completely before you attach the back.

3 Using the encoded printers' marks on the PDF, trim the document, score it, and fold it.

4 When your comp is complete, think about which parts of the product you would discuss at a large presentation. Photograph your comp on a seamless white background and upload the image. Select two details of your project from the native file and create large detail images that explain your talking points. Then create presentation boards or an electronic presentation for a meeting.

◉ PAPER SAMPLES

1 Collect as many examples of print techniques on various stocks as you can. Try to collect examples of effects as well, such as stamping, embossing, and die cutting. Cut them into 3½-in (9-cm) squares, or as close to that as you can without destroying the sample.

2 Score them across the top, ½in (12mm) down, to make a flap, and paste the flap into your sketch book, leaving the bottom free. You will be able to feel them for weight and surface texture and use the swatches as inspiration when you are brainstorming. Visit a local paper merchant and request sample books. Build a library of coated and uncoated samples that you can use as references.

◉ TEST SHEET

Find two images: a photograph and an illustration (preferably one with only a few colors, like a logo).

1 Open the photo in Photoshop and go to Save For Web and Devices in the File menu. You will see the image with a variety of controls to the right.

2 Explore the drop-down selectors, choose between JPG and GIF, and modify the settings for each format to see how the image is re-rendered. Watch the file size change in the lower left as you make adjustments.

3 Repeat the process with the illustration and make a note of which option best suits each image.

7 WEB AND INTERACTIVITY

If you assemble a group of website designers and ask them to provide concrete perspectives that relate to designing for the web, you will often get the same response: "Well, it depends."

For newcomers to the field, this vacuous response elicits more frustration than comprehension. But, at the core, this is the essence of what makes designing for the web so exciting. Each client brings with them new material, with varying project goals and functionality requirements. While some projects require the active participation of a full development team, most are the collaborative product of a few key members, or perhaps a well-rounded individual. Therefore it is increasingly common for a modern website designer to not only have a working familiarity with the varied steps of a website's development process, but also to be ready to take the lead and make sure that each step is accomplished successfully.

How many different development roles will a website designer be expected to command on a given project? Well, it depends.

PART 2 | PRACTICE

UNIT 7 | WEB AND INTERACTIVITY

MODULE 1 | **Project development process overview**

Current website development processes can vary greatly from individual to individual and from firm to firm. However, to ensure that a project runs smoothly for all parties involved, including the client, it is essential that you develop—and follow—a structured game plan, broken down into phases and related steps.

The planning phase

The planning phase in a website development project is the most crucial, because these initial steps serve to define the process for the entire project.

Review Initially, the designer and client should get together to define the client's goals, establish who the target audience is, and discuss required specific features and/or functionality of the site. You should work together to establish the metrics for which the site's success will be determined—such as increase in site traffic, sales, contact, or social media reach—with the goal of maximizing the return on the client's design investment (RODI).

Content gathering The next step is to summarize the information that will be presented on the website. Include the site content (text) as well as defining the visual elements (logos and branding elements, imagery).

Flowchart A flowchart is a graphical representation used to display the overall scope of the website. It defines the elements that make up the site's navigational structure (shown as boxes, one per page), as well as the structured flow of traffic through the website (the lines connecting the boxes). It is the crucial foundation for a successful website.

Software, technology, and resources You will need to determine and identify the programming format in

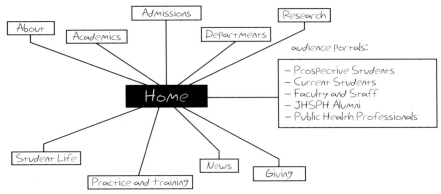

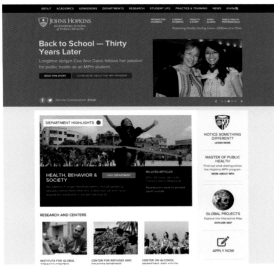

Flowcharts

These are used to document the anticipated site structure. Flowcharts can be subject to numerous revisions before the project begins. Pages are added (or removed) and topics can be combined on the same page, as logic dictates.

which the site will be developed. Anticipate the range of devices on which the site will be viewed, then summarize additional resources that may be required (web font usage, stock photography, etc.), which may add expenses to the overall project rate.

Training requirements If instructional documentation, phone support, or onsite training will be required in order for your client to maintain their own website, this should be defined in the initial planning phase, as it will add additional time to the project's development.

Contract The contract is the end product of the planning phase. Extra care should be taken to make sure that all items discovered and defined in this phase have been factored in to the project's development framework. Successful contracts clearly define the goals, deliverables, roles, timetable, flowchart, copyright, and financial information for the project.

The design phase

The design phase uses the information that was gathered in the planning phase and brings it forward to define the appearance for the final project. Generally speaking, traditional websites are developed around two to four different layout variations, or templates: one for the initial (home) page, with one to three additional, standardized layouts for the project's interior pages, as dictated by the varying types of information that will need to be displayed throughout the website.

THE CLIENT QUESTIONNAIRE

In most cases, project information is obtained by leading a client through a web-development project questionnaire, of which many can be found online. They are usually grouped by category, such as general questions, functionality questions, and design questions. Avoid using technical lingo, which may confuse your client; for example, instead of asking "Do you require an e-commerce solution?" try "Do you plan on selling anything on your website?".

SEE ALSO: SCHEDULING, ORGANIZING, AND FINALIZING, P26

GLOSSARY

Content management systems (CMS): The structured framework of a dynamically driven website.

CSS (Cascading Style Sheets): The code that controls the appearance of features of the website.

E-commerce: Websites created with the goal of selling products online.

HTML (Hypertext Markup Language): Elements that form the building blocks of all websites.

Metrics: The strategy for measuring the success, or failure, of a project's goals.

RODI: Return On Design Investment indicates the success of a project in relation to the project's unique goals.

Site map: A recap of the website's navigation structure, intended to direct viewers to a specific page within the website structure.

Wireframe: An under-designed representation of the layout structure of a website's main pages.

404 Error page: The web page that is displayed as the result of a broken link. If not specified, the web host's default 404 Error page will be displayed.

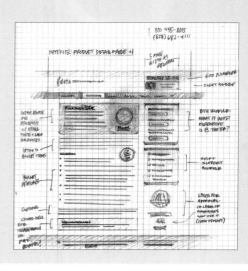

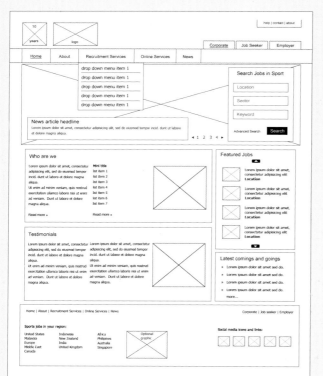

Wireframe process

As this illustration shows, a wireframe serves as a visual blueprint that represents the framework of a website layout. It is an effective process for efficiently exploring alternative relationships for content arrangement, without focusing on the details related to specific stylization choices.

CLIENT REVIEWS

Holding client reviews at specific points within the design phase will generate important feedback on approaches that might have been overlooked in the initial discussions. Having your client sign off on specific steps within the design phase before moving forward to the next step will keep the project on track—and justify any additional development expenses should they change their mind and want to proceed in a revised direction.

Wireframing This initial step in the design phase defines the visual structure of a web page's layout. Start by creating a series of purposefully underdesigned compositions, drawn with lines—similar to an architectural floor plan. Focus on the inclusion of all required elements, as well as their proportional relationships within the overall composition. Resist defining specific visual choices, as they will be defined in the next step of the design phase.

The dimensions of a website The ideal size for a website composition can vary, based on current trends, the target audience/device preferences, and even your

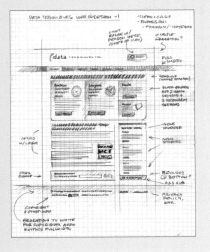

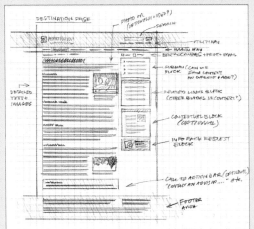

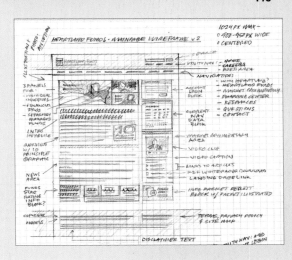

client's preferred method for viewing online content. Visit www.w3schools.com/browsers/browsers_display.asp to view current trends in screen resolution.
[Client review. Revise as necessary. Client sign-off]

Design mock-ups With the desired wireframes selected, the process moves forward to focus on stylizing the elements of your visual composition. Layout compositions are traditionally developed in layered Photoshop documents. Completed files are then exported in (flattened) JPEG format for presentation to the client.

Final compositional layouts Once the initial mock-ups have been approved, they can be refined, with a stronger focus on establishing and maintaining consistency, down to the pixel level. In this step—especially if it was not present or readily available in the mock-up step—the actual content should be incorporated into the layouts. It is quite common to discover that adjustments need to be made before moving forward; for example, allocating more space for longer headlines.
[Client review. Revise as necessary. Client sign-off]

Documentation Between final approval and the beginning of the production phase, the website designer may be called upon to generate documents that clearly outline the specifications of the project to the programmer, in addition to the layered Photoshop files. This additional documentation can include the following items: wireframes annotated with pixel dimensions; type styling outline, which defines the type appearance (typefaces, sizes, line spacing, color use, attributes); and functionality diagrams, which define link behaviors.

The development phase
The development phase consists of the bulk of the programming work. The specifications defined during the design phase are used as a roadmap for the website's development.

⬆ **Compositional Sketches** Rough sketches not only serve to quickly detail the elements that need to be included in composition, but also the visual relationships among these elements.

404 ERROR PAGES

Misdirects happen. Sometimes they may arise as a result of a linking error or from a removed page. Other times, they can come from a viewer who mistyped the address of a specific web page. While often overlooked as a required element of a website project, a "404 Error" page should be created in order to get your viewers back on track. This page can feature a recap of your site's navigation structure (site map) and also the contact details of your developer.

PRESENTATION IDEA

Present your designs within a mocked-up browser window to convey a sense of realness to your client. Browser templates can be found online, or you can take a screen capture of your preferred browser window, replacing elements with your own designs.

⬆ Embrace the scroll

When designing for print, artists make use of the entire canvas. On the web, the layout expands and contracts, defined by the content being presented on each page. Sometimes the content fits neatly within the browser window. Other times, as in this example, the visitor would instinctively scroll in order to discover the full scope of the presentation.

Image prep Image prep involves cropping/resizing supplied or purchased images for insertion within the layout, then optimizing the resulting files in order to generate smaller file sizes that help ensure faster page download times.

Coding Most websites are created using a foundation of HTML and CSS code. HTML (Hypertext Markup Language) is similar to the architectural structure of a building, defining the foundation, wall placement, and so on. The CSS (Cascading Style Sheets) is the code that controls the appearance of features within the building, equivalent to wall color, furniture placement, and inclusion of decorative elements.

Additional functionality As defined in the planning phase, the project may require additional programming. For example, if the website content is controlled by a content management system (CMS), additional code—typically PHP (Hypertext Prepocessor) or ASP (Active Server Pages) code—will need to be inserted within the HTML template structure so that the web page can "call" content from the website's database (text and images) for display on the page when it is viewed in a web browser.

Content integration For smaller websites this step will not be time consuming, because the information will be copied and pasted from a supplied text file and inserted into a web page template. For larger or e-commerce-based websites this step can involve significantly more work; for example, sizing numerous product images or creating inventory listings for inclusion within the e-commerce platform.

Test and verify Using the flowchart as a roadmap, walk through each page of your website to make sure that it functions correctly. It helps to have a fresh pair of eyes to assist you in this step. Test using current browsers (Chrome, Firefox, Safari, IE), platforms (Mac/PC), and devices (desktop, laptop, tablet, smartphone).

The launch phase
The purpose of this phase is to prepare the site for public viewing.

Upload to client's web server Developers usually create a website in a testing, or production, environment, at a different web address from the client's actual web address. Once the website is ready to be launched, the files must be adjusted for the move to the final storage location, the client's web server (or "host").

Code adjustments If the project requires the inclusion of third-party code, such as Google Analytics (for tracking site statistics), it will be inserted after the site has been uploaded to the client's web server.

Testing A final round of usability testing should be conducted. Again, a fresh pair of eyes from individuals not familiar with the project will help point out issues that might have been missed in the project's development. [Client review. Revise as necessary. Client sign-off]

The post-launch phase
This is the final step in the web project's development, when the designer provides a "clean" hand-off of the project to the client. It represents the closing of the project development contract, so be prepared to process all last-minute client requests and make sure that all contractual obligations have been met before you define the project as being complete.

Depending on the type of project, the post-launch phase could include the following:

• **Packaging source files** This task involves organizing and assembling all files to be returned to the client, such as stock photography images, font purchases, and working Photoshop and Word documents. Include a site map of the final site structure, a summary of the project's technical requirements—including languages used, web fonts, and style documentation—and a separate listing of site access passwords, since one site may require different multiple passwords, including passwords to third-party services such as hosting and social media.

• **Documentation and training** If the site is going to be maintained by the client, the developer must compile and document the process for the client, including access to passwords and technical instructions for

⬇ ➡ Concept to execution This student's senior thesis project began following the developmental structure of a traditional web design project. Rough sketches were used to define the main navigational structure, as well as desired features and visual imagery. A series of compositional grid systems were explored and the most successful approach was brought forward to create the final website.

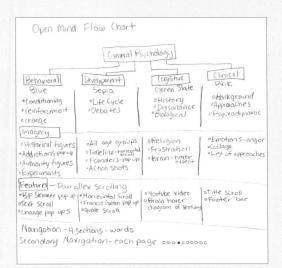

processing site updates. If personalized training or phone support has been specified as deliverable within the project's development contract, it takes place at this step.

- **Satisfaction check** Immediately following the initial website launch, most clients will begin receiving feedback from associates, clients, and friends. Follow up a few weeks after the launch to make sure that your client continues to be satisfied with your work. A little extra effort here will serve to solidify a positive experience and increase the likelihood of client referrals. Additionally, because you have adopted this step into your project development process, you can incorporate a rough estimate of support into the original project pricing.

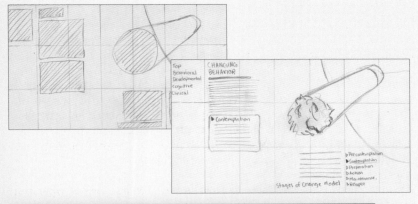

⬆ Creating visual flavor As part of the development of this online product brochure, Brolik Productions was also responsible for generating the visuals. A studio photographer was contracted to take the product images. Stock imagery of apples and orchards were acquired—and further modified—to visually reinforce the messaging present within the site dialogue.

PART 2	PRACTICE
UNIT 7	WEB AND INTERACTIVITY
MODULE 2	**Project structures**

It often falls on the designer to define the appropriate project structure in the beginning, since decisions will cascade into both the design and development processes. Your clients may often cite buzzwords relating to what they want, but it is your role as the designer to listen and decipher what your client actually needs. This module looks at a range of project structures that may define, or be combined to define, your client's project.

Brochure

This is the most straightforward type of web project. Brochure websites are usually the result of a rapid deployment, meeting the goal of quickly establishing an online presence. Branding and visual imagery are in the forefront, since the text-based content is typically less developed. Technically, we're referring to static content, HTML and CSS.

Portfolio

An online portfolio shares many similarities with online brochures, with an enhanced focus on presenting the visual examples. Clicking on an image in an online brochure may take you to a page with product details, whereas clicking on a portfolio image may simply display a more detailed view in the same screen.

Event/campaign site

You may be asked to develop an event, or campaign, website, which corresponds to a strategic marketing push or to promote an upcoming event such as a concert, lecture, or exhibition. These websites typically have a short shelf life, because they are usually attached to a specific date or campaign life cycle. These sites focus on the visual branding, with the addition of actionable items such as submitting RSVPs or purchasing tickets.

Blog

A weblog is an online journal of posts, or news items, presented in a linear, dated format. Blogs often utilize a content management system (CMS) in order to display the site content dynamically, and, by employing the option to allow your site visitors to comment on specific blog posts, you can engage your viewing audience in an evolving conversation.

Community

Community sites are focused around a need to share information and/or support for a specified interest or topic with their member audience. These sites have the goal of engaging their members to interact with each other by submitting comments, user reviews, and aggregated content through social networking and message boards.

News/reference

A news site is highly driven and based upon information. It is usually controlled by a CMS and can feature an editorial structure for managing content inclusion (contributor, editor, moderator levels). News sites are typically monetized by advertising placement. Banner ads, badges, and buttons are designed elements to be included within the layout structure.

E-commerce

Websites created with the goal of selling products online offer the benefit of being open 24/7, reaching a wider audience than an actual storefront location. These sites can be created from a range of solutions, from Google/PayPal shopping cart buttons to customized CMS, connected to a merchant gateway (merchant account) featuring a layer of SSL security. E-commerce sites can incorporate many UI display components such as cross-promotional banners, used for "You May Also Like" and "Recently Viewed" listings. Popular systems include PayPal, Google Checkout, Magento, and Zen Cart.

GLOSSARY

SSL (Secure Sockets Layer): Provides communication security over the Internet.

UI (User Interface): Where interaction between humans and computers occur.

⊕ **SEE ALSO:** PROJECT DEVELOPMENT PROCESS OVERVIEW, P142
WORKING WITH CONTENT MANAGEMENT SYSTEMS, P173

POPULAR CONTENT MANAGEMENT SYSTEMS (CMS):

WordPress An open-source CMS with a reputation for being easy to use. Websites can appear as linear, post-based blogs, or as the administrative back-end for more traditional websites.

Joomla Best for medium-sized sites that don't require a lot of complexity. Extensions—free and commercially available—add enhanced functionality to the default system.

Drupal Used in larger websites that require more complex features. Enhanced functionality is added by installing modules. Has a steeper learning curve, so most designers on Drupal-based projects team up with a developer.

1

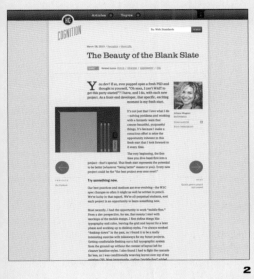

2

3

4

5

6

1 Dark, not black Site visitors prefer reading dark paragraph text on a light background because it is easier on their eyes. However, this layout does not feature an abundance of text, so they made the decision to break from the norm. The sophisticated use of a dark gray field (instead of black) provides enough visual contrast for the white text to be easily read.

2 Editorial structure Blog content is intended to be read. This blog echoes layout styles common to printed publication design, with a strong visual hierarchy, the use of a playful grid structure, thoughtful typography, and the flourish of using an initial capitol letter to lead off the first paragraph.

3 Communicating visually When presenting an online portfolio, your selected work examples should do the talking.

4 A full home page The home page of a news website serves as the gateway for presenting site content. A variety of topics are being presented to a wide audience within a limited space. A structured grid system with clearly delineated content areas is used to organize the presentation of information. Content rotators and tab-based navigation structures are used to efficiently group similar content within the available space.

5 Featured images The pairing of a featured image with a specific article topic serves to visually reinforce the subject matter of the article. It is presented at a large scale on the home page to visually convey that the website is fresh, with new content. On the interior pages, the featured image can be presented in thumbnail form for category listings or as the main visual accompanying the full article.

6 Keeping it simple For e-commerce projects, a successful user experience would provide clear access to review the available products and complete the purchase in the shopping cart. Access to review the shopping cart is usually located in the top-right corner of a web-page layout and remains present on each page of the site.

PART 2	PRACTICE
UNIT 7	WEB AND INTERACTIVITY
MODULE 3	**Web tools**

As a web designer you will be relied upon for your production and technical skill sets, in addition to the strategic creativity that you bring to every project. Whether working on your own or in a collaborative environment, you will need to keep abreast of software and technological advances; maintain clean and well-organized source files, and possess a working knowledge of current code standards.

In the absence of any industry-defined absolutes, there are two perspectives that remain constant. When generating a great product, use whichever applications you deem necessary. Then, when the time comes to hand over the files to the development team (the "coders"), these files should be layered Photoshop documents.

Adobe Illustrator A vector-based drawing application for creating graphics that are used in print and/or on the Web. Web designers use this application for the rapid creation of wireframe layouts and flowcharts (exported and shared with the client as PDF files).

Illustrator can also be used for rendering graphics that are incorporated into websites, such as logos or icons, because it's more efficient and intuitive to create complex graphics in Illustrator than it is in Photoshop.

File set-up: RGB color mode, with "pixel" as the unit of measurement, and 72ppi (screen/web resolution).

Create your artworks in Illustrator at the size they will be used, paying special attention to generating shapes that remain within the pixel-based grid structure. Then copy your artworks from Illustrator and paste into Photoshop as "Smart Objects," which preserves their ability to be edited or updated at a future time.

Adobe Fireworks Fireworks is a vector-based rendering application, developed to only create artwork that will appear online. While the shapes remain vector based, the preview is pixel based. This facilitates the creation of pixel-perfect artwork.

File set-up: By default, all Fireworks documents are set up in RGB color mode, with pixel as the unit of measurement, 72ppi as the resolution, and the desired length-width dimensions.

For generating web layouts, Fireworks has a "States" feature, a saved selection of user-defined layout snapshots (showing/hiding elements within the layers panel) that help the coder of the site see how layouts would change based on rollover states, drop-down menu appearance, varying page content, and so on.

Adobe Photoshop Despite the preferences of the individual designer, the person who will be responsible for "slicing up" and coding the web page layout will primarily have a working familiarity in using Photoshop. Industry-wide, this is why most request that the final files be supplied in a layered, Photoshop (PSD) file.

File set-up: RGB color mode, with "pixel" as the unit of measurement, and 72ppi (screen/web resolution), and the desired length-width dimensions.

Layered PSD files can often grow to more than 100 layers, with elements present across different views. Even when relabeling and organizing your layers into a coherent structure, it can be quite complicated to work with the file. Photoshop's Layer Comp feature (similar to "States" in Fireworks) lets you take snapshot views depicting which elements are visible/hidden when viewing a specific web page.

🔘 **Adobe Photoshop**
As with the other Adobe applications, the appearance and positioning of the palettes, toolbars, and document windows can be adjusted to suit your individual preferences. The default layout is optimized for working on a laptop, but can be expanded to take advantage of larger monitor sizes.

✴️ **Photoshop file etiquette**
This website offers a valuable lesson in organizing and labeling your Photoshop files for working in a collaborative environment.
www.photoshopetiquette.com

✴️ **Adobe TV**
Online video tutorials relating to all Adobe products. An excellent resource for discovering features that have been added to recent software releases.
www.tv.adobe.com

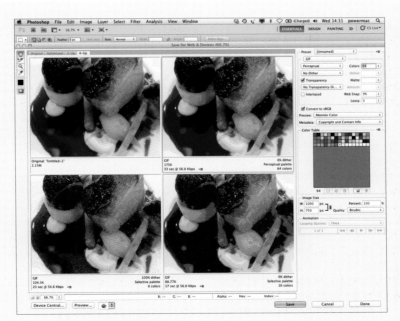

Illustrator is an ideal application for modifying letterforms. Live, editable text can be converted into vector shapes and further modified to create unique visuals. In this example, designer Louise Carrier meticulously works on the positioning and shaping of the branding element for The Natural Rug Store, infusing a unique visual style.

Using Illustrator

Louise Carrier uses Illustrator to generate vector-based illustrations that can be used for a variety of applications—scaled larger or smaller with no loss of image quality.

GENERATING PIXEL-PERFECT ARTWORK

Illustrator will let you render graphics that can break from a pixel-based grid. For example, if you created an icon that was 20 by 20 pixels and, later, manually resized it using the bounding box, the resulting dimensions may become fractions of a pixel (30.565 by 30.565 pixels). While it may look fine in Illustrator, when you placed the artwork into Photoshop (or export it for the web), the artwork will become aliased (or feathered), as opposed to maintaining a crisp edge. Web designers maintain a pixel-based grid in Illustrator by working with the grid turned on (View > "Show Grid"), based on one-pixel integers (Illustrator > Preferences > Guides & Grid > "Gridline every: 10px/subdivisions: 10"); using the dialogue box to define the desired width/length dimensions of rendered shapes; and reviewing the dimensions in the Properties panel to make sure that any resized shapes remain comprised of solid integer values.

EXPORTING GRAPHIC ELEMENTS

Until you get a feel for which specific file format you should use, you can take advantage of the "Save for Web" export feature in the applications above to preview the visual results, while making sure that the file size stays as low as possible. The file sizes of images included in a web page layout will have a direct impact on a web-page's loading time.

GIF and PNG Traditionally used for buttons, logos, and simple artwork, GIFs tend to yield smaller file sizes, while PNGs tend to provide better visual results. Both of these file formats support transparency (if needed). GIF also supports animated content (banner ads).

JPEG Primarily used for optimizing photographic images. Usually, the default 80% quality setting generates the best result without loss of image detail. Avoid using a 90% or higher quality setting, since this may actually increase file size.

Visual Compression

Photoshop's "save for web" feature gives you the ability to review different image compression options to see how they will affect your original image. Using their "4 up" display tab (as shown), you can visually compare the compression results and the corresponding file sizes. Your goal is to reduce the file size as much as possible without reducing the visual integrity of your image. Additional features available in this interface include image resizing, as well as image compression to match a specified file size—typically used for creating banner ads.

Coding

Web pages are usually made up of textual documents, which are annotated in a specific manner indicating to the web browser how they should be displayed—this is known as coding. The most common language used is HTML. Extra stylistic methods such as CSS and JavaScript can be applied along with HTML to improve the look and feel of web pages.

HTML and CSS To use an architectural reference, the combination of HTML and CSS creates a complete house. The HTML represents the structure of the building, while the CSS is used to define the visual appearance.

Designers new to the field should endeavor to learn HTML4.1 and CSS3, since these coding structures have been with us for quite some time and it is likely that you will come across them in your workload.

CSS code is more versatile (and more complex) than HTML, but CSS cannot live alone without the HTML. It would be like trying to paint a wall that does not exist.

CSS has evolved over the years to not only define the style elements of a specific web page, but to be use as an external library of stylistic definitions for an entire website. This strategy allows developers to make modifications quickly, and have them applied globally.

While "living" in a separate file, the use of CSS also helps speed up the loading time of a web page, reducing the amount of code that the viewer's browser must download for each page.

The newer HTML5 builds on the HTML4.1 code structure, while organizing the code differently, based on revised semantics, as opposed to the traditional structure of "head," "body," and so on. HTML5 also adds enhanced animation that is controlled programmatically—replacing the reliance on Flash animation for effects such as sliding elements, color cycling (buttons change color using a timed easing process as opposed to abruptly swapping), and 3D extrude effects.

JavaScript framework MooTools, Scriptalicious, and jQuery are lead examples of libraries within the JavaScript framework. Extensive, external scripts are referenced via your HTML file using a short annotation. Animated slide shows, Apple-style touch interactions, and display/hide content options are examples of functionality that can be added to a website.

Flash/ActionScript Flash is a timeline-based application that can be used for animating vector content. It is supported by a robust back-end programming language called ActionScipt. For a long time, animation and design in Flash were considered essential skills for web designers and developers, and it is still widely popular. Today, emerging languages/formats such as HTML5, CSS, and JavaScript are gaining traction in creating presentations that used to be only feasible in Flash. However, learning to use Flash is still an important skill, not only to produce Flash content but also to understand the concepts and practice of timeline-based animation.

```
<!DOCTYPE html>
<html>
<head>
    <meta charset="utf-8" />
    <title>Title</title>
    <link href="css/html5reset.css" rel="stylesheet" />
    <link href="css/style.css" rel="stylesheet" />
</head>
<body>
    <header>
        <hgroup>
            <h1>Header in h1</h1>
            <h2>Subheader in h2</h2>
        </hgroup>
    </header>
    <nav>
        <ul>
            <li><a href="#">Menu Option 1</a></li>
            <li><a href="#">Menu Option 2</a></li>
            <li><a href="#">Menu Option 3</a></li>
        </ul>
    </nav>
    <section>
        <article>
            <header>
                <h1>Article #1</h1>
            </header>
            <section>
                This is the first article.  This is <mark>highlighted</mark>.
            </section>
        </article>
        <article>
            <header>
                <h1>Article #2</h1>
            </header>
            <section>
                This is the second article.  These articles could be blog posts, etc.
            </section>
        </article>
    </section>
    <aside>
        <section>
            <h1>Links</h1>
            <ul>
```

| Header |
| Nav |

Section	
Article	Aside
Article	

| Footer |

⬆ **Website structure**
This diagram stows the typical organizational structure of an HTML document.

⬅ **Website code**
HTML code is an organized structure of opening and closing tags that tells your browser how to present your site content.

✱ **Code academy**
A highly regarded resource providing free, step-by-step, online courses in Web Fundamentals to introduce novices to coding using HTML and CSS.
www.codecademy.com

➕ **SEE ALSO:** FLOWCHARTS AND WIREFRAMES, P158

Dreamweaver Adobe Dreamweaver is the HTML/CSS editor of choice for creating web pages. It remains the industry standard because it generates the cleanest code.

InDesign Adobe InDesign, a vector-based application for creating multi-page documents, can now be used to produce iPad apps. Apps can include audio, video, touch-based interaction, alternate layouts (based on device orientation), and other interactive features.

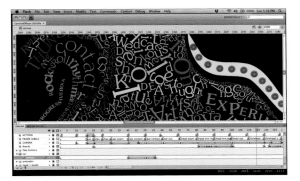

◀ **Adobe Dreamweaver**
The Dreamweaver interface can be adjusted to preview the appearance of the web page, a code-only view, or a combination of both.

▲ **Adobe Flash**
The Flash interface has a focus on creating content based on a timeline. Visual elements are placed on "the stage" (the document area) and their behavior is controlled via the settings in the timeline.

CODERS VS PROGRAMMERS

Within the industry, the people who make web pages using a combination of HTML and CSS are referred to as "coders." Web designers are expected to have a working familiarity with HTML and CSS code.

Professionals who work in different programming languages, usually more complex in structure and relating to enhanced functionality, are referred to as "programmers". Examples of these languages are .PHP, .NET, .ASP, JavaScript, and C++.

FILE-NAMING CONVENTIONS

When creating graphics for the Web, all files should be named using criteria that both facilitate proper image indexing by the search engines and correspond with accessibility requirements for special needs visitors. Naming your source files properly will save you from having to rename them each time you export your images.

- Always use lowercase letters.
- Never use spaces.
- Use a hyphen (-) to separate word combinations.
- Use an underscore (_) to separate concepts.
- Do not use periods, commas, or any other characters.
- Use keywords and/or descriptive phrasing that corresponds with the project's established taxonomy.
- Source files can also be dated (012313) when maintaining version control is a concern.

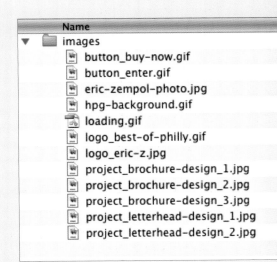

PART 2	PRACTICE
UNIT 7	WEB AND INTERACTIVITY
MODULE 4	**Initial consultations**

Web designers are usually invited to preliminary client consultations, where they can provide insight into the project's development based on their previous experiences. They assist in defining the technical requirements and content organization, in addition to visual approaches.

MEETING TIPS

- Limit the number of detailed questions you ask. Most clients won't be prepared to focus on specifics at this time.
- Avoid relying on technical jargon.
- Take thorough notes. Nothing communicates the fact that you value your client's time more than pausing to document the points they are discussing.
- Actively listen. Ask your prepared questions and listen to your client's replies. Brainstorm on your own time as part of the proposal process.

These meetings—usually limited to an hour-long discussion—can take place in the agency, at the client's location, or via conference call. The purpose of this initial discussion is to meet the client and understand their goals for the project. Follow-up meetings may be required to address specific items, but the focus of this step is to clearly define the project requirements for the development proposal.

Preparation

Before you attend the first meeting, make sure you have a basic understanding of the project. Different project structures (see pages 148–149) will require that you ask different questions.

Prior to the initial consultation, it is common to ask clients to submit six websites for review.

- **Three competitor websites**
  In reviewing these sites, as well as the comments on what the client liked/disliked, a designer can see how high (or low) the bar has been set for defining the anticipated complexity of the project. The designer can also reference technical features, such as banner advertising, e-commerce functionality, social media integration, and mailing list opt-ins, which will be discussed in the initial consultation.

- **Three aesthetic reference websites**
  These websites are supplied to efficiently communicate the client's thoughts on the visual styling of their own project. As with the competitor websites, a short dialogue should be supplied that

defines what they liked/disliked about the designs. While the goal is not to replicate an existing website, a designer can use this information to derive appropriate design cues, such as color palette, layout structure, typographic styling, and use of imagery.

Consultation topics

Project goals Ask questions that guide your client through explaining who they are and defining their current business challenges.
- What is the website supposed to do for your business?
- What sets your company apart from your competition?
- Is clearly defining the benefits and features of your organization a challenging task?
- Who are the decision-makers on this project?

Metrics/RODI Understanding how a client will determine the success of their project and the return on their design investment (RODI) will help you determine the items that will require your focus.
- Increase in sales? Social media following? Site traffic?
- Increase in email newsletter registration?
- How will clients find your website?

Technical requirements Use "plain-speak" to ask questions that define the technical features for the project. From reviewing the competitors' websites, you should have compiled a basic list of items that will be discussed. In addition, you can draw from your own expertise to recommend new features and approaches that may benefit your client.

- How do you currently communicate with clients?
- How often will your website need to be updated? By whom?
- Will you be selling items directly from your website?

Scope The size of a website has a direct impact on the project pricing. Guide your client through defining the different sections and subsections of the site. For reference, it can help to review the navigational taxonomy of their competitors' websites. This will serve as the first step for creating the initial flowchart (see pages 142–143).

- Define the sections and subsections of your website.

Additionally, determining your client's level of preparedness will assist you in scheduling the project's development, by clearly defining the client-supplied deliverables.

- For a new site: how much time will you require to generate the dialogue (text) that will be presented throughout your site?
- For a site redesign: how much of your current site dialogue/imagery will remain the same (or be changed) in the revised site?
- Will your website require photography/illustrations? Will you be supplying these items or will you require my assistance?

Turnaround You should have an idea of a comfortable development timeframe for developing a project at your own pace. If you do not, make an estimate, then triple it, to include time for unforeseen delays, as well as client delays. A shorter turnaround time requires that you be more aggressive in managing the development of the project.

- Do you require the site to launch by a specific date?
- Is this date flexible or does this date correspond with an event?

Budget Don't be afraid to ask this question before you go through the process of crafting a thoughtful proposal. Some clients will be up front about their budget range. Some will have no idea. Others will prefer that you define your pricing range—so you should give this some thought prior to your initial conversation.

Closing the meeting

The meeting closes with a recap of the current actionable points.

The designer follows up by emailing a list of questions that the client was not able to answer. The designer also explains the next step, which could be a more detailed conversation or submission of the project proposal, which incorporates the points raised in the client consultation.

Smashing idea
SmashingMagazine.com offers many resources that relate to questionnaires and project checklists, specific to varying project structures.

The Plan B
If the client's budget is unrealistically low, be prepared to offer an alternative solution, such as a DIY service from a web host (or WordPress.com). It's not only polite, but it's good business. Once they grow frustrated by the limitations, they will often return to you.

PART 2	PRACTICE
UNIT 7	WEB AND INTERACTIVITY
MODULE 5	**Information architecture (IA)**

The information architecture (IA) of a website is a major component of designing the overall user experience (UX). It is a balance of the intrinsic nature of a website and established user expectations, combined with your client's overall goals. This is the practical and functional expertise that a web designer brings to a website development project and has a strong impact on the perceived success of the endeavor.

Define the critical pathways

Defining the critical pathways of a website involves understanding the goals for the project and making them clear to your site's audience. This could be in the form of presenting clear calls to action within the page layout. Or it could be guiding your viewers through the navigational structure in order to quickly locate the content without forcing them to "click" through an excessive number of pages.

Establish structure and visual hierarchy

Divide your layout into clearly defined content areas. Create visual relationships by grouping themed items together (for example, a list of recent news items).

Vary the scale of your type. The traditional size for paragraph type should be 11–13 points. Headline and subheading type should be presented proportionately larger, in order to make it stand out. Limit the use of bold or italic formatting, only to provide occasional emphasis within paragraph text.

Avoid presenting too many different navigational options, which may leave your audience confused about which link they should click on next. Instead, use visual cues (such as prominence, positioning, and/or scale differences) to visually guide your audience through your site's navigational options. Group similarly themed, secondary pages together into subsections and present them using a drop-down (or fly-out) navigational structure.

White space is your friend. Controlled and generous vertical white space within a web page layout is your best friend. It segments content areas and helps to control visual noise within your compositional structure.

Create polite user experiences

A "polite website" reacts the way your audience expects it to behave.

When users click a hyperlink, they expect a new web page to load in the same browser window. If your navigation element launches a new browser window (pop up) or abruptly launches an application like Adobe Acrobat (or your email client), it is considered polite to warn your audience what to expect when they interact with that specific link.

View Application Form (PDF)
View Full Article (via pop-up window)
Email Us: info@website.com

Vary the color of visited hyperlinks to let visitors see where they have already been within your website. Avoid using the underline decoration style for non-hyperlinked items.

Let users control their own audio/video experience. Don't force audio/video elements to auto-play as the page initially loads. Give your viewers time to adjust their speaker volume before they choose to press the play button.

Direct access

A successful e-commerce website's structure reduces the need to click through multiple pages in order to locate a specific item. In this example, an additional subnavigation structure is presented on the left, where similar products are grouped together by category.

Experimental navigation

Ndali.net features a color-coded navigational structure that is oriented on the vertical access. This characterful example serves as a reminder that it's ok to break from traditional website structures, as long as it doesn't negatively impact the user experience.

Usability

Jakob Nielsen is widely recognized as an authority in web usability. His website presents findings from many usability studies. www.useit.com

Present digestible content

While writing site content rarely falls on the shoulders of the web designer, it is often your responsibility to guide clients in crafting dialogue for their web sites, as there are differences from writing for the web versus traditional media.

Online audiences are on the hunt for information. They approach a web page by scanning through the content, starting with the taxonomy of your navigation structure, continuing through your series of headlines and subheadings, and eventually landing on the desired paragraph content.

- Use descriptive keywords in your navigational taxonomy. Avoid using generic names like "products" or "services." Select words that more accurately describe the products and services that relate to your client's business. For supporting information (contact, about us), it is considered appropriate to employ the traditional naming conventions.
- Use visual devices like headlines, subheadings, lists, and call-out text to guide your viewers through the information.
- Be up front in your dialogue. Have the first two paragraphs of a page contain the most important information that your viewers are hunting for. Stay on point by defining what the product/service is,

what it is used for, and how it will benefit your client's site visitors.

- Review your site dialogue and infuse it with relevant keywords. Within reason, limit the amount of pronouns—he, she, it, they—in favor of including the actual names. This will help your site generate higher organic rankings from the search engines.
- Keep your paragraph text short and concise. Avoid compound sentence structures. Divide long paragraphs of text into smaller groupings of sentences.
- Use bulleted (unordered lists) or alphanumeric lists (ordered lists) to allow your audience faster access to the information they are seeking. Additionally, these lists facilitate comprehension between groupings of similarly themed items (bulleted list) or an implied sequential order (lettered/numbered list).

Be inspired

Innovation in web design is driven by the desire to create a better user experience (UX), not just change with the goal of appearing to be different. Review the websites that you visit most often and question everything. Look for patterns and similarities. Adopt (or reject) trends as you deem appropriate.

⬆ Creative break

Designer Nelson Balaban's design for Desfiacoco's online brochure creatively breaks from the traditional layout structure. A significant amount of the layout has been dedicated to the header, as the website also serves to announce the company's rebranded visual identity. The content in the lower part of the layout features parallax scrolling—where content scrolls sideways, as opposed to scrolling down in the browser window.

ⓘ Reduce the number of clicks

Try to limit the number of links that your typical viewer would have to click through in order to get to the information you want them to have.

PART 2	PRACTICE
UNIT 7	FUNDAMENTALS OF COMPOSITION
MODULE 6	**Flowcharts and wireframes**

**Flowcharts and wireframes
enable both designer and client to visualize
the structure of a website and throw light on
possible problems. It is recommended that both
are tackled before the project begins and are
included in the project development contract.**

Flowcharts

In the initial planning phase, flowcharts are created to illustrate the navigational structure of the website, the critical pathways for the site audience, and to define the overall scope of the project. These foundation elements are used in establishing a meeting of the minds between the designer and the client.

Experienced web designers will caution you not to skip this step. Having a visual representation of the website's structure will facilitate discussions relating to detailed considerations that clients may not be able to immediately grasp.

Navigation structure By presenting a flowchart with the defined navigational structure, the client can review the specific taxonomy, the presentation order of the links as well as the distribution of content among primary, secondary, and tertiary page structures.

For example, does a primary page ("our services") present an overview of the content found on the secondary pages (each of the services)? Or will it serve as the first page for the section (service #1) and provide links to the other, secondary pages?

Critical pathways Every website has a purpose and the clients goals for their site should have been defined clearly in the Q+A phase, via the Client Questionnaire (see page 143). In creating a flowchart, the designer's goal is to limit the number of pages that a visitor must view before arriving at the desired content or call to

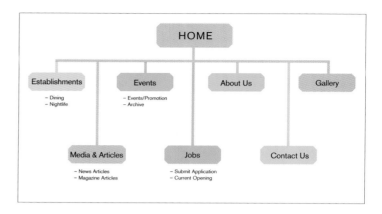

⬆ ⬇ Critical pathways

Working with flowcharts and diagrams to help visualize the hierarchy and connections between different pages or areas might seem unnecessarily excessive. However, this is a simple and valuable way of making sure that all aspects of the common-sense organization of your site have been fulfilled and nothing is accidentally overlooked. Working in this manner helps to explain planned connections to your client and also helps to confirm the minimum number of steps necessary to get from one page or area to another. This is an important factor, since you don't want your client to lose their audience within an overly complex navigation system.

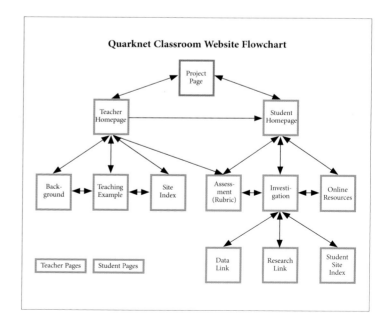

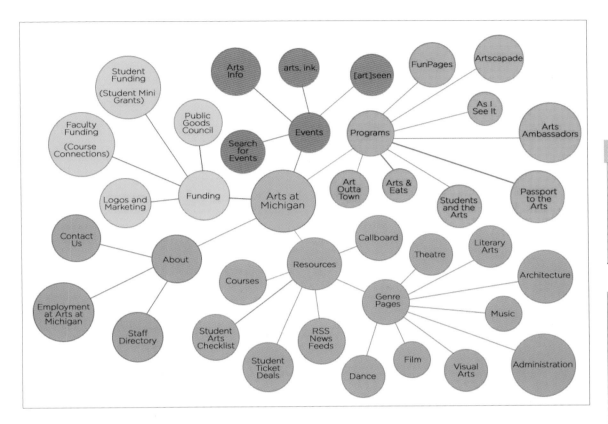

action. A generally accepted rule of thumb is three clicks or fewer. However, some calls to action can be incorporated, globally, into the site layout. For example, it would be more efficient to list out the desired contact information on every page, as opposed to isolating it on the "contact us" page.

Project scope In providing a visual representation that defines the size of the project, all parties involved will be able to review the anticipated scope. If the project is amended—as they often are—both parties can refer to the previously approved flowchart to discuss how this may affect project pricing and turnaround.

⬆ **Communicating visually** Flowcharts are an efficient way to communicate the scope and organization of a web project. This example uses color to define related sections, and change in scale to identify the critical pathways within the website structure.

⊕ **SEE ALSO:** PROJECT DEVELOPMENT PROCESS OVERVIEW, P142

➡️ **The grid**

A 12-column grid is a common starting point in a website design. By aligning elements to a structured grid, the coders will have an easier time bringing your project to fruition.

➡️ **Establishing visual hierarchy**

Define content regions for the elements of your layout. Balance spatial relationships with the goals of presenting content in a hierarchical form.

🔽 **Incorporate text and navigational elements.**

Consider the critical pathways through the website. Guide your audience through these pathways by making options clear, using changes of scale and visual prominence.

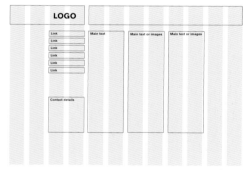

Grayscale values

🔽 Assigning corresponding grayscale values will help you check to make sure that you are presenting your content with the appropriate level of contrast. As color palettes can be modified as project development continues, you can refer back to your grayscale wireframe to determine the appropriate values that will work with your layout.

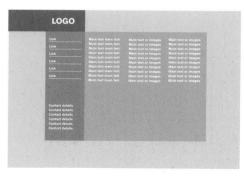

Wireframes

The wireframe is a purposefully under-designed representation of the layout structure of a website's main pages. Similar to an architectural blueprint, it incorporates all structural elements, as well as defining the visual hierarchy and their proportional relationships within the layout. With a reduced focus on visual style choices, both the designer and the client can have productive discussions that relate to the layout structure without getting stuck on visual distractions such as typefaces or color choices.

Traditionally, wireframes are created in Adobe Illustrator, because designers are already familiar with it, approaches can be revised quickly, and the artwork that it generates can be imported directly into Photoshop when they are ready to begin the visual design process.

Start with a grid Most web designers use the 960 Grid System, a streamlined approach to web development using common dimensions based on a width of 960 pixels, which can be divided into a series of equal columns (8 columns, 12 columns, 16 columns).

Add regions Insert a series of boxes into your grid that will define the different content areas of your layout, from logo and navigation placement, through the body content, down to the footer area. These boxes should serve to define the proportional relationships between content within your layout.

Add typography Define the visual hierarchy between type elements within your layout. Create proportional relationships among your headline and subhead type to guide your viewer through the content. Mix it up and establish a flow. Traditionally, lines (instead of actual words) are used to represent lines of smaller, body copy.

Add links Define the interactive elements. Will the main navigation menu feature drop-down menus? Will the layout feature buttons, text-based links, or a combination of both? At this step, you're not defining the visual appearance of these links, just their form.

Incorporate grayscale values Your last step in the wireframe process is to assign grayscale values to your content. This step will help you determine the visual

strength of your elements without having to focus on the color palette. This will also help you assign colors, later, based on their relative values.

Don't be afraid to experiment. The purpose of the wireframing process is to quickly discover what isn't working and make adjustments.

High-definition wireframe (optional) A hi-def wireframe means adding additional details without getting too specific on the visual elements. It usually refers to inserting actual text to determine ideal type sizes, line lengths, and leading.

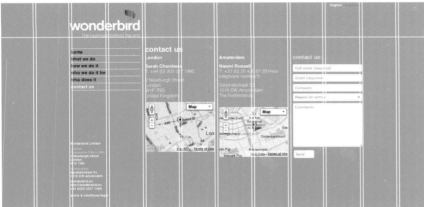

12 Column grid The design of Wondebird by Rebecca Foster illustrates well the scope and flexibility of her selected 12-column grid. She uses consistently 2 columns for left- and right-hand margin spacing throughout. From page to page, as she accommodates different kinds of information and imagery, Rebecca allows detail to extend across varied column widths as appropriate to the information in hand.

TESTING RESOURCES

There are several online resources that will help you troubleshoot your work by validating the HTML and CSS code structure, or by checking your website's navigational structure for broken links. The World Wide Web Consortium (W3C) is regarded as the leading markup validation service. validator.w3.org/

PART 2	PRACTICE
UNIT 7	WEB AND INTERACTIVITY
MODULE 7	**Common elements of a web layout**

Above the fold

Below the fold

All web pages have certain elements in common. These features make up the basic building blocks of a web page.

Before getting down to building and assembling the elements of a web page, let's take a moment to identify the structural zones common to most website layouts. The top area of a website is often referred to as the header. It usually contains a few key elements, such as branding visuals and the main navigation links. Immediately below the header, you have the body area. It is within this area that content will be changing as you navigate through the pages of the website. And at the bottom of the web page, you have the footer area. It typically contains items relating to site ownership and a recap of the main navigational structure, eliminating the need to return to the top of the page to access the links.

Page title The descriptive title for the website also identifies the specific page that is being viewed. It is presented at the top of the browser window, or in the browser tab; in the user's bookmark list (if they bookmark the page); and serves as the identifying page title within the search-engine results.

Favicon This is a small, branding graphic that appears to the left of the web address.

Header The top area of a web layout. It typically features the company logo in the top-left or center position. The upper header area can feature call-out navigation elements such as login/logout for websites that require user registration, or provide access to shopping cart details for e-commerce sites.

Main navigation/top nav/left nav The main navigation is usually located horizontally across the top area of the screen, under the header. This design pattern (trend) is popular because the abundance of space across the width of the layout usually affords the ability to add additional links to the navigation, as needed, over time. An alternative is to present the main nav, stacked vertically, along the left side of the web layout. However, this design pattern is becoming less popular as designers prefer to position the subnavigation links in this column space.

Drop-down navigation/fly-out nav As their names imply, these methods of subnavigation represent ways to visually organize related links, based on the site's organizational structure. Initially, the drop-down menu is revealed (on hover/rollover/tap) to show a series of secondary pages associated with the main navigation link. From those options, related tertiary links are displayed, flying out to the right of the drop-down list. An alternative to the drop-down, which features a full panel of stylized content ranging from subnavigation links to social media feeds, is called a mega menu.

Breadcrumb navigation This is a navigational wayfinding element, usually located below the header, presented globally, throughout a website. It helps communicate where the viewer is currently located within the site structure, while providing clickable access to return to a main page. It is most useful in sites that feature a navigational structure that goes at least three levels deep. On websites that feature only a primary or secondary navigation structure, this element would be superfluous.

Feature panel slider This image slide show is a visual marketing device that can be used to serve a variety of purposes. Most often it is used to spotlight new products or updated site content, to keep the site looking fresh. Or, it can be used to visually communicate a marketing message, such as product benefits, ease of use statements, and so on.

⬆ Extending "below the fold"

As this website example demonstrates, site content often continues past the bottom of the browser window, revealed as the visitor scrolls down. Web designers have a sensitivity to place important elements within the top of the website layout, so that they are visible when the page initially loads. Site visitors take visual cues from content being cut off at the browser window, as an indicator that they should scroll.

✱ Learn the lingo

www.motive.co.nz Designers rely upon an ever-increasing list of terminology to communicate among collaborators and also with clients. Where there are many glossaries available for review, we recommend this list as a great starting point, compiled by the design firm, Motive.

Structure with variety The Everlast.com website employs a fixed-width, centered layout, with a stacked navigation along the left side of the page. This structure is consistent throughout the website. Large photographs are employed as background images to add bold visual interest as viewers navigate through the website.

Body area The body area presents a series of content and subcontent that is specific to the type of website being developed and/or the specific page being viewed. Most websites organize content presented within the body using a vertical column structure, ranging from two to four columns.

Call-out/call-to-action elements Pull quotes, special notices, and/or buttons with calls to action are usually positioned within the body area, above the fold.

Below the fold Pulled from newspaper terminology, "below the fold" refers to content that appears lower on the screen, which viewers do not immediately view when the page loads unless they choose to scroll down. While once it was a firm belief that viewers rarely thought to scroll down a web page, we now know that most do. Usually a visual cue, such as content being cut off, serves as a subtle indicator that the viewer should scroll down.

Inline text links Text-based links interspersed through the body copy to facilitate cross-linking among the website's pages, based on topic relevance.

Anchor link/jump link/top of page link
A navigation element that, when clicked, directs the viewer to a specific area of a web page. Typically used on pages that present an abundance of dialogue, such as FAQs, or to give the viewer quick access to return to the top of the page without having to scroll.

Footer This area identifies the lower section of a web page. Content in this area is presented globally throughout the website. It can repeat the main navigational elements that are presented at the top of the page, removing the need to scroll to the top in order to continue. Some websites utilize this area to present dynamic content, such as social media feeds, recent news, recent comments, and/or special anouncements. Corporate websites usually include a series of required, subordinate links to such topics as legal notices, disclosure details, site map, and so on. Additional elements often found in the footer area include address and contact information, dated copyright statement, and developer credit—free advertising.

Multiple navigation sources This website features a combination of both a horizontal navigation bar and side stack of navigation links for navigating within the current section of the website. Blogs, like this web page, usually feature category lists of similarly themed posts. E-commerce websites usually use this side area for refining product searches, based on specific categories, product attributes, price ranges, and so on.

PART 2	PRACTICE
UNIT 7	WEB AND INTERACTIVITY
MODULE 8	**Designing for the web**

Designing for the web is often a clever mixture of reflecting client goals, understanding user expectations, keeping up with current trends, and infusing the project with your own insights and creativity.

⊙ Web trends

The inclusion of a large slideshow element on the upper part of the home page is a popular trend for communicating the purpose of the site, reinforced with imagery. An alternate method for using this element is to spotlight new content, so the site looks fresh to repeat visitors.

⊙ Style boards

Presenting varying stylistic design options—independent of a website's structural layout—is a popular strategy for keeping the focus of the discussion on the stylization options such as color palette, typefaces, navigation, and image appearance.

COMMON LAYOUT STRUCTURES

◉ Fixed-width layout

Most popular among contemporary websites, this layout structure features a defined pixel width, typically positioned within the center of the browser window.

◉ Liquid layout

This layout is designed to be fluid and repositions the elements in response to the width of the browser window.

◉ Floating layout

This layout is based on a fixed width and height within the browser window. Typically, the background remains visible on at least three sides (left, right, lower) and the need to scroll to view content has been eliminated. Popular among high-end retailers, or as interstitial landing pages, this layout style can be problematic over time, since space can be limited.

Client goals

In your initial consultations for the project (see pages 154–155), you will have defined the client's goals and reviewed the expected scope of the website. With the flow chart on hand (see pages 158–159), these points of information are brought forward to define the critical pathways of how the visitor moves through the site.

User expectations

The foundation of web design is rooted in adopting globally accepted sets of behaviors. Novice web designers may feel restrained by following these behaviors, but their acceptance and continuation serve to deliver a consistent user experience as visitors interact among different websites; for example, when the branding element in the header is clicked, the viewer is taken to the home page.

Web trends

The Web is fueled by innovation. Trends are often rooted in logic: a clever solution that repeatedly springs up across the Web because, frankly, it just makes sense. An example of a current trend is the inclusion of

Critical pathways: Defining the desired route of a website's audience, as it relates to taking an action (purchasing, contacting, registering, etc.).

Drop-down (menu): A navigational element that is revealed when a visitor clicks a main navigational link to reveal related links (subsections) that are displayed below.

Fly-out (menu): A navigational element that is revealed by extending out to the side of a main navigational element.

Layer Comps (Photoshop): A feature that allows the user to record which items are viewable in a complex, multi-layer document.

Style board: A presentation of proposed website stylizations for review by a client, independent of the overall website structure.

Tool tips: A message that displays when a user hovers with a mouse over a linked element.

---

a slideshow feature on the home page. While the size of this element can vary, it serves as a visual device for informing the viewing audience about what the company does, or it can be used to spotlight new content. Either way, it is substantially more appealing than reading paragraph content. Of course, not all trends should be followed blindly: this is where your own aesthetic judgment as a designer comes into play.

Layout structures

The most common layout structure is a fixed-horizontal layout, usually centered within the screen, whereas vertical positioning is more fluid, dynamically expanding and contracting to accommodate varying amounts of page content. Alternative options include: proportionate width, such as 80% of the browser window; full-width, 100% of the browser window—not very popular; flush left, a fixed-width layout aligned to the left side of the browser window—also not very popular; and fixed horizontal and vertical, a "floating" layout that is popular among online retailers but extremely challenging to maintain in the long term, since content presentation needs may evolve over time, requiring more vertical space.

Where to start?

The generally accepted starting place for designing a website is to focus on the traditional "laptop view" at 1024 pixels wide (at screen resolution/72ppi).

Designers usually create a Photoshop document that is 1200 pixels wide by 2500 pixels tall, with an understanding that they're not designing to fill the entire canvas vertically. Some pages will require the insertion

of a lot of content, and this height means you don't have to reposition items later on. The more space you dedicate to the elements at the top of a website layout, the more information you will be pushing below the bottom of the browser window, requiring your site visitors to scroll to reveal. A header (with navigation bar) over 200 pixels tall would be considered excessive. Most website designs are compact, using less than half that height.

Grid structures

The compositional grid (see page 160) is a design concept that is pulled forward from traditional, print-based graphic design. In web design, a vertical grid structure is used to provide visual consistency and make the transition from design to programming phase less complicated.

The compositional grid (see page 160)

SUPPLYING CLEAN FILES

In an agency environment, most likely you will be supplying your layered Photoshop files to a team of coders. Keep your files organized. Name your layers using a consistent system. Delete unused layers. Organize related content into named folders.

If you find yourself lost and hunting through layers, most likely your developer may also. Use the Notes and Layer Comps features to define complicated items or settings.

Start with paper

Work out your concepts on paper before you move ahead to use a computer. Identify all regions where content will be displayed and the amount of visual real estate that specific elements will require.

SEE ALSO:

FLOWCHARTS AND WIREFRAMES, P158

E-commerce
E-commerce websites are regularly updated with revised inventory listings, notifications of sales, and featured product announcements.

Corporate Corporate websites are frequently updated to present revised content such as recent news items, press coverage, new business initiatives, and job listings.

Restaurant Restaurant websites are updated to reflect amendments to the menu, coupons, and to promote upcoming special events.

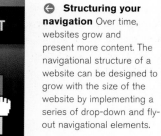

Structuring your navigation Over time, websites grow and present more content. The navigational structure of a website can be designed to grow with the size of the website by implementing a series of drop-down and fly-out navigational elements.

The 960 Grid System is the leading system, because it can be divided evenly into 12 and 16 columns. The width of website layouts using this system is 960 pixels. The additional space would be used to display the background.

Web typography

Type presentation online is more fluid than its print-based counterparts. Current technological advances in web design now afford designers the ability to present more thoughtful type solutions.

The width of paragraph text is controlled by defining a fixed width for the type container, typically reflected in your grid system. If your visitor decides to increase the viewing size in their browser settings—and they will—the content will reflow accordingly.

With the advent of web fonts, designers have access to an ever-increasing library of typeface options that have been optimized for onscreen viewing. Gone are the days of laboring to create pixel-based graphics with typeset words. This is the era of quickly swapping in new typefaces (globally, via the CSS) to text that can be understood and indexed by the search engines.

Design to evolve

Unlike designing for print—where the project is considered complete when the files are sent to the printer—web design projects will continue to evolve over time. A designer must plan ahead for revisions, including the insertion of additional content, new pages, and revised project goals. Failure to do so may require that the site be completely reengineered at a later date in order to accommodate the requested adjustments.

It is because of this anticipated growth that a web designer should focus on a template-driven approach, distributing content consistently across a series of structured layouts.

It would be unheard of—and quite expensive—to design a 24-page website where each page features a completely different layout structure. The traditional route would be to design a home-page layout and one (or two) interior pages. The presentation of content and imagery can be adjusted per page, but the overall structure remains consistent with the established template structure.

Responsive web design

Responsive web design is the innovation whereby the elements within a layout are modified in response to the device on which the site is being viewed. Primarily, this feature is controlled by the back-end coding of the website, which calls a media query to apply the appropriate CSS code to reposition the elements accordingly.

Developing a responsive website often stems directly from the client's request. It requires more labor than a traditional project and this can affect the overall project pricing. Responsive website designs will require the artist to create multiple versions of their designs (separate PSDs), which can be reviewed by the client, and eventually submitted to the coding team.

✴ Web font services
Google Web Fonts: www.google.com/webfonts
My Fonts: www.myfonts.com
Font Squirrel: www.fontsquirrel.com

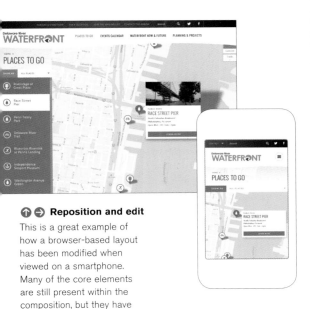

⬆ ➡ Reposition and edit
This is a great example of how a browser-based layout has been modified when viewed on a smartphone. Many of the core elements are still present within the composition, but they have been re-arranged to accommodate the smaller viewing screen. Some elements, such as the location photograph, are removed in order to reduce visual clutter.

➡ Responsive design
A responsive design can reposition elements to the orientation of the device, portrait or landscape view.

TYPE TIPS

- Audiences prefer dark body text on a light-colored background, as opposed to light text on a dark background, which tends to "burn" into your retinas.
- Use solid numeric integers for the type that you specify in your Photoshop document. The typical size for paragraph text is 12 to 13 points, with an open leading of 16 to 18 points.
- The width of a paragraph should be limited to "an alphabet and a half" (between 20 and 40 characters is ideal).

- While not an absolute, usability experts recommend using a sans-serif typeface, such as Helvetica, for paragraph text and a complementary typeface of your choosing for heads and subhead systems.
- Avoid applying the attributes bold and/or italics to entire paragraphs. Instead, limit these to occasional use in order to highlight specific elements within the paragraph text.
- Avoid using underscore formatting for non-linked text.

RESPONSIVE DESIGN AND DISPLAY SIZES

At the publication of this book, the current display sizes are:
- Desktop (1600 pixels wide)
- Laptop (1024 pixels wide)
- Tablet (768 pixels wide)
- Smartphone (320 pixels wide)

A traditional (non-responsive) website, when viewed on a smartphone, might be revised to maximize the viewing experience on the smaller screen.
- Reposition/resize the brand mark (logo) and, perhaps, align it to the center.
- Condense a main navigation bar into a scrollable drop-down menu.
- Remove rollover effects, because there is no cursor to roll over content.
- Space out links to avoid accidental activation.
- Adjust the alignment of subhead titles to be centered within the screen.
- Adjust images to fit in the screen by cropping or proportionately scaling them down (or a combination of both).

- Reposition multi-column content into a single-column view by stacking elements.
- Display content focused on the smartphone user's anticipated needs; for example, a restaurant spotlighting their hours of operation and reservations number on the home screen.

To review how a responsive website could behave, visit the larger websites you view most often from your computer. Resize your browser window, making it narrow. Responsive websites will reposition the elements in order to maximize the screen view. Traditional websites can still be viewed on these devices, but require the viewer to "pinch-to-zoom" the site in order to get a better view.

Documenting the details

In a web design project, the list of elements that need to be designed (and specified for the coding team) can grow to be quite large. Some elements may not be an anticipated factor in the site launch, but will need to be added at a later date. The following list can be used to make sure you have defined the traditional elements of a website.

Main navigation

Traditionally, the main navigation of a website will appear horizontally across the top. Design for growth and leave space to add an additional navigation link or two.

- Positioning
- Alignment (aligned left, centered, indented)
- Text appearance (typeface, size, color, spacing, etc.)
- Background appearance
- Active link appearance
- Graphic elements (vertical dividers or a triangle—typically used to identify the availability of submenu links)
- Drop-down submenu appearance (text appearance, horizontal rules, background color, background opacity, graphic element, etc.)
- Fly-out sub-submenu appearance

Background

A subtle tint is preferred over stark white.

- Solid. Pattern. Gradient
- Alignment
- Locked into position or scrollable?
- Blend image to solid background color
- Does the background vary by page?

Vertical positioning

- How will the layout reposition when the browser is resized?
- How much vertical space should be placed between elements?
- What is the shortest vertical layout size?
- How much space will be consistently above the footer content?

Footer content

- Appearance of hyperlinks
- Appearance of text (copyright statement)
- Additional elements

In-line hyperlink states

- Link appearance (typeface, size, color, underline, etc.)
- Visited link appearance
- Active link/tab appearance
- Hover link appearance

Navigation button states

A website could feature a wide range of visual buttons, from "Read More" links to form submit, to adding items to a shopping cart.

- Default button appearance (height, width, color, padding, corner radius, typeface, size, type color, drop shadow)
- Hover button appearance
- On-click button appearance
- Disabled button appearance (typically displayed with incomplete forms)

Submenus

Submenus are usually stacked on the left of interior pages, for navigating within a subsection.

- Interior page position (right column, left column, horizontally under top navigation)
- Styling (typeface, size, color, background, graphic elements, etc.)
- Active link appearance
- Fly-out menu appearance (for sub-submenu)

Text styling
- Body (typeface, color, size, line spacing, bold/italic, etc.)
- Headings (H1, the largest, to H6, the smallest)
- Paragraph spacing
- Lists (ordered—with numbers/unordered—bulleted)
- Quote appearance
- "Read More" link appearance
- Excerpt text appearance (and length)
- "Top of Page" navigation link

Horizontal rule
- Appearance (weight, color, etc.)
- Spacing (above/below)

Image styles
You will notice a trend to display images in a wide format. This is more common than displaying tall-formatted images, because it reduces the amount of vertical space within the layout.
- Display sizes
- Cropping. Scaling
- Corner radius
- Drop shadow
- Padding
- Caption text appearance (typeface, size, color, line spacing, etc.)

Tables
Tables offer a way to pre-format structured content such as charts.
- Border
- Background color. Alternating
- First column, first row appearance
- Padding
- Typeface. Type size
- Price comparison chart

Banner advertising
- Display sizes
- Number of ads presented within the layout
- Location of ads (header, side column, footer, with content, etc.)

Forms
A form can be used by visitors for sending a message or submitting a request, such as joining an email list.
- Overall appearance (background, border, padding, spacing, alignment, etc.)
- Types of input fields (text field, multi-line text field, check box, radio button, drop-down menu, etc.)
- Text label appearance
- Required fields
- Submit/reset button text
- Validation/error message (location, text appearance, message)
- Destination of form content (email, database, etc.)

Animated content
- Buttons/button transition appearance
- Tool tips
- Image slideshow
- Lightboxes (title and caption display, previous/next icon, etc.)

Social media
- Twitter feed appearance (text styling, link appearance, Twitter logo/emblem, etc.)
- Facebook badge appearance (include "Like" button, display fans, number of fans, include "Like" total, show recent post feed)
- Flickr badge appearance (number of images, thumbnail size, etc.)

PART 2	PRACTICE
UNIT 7	WEB AND INTERACTIVITY
MODULE 9	**Mobile application design**

On an increasing scale, web designers are invited into mobile applications (apps) development to work on projects that are extensions of a client's existing brand. Be it smartphones or tablets, our clients are moving into an exciting new arena and taking us along for the ride.

App categories

Currently there are three categories of apps that a designer could be assigned to work on. It is crucial to understand the difference among the categories as the development process can be quite varied.

Native apps These apps are software developed to run on a specific operating system (Mac, Android, Windows Mobile). A designer working on a native app project would be collaborating with, at least, a programmer (of C++) for the project. In order to be approved for inclusion into the marketplace, native apps must first comply with a firm set of development guidelines, as defined by the individual device manufacturer. While that may seem limiting to a designer, the focus is on maintaining a consistent user experience from one app to the next.

Web apps A web app lives on the Web. Think of it as a mini web page that has been optimized for viewing on a mobile device. When the app is launched, it subtly loads in the mobile device's browser window—you will know by seeing your browser's bookmark/navigation bar at the bottom of your device screen. Using a JavaScript framework, such as jQuery Mobile, you can incorporate a similar touch-optimized framework that is present in native apps.

Web apps offline These web apps do not require Internet connectivity in order to function. They run locally—all of the supporting web files are included with the app's download.

← **Retromatic app** The Retromatic app echoes the structural foundation of the GUI established by Apple for native apps. Note the size and positioning of major buttons are consistent, while the visual stylization of these elements has been customized for the app.

APP icons Icons are the main branding element for an app project. The rounded corner is applied automatically by the device manufacturer. The glossy highlight is also a default appearance, but this setting can be deactivated programmactically.

The SimsUShare app icon has been designed to take advantage of the rounded corner display of icons within the app marketplace.

The Retromatic app icon features a hand-crafted aesthetic that echoes the stylizations that can be created with the app.

The Haunted Edinburgh app icon is modified for use in other haunted cities by changing the color of the skull graphic.

Tableware icon A successful icon is visually distinctive and communicates the theme of the app.

Device GUI This is an example of Apple's GUI for their iPhone. These elements reflect the structural relationships and common interactions involved with app usage.

Designing apps

The app development process usually begins before the designer gets involved. The project's producer compiles a project script, or content document, that defines the content that will be displayed on each screen; the navigation and interaction behaviors; specific programming requirements; and lists out required graphics. The more experienced the project's producer is in the field of app development, the more insightful this foundation document will be.

The most efficient method of learning to design apps is to seek out user interaction (UI) kits that are available online and review the range of elements that are typically included. This is also a great way to familiarize yourself with the specific terminology relating to device-specific elements, behaviors, and features.

If you are designing a native app, it is strongly recommended that you go to the source and review a UI kit that has been produced by the device's manufacturer (Apple, Android, etc.). If you follow their well-documented guidelines, your design decisions should not negatively affect the app approval process.

Modifying the user interface (UI)

Review the apps that you use most frequently and take note of design patterns for how you interact with the app. For example, where are the "Cancel" and "Done" buttons placed? If echoing the positioning of these items would lead to a more intuitive user experience, why break from standard conventions?

When first viewing a sample UI kit, take note of the design specs for major elements (screen size, required

Kew app The Kew Gardens app was developed to help visitors find their way around the 300-acre park. Visitors can use this educational app to see what's currently in bloom and dig deeper into Kew's scientific and horticultural endeavors.

screen elements, and so on), then focus on the detailed elements. Use supplied button examples as a reference for appropriate sizing. Feel free to retain or modify the button color/appearance as you deem appropriate.

Many UI elements are available to a projects programmer as "components," preprogrammed for easy, plug-and-play insertion into an app. Modifications to these elements, while possible, may require additional development time. It's best to review what is possible with your programmer before you begin presenting your concepts to the client.

Supplying art files

As with a website design, you will most likely be working from a layered Photoshop file throughout the design process. This file should be thoughtfully organized and take advantage of Photoshop's Layer Comp viewing feature, offering a preview of each screen, as defined in the project script/content document.

If your app is designed to respond to changes in the device's orientation, you will be specifying the positioning in two separate Photoshop layout files: landscape and portrait.

App icon design

The icon created for an app is its principal branding element within the consumer marketplace. The concept should be unique and visually represent the utility of the app. As with logo design, you should investigate similar apps to make sure that you are not supplying a graphic that is too similar to an existing app.

You will be supplying the icon artwork, in .PNG file format, to your programmer for inclusion in the app. These files are then converted into an .ico file and included within the app submission. Typically, you will be providing your icon artwork at multiple sizes, from quite small (device view) to large (store view). You may want to review each icon to make sure that each graphic retains its visual impact at each size.

Citing Apple as a reference, they request five different sizes for use on the device screen, in their Spotlight app, and also in their App Store display. This increases to ten icons if you include a set for their devices with Retina Displays.

Your icon's rounded corner styling is rendered automatically by the device. The glossy "gel" overlay is also automatically added to your icon, but your programmer can remove that feature, programmatically.

DESIGNING FOR REGULAR AND HIGH-DENSITY DISPLAYS

Apple's high-density Retina Display squeezes double the pixel resolution into their device displays. Creating artwork for both regular and high-density displays will require the designer to deliver two separate Photoshop files, one at the standard size (dimensions vary per mobile device) and another for the high-density display that has the document canvas shown at double the size (note: both files remain 72ppi). If you set up your working Photoshop file correctly, the process of creating the second file is as easy as revising your document's image size and performing "Save As" to create the second document.

If you are unsure about which size you should design first—big version or small—start by asking yourself if there will be photographic imagery in the presentation. If the answer is yes, then design around the larger size—increasing the scale of placed images within Photoshop will make them blurry/pixelated. Next, you'll want to set up your file using vector shapes, created in Photoshop (or imported as "Shapes" into Photoshop), and use the layer styling effects to apply color, bevels, and shadows, because vector art will scale without distortion.

And finally, because you will be either reducing by half or doubling your document's dimensions, you want to use even integers in your measurements. Rules, shapes, spacing, point sizes for your text, everything should be divisible by two. This will eliminate the need to revise your second document to achieve a pixel-perfect layout.

PART 2	PRACTICE
UNIT 7	WEB AND INTERACTIVITY
MODULE 10	**Working with content management systems**

An increasingly popular option for creating an online presence is to use the structured framework of a content management system (CMS), which is a software application that resides on your web hosting account. The CMS serves as an intermediary between the database—where text and images are stored—and the predesigned, dynamic layout structure of the website.

Designers like working with CMS because they spend less time wrestling with programming code, which affords them more time to work on the appearance and overall content organization of a website.

Clients like working with CMS because it allows them to independently process their own site updates without needing to adjust the programming code. The website can be edited by logging into the browser-based admin, often referred to as the dashboard. This is a password-protected micro-site that allows you—or a designated site administrator—to create new or modify existing content.

Designers often refer to CMS projects as theme integration projects. The project typically encompasses installation of the CMS; selection of a theme; the application of functionality and visual customizations; the integration of the site content; and training and occasional maintenance.

Platforms

There are many CMS platforms available, ranging from proprietary systems to open-source, free options. WordPress.org is the most popular open-source option for small to mid-sized websites. Others to consider include Joomla.org, Drupal.org, and LightCMS.com.

CMS Installation

CMS applications are typically installed into the clients' web hosting account. Most web hosts usually provide automated installation of the major CMS systems (WordPress, Drupal, Joomla). This set-up process creates the database, where text and images will be stored, and defines the admin/password credentials to access the system's dashboard.

Protect the site

When working with CMS projects, always assign complex passwords to the database and also for the admin access. This will help prevent attacks from hackers. Try using a random password generating service, such as www.random.org/passwords.

⬇ **The dashboard**

The dashboard is WordPress' browser-based interface for editing a website. Administrators can log in and edit pages or post news items, as this example demonstrates.

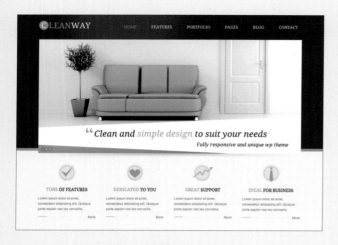

⬅ **WordPress corporate themes** Many corporate themes are available commercially, often subcategorized by company genres (for example, nonprofit, entertainment). Many visuals can be customized for each client's specific needs. If more customization is necessary, the client may consider the development of a fully customized theme, which would not only require the design but also the related PHP/CSS coding.

⬅ **WordPress portfolio themes** In addition to having a different appearance, portfolio themes often feature a different type of interaction. On a corporate site, you might click an image and be taken to a specific web page or article. Clicking an image on a portfolio website may simply present the image at a larger size within the same browser window.

⬅ **WordPress special event themes** WordPress is a popular option for websites that will be used to promote a special event. Typically featuring a short life span, these websites can be modified with relative ease, with faster turnaround, and at a reduced price point because it's less labor-intensive to produce than a customized WordPress theme.

Selecting themes

A theme is a collection of predesigned web-page layouts around a centralized concept, where the arrangement of the pages' structure has been specified by the theme's author. A theme may feature a series of page layouts for different content areas of the website, such as home page; about us page; blog page; contact page; gallery page; portfolio page; full-width layout; and two-column layout.

Many commercially available themes are highly customizable, giving the designer the opportunity to make adjustments to ensure the resulting website is unique to the client. For larger projects, a designer might partner with a programmer to create their own theme, from the ground up, based on the project's exact requirements.

Installing plugins

The functionality of the basic CMS structure can be enhanced by adding plugins, also referred to as widgets or modules. A plugin could be comprised of a contact form, a social media feed, banner ads, weather forecast, live chat, recent post summaries, dated post archive list, keyword-based tag cloud, and testimonials, and may automatically add social media "like" buttons to a web page's layout. Most CMS systems offer a wide range of plugins for free. Additional plugins may be available from commercial entities for a nominal fee.

Visual customizations

While themes are highly customizable—allowing you to adjust logos, colors, background visuals—they are not absolutely customizable. A certain degree of flexibility is required. In architectural terms, instead of asking an architect to include two dining rooms in a home's floor plan, a compromise would be to add a table into the kitchen area. In the end, the goals have been met (dining in two different areas). Most visual customizations can be specified via the theme option settings, while additional stylizations can be controlled by amending the CSS (Cascading Style Sheets) code with exception, or child, elements.

Integrating site content

Define the navigational structure of the site using the flow chart as a guide to the established taxonomy, then create the required pages for the website, inserting the specified text and imagery. Crop/resize images as necessary. Define the categories for the news feed or blog posts—these dated entries are usually referred to as posts—and generate a range of initial posts, so as to populate the website with visual examples.

Training

If your client will be editing their own site, it is reasonable to provide a certain level of training or orientation in working with the dashboard. Often, designers will create a customized user manual that identifies specific elements within the layout and the corresponding instructions on how to update the content, since the process can vary per theme.

Maintenance

CMS and plugins are routinely updated with security patches. You should be regularly processing these updates as you are notified by the system. Comments to blog or news items should always be moderated, to prevent comment-spam from appearing on your live site. Security plugins and/or site monitoring services should be utilized to prevent potential security attacks.

⊕ **SEE ALSO:** PROJECT DEVELOPMENT PROCESS OVERVIEW, P142

WORKING WITH CONTENT MANAGEMENT SYSTEMS, P173

BANNER AD DESIGN, P176

TIPS ON SELECTING THEMES

- **The newer the better** Updates to CMS systems usually feature new innovations, in addition to security patches. Themes released (or updated) within the last six months usually take advantage of current innovations.

- **Focus on functionality** Avoid selecting themes that have been created for different intended uses, because they may feature different navigational behaviors. For example, a "portfolio" theme may be structured so that when you click on a thumbnail, a larger view is presented. Conversely, in a "corporate" theme, clicking on a thumbnail would launch a new web page.

- **Note the widgetized areas** These spaces are designated locations within the structured layout of a theme. Typically located in the bottom portion of a website, widgets offer the ability to add one to four columns of useful information, ranging from contact details to spotlighted links and social media feeds. The narrow column of a two-column page layout is also typically a widgetized area, expanding in height to correspond with the number of elements you assign to the column widget area. Typically, side column widgets include subnavigation links, search box, archives list, banner ads, etc.

- **Review the customer** reviews, documentation, and message board comments, if available.

GLOSSARY

Categories: A taxonomy structure for designating dynamic content (posts) to appear in similar, or different, news feeds within a site. Can be used as search criteria for displaying similarly themed posts.

CMS: Content management system. The structured framework of a dynamically driven website.

Dashboard: The administrative back-end for a CMS.

Plugin: A WordPress term for an element that adds a functional enhancement to the basic CMS structure. Also referred to as widgets and modules.

Tag cloud: A keyword-based navigation element where keywords can be selected in order to refine search criteria to display similarly themed posts.

Widgetized areas: Locations within a CMS theme where plugins and widgets can be inserted into the physical layout. Typically, these are located within the side column and lower (footer) area of a web page.

THEME AND PLUGIN RESELLERS

ThemeForest.net

WooThemes.com

Themezilla.com

ElegantThemes.com

GraphicPaperPress.com

WPMUdev.org

CodeCanyon.net

WORDPRESS.ORG VS WORDPRESS.COM

WordPress.org is the open-source application that you install on your web server. It's yours to edit as you like. You have access to customized themes and plugins. However, you are responsible for processing occasional software and plugin upgrades.

WordPress.com is a commercial entity. It's free to start, but many enhancements are available via paid, "premium upgrade," options. You are required to pay to have sponsored adverts removed, pay to be able to edit the visual styles, and pay to access "premium themes." Software updates are processed on your behalf.

PAGES AND POSTS

At the most basic level, a page is considered to be an individual web page within the website's navigational structure. A post is an individual item (for example, a news announcement or blog entry) that is presented in linear, dated format within a page.

PART 2	PRACTICE
UNIT 7	WEB AND INTERACTIVITY
MODULE 11	**Banner ad design**

Online advertising fuels the continued development of the Web. The revenue generated from placing banner ads on websites can be impressive. Equally impressive can be the number of sales leads generated by a successfully designed campaign. At some point, most web designers are called upon to design web layouts that incorporate banner ad placement, or to create designs for banner ad campaigns.

Campaign models

In a website development project that features banner advertising, it is important to understand the differences in campaign models, because they can have an impact on the overall website layout. A web designer would consult with their client for specific instructions relating to the number of banners, the requested dimensions, and banner placement within the layout.

Cost per M (CPM) The "M" stands for 1,000 impressions. In this model, advertisers pay based on how many times their ad has appeared to the viewing audience.

Generally speaking, this option is the least expensive for advertisers and, therefore, quite popular. Sites that follow this model usually have a large number of banner ads placed within each layout, so they can maximize advertising revenue.

Cost per click (CPC) Cost per click allows advertisers to pay only for the targeted leads they receive from visitors who have clicked through their ad. For the designer, this means that there can be a fewer number of banners incorporated into the layout.

Designing banner ad campaigns

As part of a banner campaign, a designer may be asked to adapt their design across a range of banner ad sizes. Additionally, they could be asked to create a series of different designs featuring different text content and/or visual imagery. This would allow the client to determine which designs work best, based on the statistics they receive on their campaign's activity.

TYPES OF BANNER ADS

Banner ads are traditionally broken down into the following categories:

- **Text based** Simple text-based ads, typically connected to an online ad server such as Google Ads that dynamically inserts the content into your web page when it loads, based on selected keywords. While these ads are not designed, designers will allocate space within the layout and insert the related HTML code.
- **Static graphics** A single, still image, usually incorporating text. Static graphics can be created in Adobe Illustrator, Fireworks, or Photoshop. The artwork would be supplied in either PNG, JPEG, or GIF file formats.

- **Animated GIF** Created using a limited amount of animation, designed to catch the viewer's attention. This art can be created and easily animated in Adobe Fireworks or Photoshop by displaying a sequence of static images, or "frames." Timing can be adjusted to further control the presentation. Animated GIFs must comply with established standards relating to overall file size, limiting the number of animation slides—usually three, since any more would exceed maximum file size—and a number of controlled rotations—typically animations are set to loop three times and stop. The artwork would be supplied in the GIF file format, or Animated GIF file format, depending on which application you are using.

- **Flash banner ads** A banner ad created using Adobe Flash allows the user to interact with the ad—for example, by rolling over the art to reveal more content. Because it is a Flash animation, it will run more smoothly than an Animated GIF and, therefore, be less intrusive. Run time is limited to 15 seconds at 24 frames per second. However, they are more expensive to develop and are not supported by some smartphone and tablet devices. The artwork would be supplied in the SWF file format.

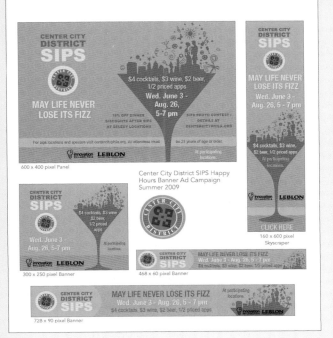

600 x 400 pixel Panel

Center City District SIPS Happy
Hours Banner Ad Campaign
Summer 2009

160 x 600 pixel
Skyscraper

300 x 250 pixel Banner

468 x 60 pixel Banner

728 x 90 pixel Banner

Banner ad elements

Successful banner ads usually
contain each of the following
items: a bold graphic with
a main focal point; a short
amount of type; a logo/
branding element; and a
clear call to action.

BANNER AD SIZES

Most websites that feature banner advertising
comply with the established, standard ad
options (defined by the Interactive Advertising
Bureau) and will provide specifications
relating to dimensions and file size limitations.
While the range of sizes continues to evolve
over time, these are the most common
formats. They are measured in pixels, at
screen resolution (72ppi), in RGB color mode,
with the maximum file size indicated.

Banner campaigns One of
the unique challenges of designing
a banner ad campaign is to create a
great composition that translates
across the different formats
(rectangle, leaderboard, badge).
Start by designing for the ad that you
consider to have the most challenging
dimensions. Then move ahead to the
easier sizes, maintaining as much
visual consistency as possible.

Useful link
**Interactive Advertising
Bureau**
This professional association
for online advertising works
to define the standards for
the industry as it changes
over time. The website is a
great resource for locating
current ad standards and
creative guidelines.
www.iab.net/guidelines

SEE ALSO:
WEB TOOLS, P150

- **Leaderboard—728 x 90 pixels (40kb)**
  A larger, more eye-catching version of
  the traditional full banner (see below).
  Usually placed at the top or bottom of
  a web page.
- **Wide skyscraper—160 x 600 pixels
  (40kb)** A tall, thin banner ad, designed
  to remain in view as the reader scrolls
  down. Usually appears in a side column,
  next to the body copy.
- **Banner ad elements —300 x 250
  pixels (40kb)** An increasingly popular
  option because it is large and typically

placed within the body copy, with the
text content flowing around it.
- **Rectangle—180 x 150 pixels (40kb)**
  This smaller ad size is popular with
  blogging sites, usually appearing in
  the side column.
- **Full banner—468 x 60 pixels
  (40kb)** Traditionally placed at the top
  or bottom of the web page. Officially,
  this once popular banner size
  has fallen out of favor and it is
  increasingly less available as a
  size option.

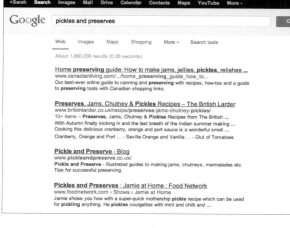

PART 2	PRACTICE
UNIT 7	WEB AND INTERACTIVITY
MODULE 12	**Search engine optimization (SEO)**

As part of any website development project, it is the designer's role to organize and structure the website in a way that helps it to be indexed properly by search engines, such as Google, Bing, and Yahoo!. The goal is to achieve unpaid, or "organic," search results.

Page title (meta tag)

Meta tags are elements within the HTML code, used by the search engines to properly index your website. Depending on the specific tag, it may or may not be visible when viewing the actual web page. A designer could develop a site without using any meta tags, but it would not perform well in the search engines.

Keywords (meta tag)

Keywords are the word combinations that web surfers use when they're performing their search queries. An initial step is to define all words and word combinations that a visitor might use to search and locate your site. You can do this on your own (from the dialogue your client supplied) or you can get them involved and ask them to compile their own list.

Page title (meta tag)

The page title is what appears at the top of your listing in the search results. This is also what appears in a bookmark list and at the top of the browser window/tab. It can be truncated, so arrange the important information first.

Bad: Your Site | Recipes
Great: Chili: Award-Winning Recipe | Your Site

Site description (meta tag)

A site description is a sentence of approximately 20 words that appears within the search results. This sentence should clearly define what information viewers will encounter on your site, using as many keywords as naturally possible.

Images

Often, viewers discover websites by performing image searches and clicking the link to view the full website. For your images to be properly indexed in the search engines, you should make some adjustments.

• **Retitle your images** Adjust the file name to incorporate keywords or relevant descriptive information. Remember never to use spaces. Use hyphens (-) or underscores (_) to separate words.

Bad: img00123-23.jpg
Great: recipe-wins-the-chili-cookoff.jpg

• **Include ALT tags for the images that you use on the website** Think of this as a caption that you add to each image, which appears in the HTML code. Spaces are fine between words.

• **Do not put important text inside images**
The search engines can't read pictures of words.

⊙ Search page results
In the search results, the designated page/site title is displayed first, followed by the complete URL, and then the site description.

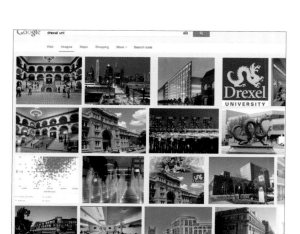

⊙ Image search results
A growing number of web viewers rely on image searches to discover websites. Make sure your corresponding artwork is presented so that it can be indexed properly in the search engines. Title the image file's name using relevant keywords, ALT tags, and descriptions (or captions).

PUTTING KEYWORDS TO WORK

Create a list of keywords (and keyword combinations) that you think site visitors would be searching for in order to discover your website. Then incorporate these keywords into your site using the following strategies:

- **Use keywords to create descriptive, human-friendly URLs** Name your web page documents using the keywords that relate to the information found on that page. Avoid using general terms or insider lingo.
Bad: www.yoursite.com/recipe.html
Great: www.yoursite.com/award-winning-chili-recipe.html
- **Use keywords in your headline and subhead text** Within an HTML structure, these elements are usually defined by <h> tags (heading tags). The search engines read the words stylized by these tags and assign them higher priority.
- **Infuse your dialogue to contain the appropriate keywords** Often clients will overlook using keywords within their site dialogue, in favor of using pronouns (he, us, it, they). Where naturally possible, keywords should be used instead. But don't go overboard. The search engines know all the tricks. Strings of random keywords within your dialogue will negatively affect your rankings.
- **Use the keyword meta tag** You can insert a string of chosen keywords into your document's keyword meta tag. However, more weight is assigned to keywords that appear naturally within your site dialogue.

PRACTICAL SEO ADVICE

For designers Never promise your client that their new site will receive top ranking in the search engines. A web designer's role is to make sure that a site looks great and is organized so that it can be indexed properly. You have no control over how popular the site will be, nor how high it will rank compared with other sites that may be paying for placement.

To put it in perspective, legitimate SEO/SEM analytics agencies can be hired to increase website rankings. They offer a multi-pronged approach, following the guidelines established by the search engines, and charge up to $20,000 on retainer.

For your clients If the designer has followed the advice given above, they will have delivered a website that will be properly indexed. There are also things the client can do to ensure the site ranks highly in the search results.

- Be aware that it can take up to one month for a website to appear in the search engines.
- What keywords are they searching for? Perhaps they are too generic and yielding too many results. Have they tried searching for keyword combinations that feature the city/town where they are located?
- Keep the site updated regularly.
- Promote your website directly to your audience by including your web address on material that you distribute regularly, from business cards to brochures and your email auto-signature.
- Create a presence using social media that drives traffic back to your website. Use status updates to keep your audience informed about new content additions and special offers from your site.
- Have you tried becoming an active participant in online forums and discussion boards? Use your expertise to share tips and advice. Establish yourself as someone people will want to do business with and they will seek you out.
- Have you considered paid placement (sponsored listings) within the search engines? Or sponsored advertising in social media, such as Facebook ads?

PART 2	PRACTICE
UNIT 7	WEB AND INTERACTIVITY
MODULE 13	**Online portfolios**

Any professional web designer needs a strong and well-conceived online portfolio and the growing list of "low-tech" options for displaying work online means that even non-web designers have little excuse for not having their work available for review online.

A successful online portfolio is a snapshot of work that reflects your abilities as a graphic designer. As with other design projects, you are designing for your target audience and addressing their needs. In reviewing numerous candidate websites in a single setting, potential employers are seeking a clear listing of skills and work experience, in addition to a complementary stylistic match for the work they produce.

Elements of an online portfolio

Your online portfolio should be clear, uncluttered, and easy to navigate. It should feature fundamental, descriptive information, including your name, field of practice, geographic area, and your current availability. You should also use it to present a summary of your professional biography, organized for easy visual scanning on screen. Include a link to download your resumé in PDF format. Finally, invite interested parties to make contact with you by including a clear call to action.

Prepare your images

Limit the number of visual examples you present in favor of providing a snapshot overview of your experiential range. You can present more examples during the in-person interview phase. Most new designers find it challenging to decide which images to include in their online portfolio. Focus on presenting work that represents a solid foundation of design—typography,

composition, color—in addition to your own aesthetic style. Ideally, your selected examples will complement the scope of work that is being produced by the companies that interest you. If that is not the case, you should work on bolstering your portfolio with new projects.

Portfolio images should be consistent in size and visual presentation. A typical size for a detailed view would be 800 x 600 pixels, at screen resolution (72ppi) and optimized for online viewing. Smaller, thumbnail views can be presented as proportionately reduced artwork or as strategically cropped designs, intended to intrigue your audience into clicking to view in more detail. Website design examples typically feature a browser "frame" and app designs usually feature the device screen view.

A subcategory navigation structure can be employed to help direct viewers through the project-type examples that relate to the work they are interested in viewing, such as publication design, identity, packaging, and advertising.

Getting started

To set yourself apart from novices or design hobbyists, you'll need your own domain name and a web hosting account. A domain name (for example, www.yoursite. com) is like leasing a car. Web hosting is like renting a parking spot for your leased car. You need both in order

⬆ Slideshow feature To reduce the visitor's need to scroll, project examples are presented in a slideshow format. Tinted thumbnail views serve as the navigational element for reviewing the additional detailed images.

GLOSSARY

Domain name: The web address for a website. It is renewed annually by the site owner for a nominal fee.

Web hosting: A designated online storage space for hosting a website and related email accounts.

⊕ **SEE ALSO:** WORKING WITH CONTENT MANAGEMENT SYSTEMS, P173

OPTIONAL PORTFOLIO ELEMENTS

- Images can be captioned with brief project summaries to spotlight details or your specific involvement within the project (for group work).
- Concept sketches and creative explorations can effectively provide a unique insight into your creative process. Select one project, present it as a case study, and use visuals to guide your audience through your process.
- Additional interests that reinforce your design skills (photography, illustration) can be included to demonstrate a broader range of skills and interests, but should be presented with reduced presence, so as not to deter from your focus on seeking employment as a graphic designer.
- Invite site visitors to connect with your professional presence across social media accounts (Linkedin, Twitter, Facebook Fan Page, Flickr, Pinterest, etc.). But, avoid linking to accounts where you represent yourself informally.
- Maintain a creative design blog (or Tumblr micro-blog) with shared insights on where you derive inspiration and comments on related design trends.

SELECTING THE RIGHT DOMAIN NAME

Start by using your own name, as opposed to laboring to conceive a clever business alias. It's easier to associate you with a web address that features your actual name. Use a ".com" domain, because people instinctively type that suffix. Select a name that is difficult to misspell or consider purchasing multiple names. You can always set your domain names to reroute site visitors to your main web address.

⬆ **Be innovative** Designer Dado Queiroz presents his portfolio in thumbnail format by creating clever icons that derive visuals from each project example.

⬅ **Lightbox feature** The "lightbox" JavaScript can be used to display detailed views of your artwork within the same browser window. It can be customized to include a title, short description, the styling of the next/previous navigation buttons, and the overlay effect on the site background.

to establish your online presence. Both are renewed annually for a nominal fee. With a traditional web hosting account you also get email accounts for your domain, which you should use for professional correspondence.

Low-tech online portfolios

Popular among non-web designers, there are a growing variety of online resources that provide designers with the ability to upload and share image examples from their portfolio. The utility-driven goal is to have the image examples available on demand, via hyperlink, as opposed to manually attaching images to email correspondence.

Your domain's settings can be adjusted to redirect your site viewers directly from your web address to a user profile on any of the following websites.

Flickr.com Although widely considered to be the most low-tech option, Flickr image galleries can be further subdivided into photo sets, based on related themes. This is more user friendly than presenting a timeline-based photo stream.

Dribbble.com, Behance.net, and Dunked.com

Dribbble is rooted in social media, allowing you to follow (and be followed by) other designers and potential clients. Behance presents uploaded project examples in a clean and standardized portfolio-style presentation. Dunked takes it a step further, letting you customize the visual design of your portfolio's appearance.

Tumblr.com Tumblr is a micro-blogging platform, intended for sharing images, links, and short text-based posts. The traditional, linear timeline format of a Tumblr page design can be amended with the application of pre-styled "portfolio theme" formatting. Typically, these commercially available theme styles focus on image-based posts, presented in a visual, grid-style format. Easy to update, each new post presents a new portfolio item. To revise the order of the presentation, you revise the date of the post.

WordPress Popular among creatives, the WordPress content management system (CMS) has a wide assortment of commercially available themes that have been specifically created for portfolio-style presentations. More complex than a post-driven Tumblr account,

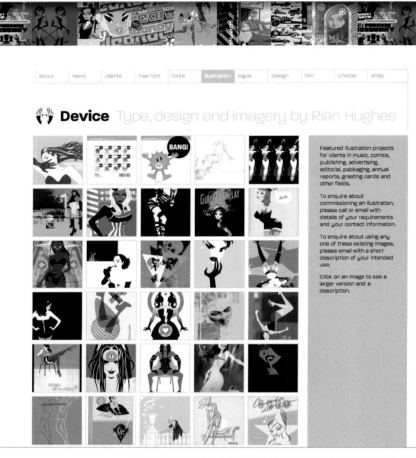

⬆ Thumbnail design
Designer Rian Hughes' website presents a series of thumbnails as cropped visuals. Intrigued viewers will click to reveal the full image.

✳ Self-promotion
Don't forget to include the address of your online portfolio on your resumé, business cards, social-media account profiles, and your email account's auto-signature settings.

⬆ Creative cropping This example presents the artwork as both an angled perspective and a cropped view.

WordPress affords you the ability to add more functionality and styling enhancements.

Traditional online portfolios

If you are seeking positions within the field of web design, the online portfolio serves as a perfect vehicle to demonstrate what you know, from HTML and CSS coding to crafting a memorable user experience. The level of design and coding should be representative of your level of technical expertise.

The online design blog, SmashingMagazine.com, features a growing list of articles showing the latest trends and case studies relating to online portfolios.

Test your work

When you reach the point at which you think you have finished your project, take a break and return with a fresh pair of eyes. Click through all of your links to check that they are functioning properly. Check that your presentation is well organized and visually consistent. Review your grammar.

Conduct a "beta test" within a small group of friends and/or family members and review their feedback. If your parents are having a challenging time navigating through your site, a potential employer may experience the same issue. Process all necessary adjustments before sharing your web address with a larger audience.

EMAIL AND AUTO SIGNATURES

Regardless of which email system you use regularly (school, Gmail, Yahoo, etc.), for professional correspondence you should set up and use an email account associated with your own domain name. Where a school email account communicates "student" and a nondescript Gmail account may say "hobbyist," your own domain serves as the foundation in creating a professional first impression.

Most email systems provide you with the ability to set up default auto signatures, where you can predefine a standardized closing signature for every email you distribute. Take advantage of this feature, envisioning it as if you are passing along a virtual business card to everyone you correspond with. Typical signature elements include name, desired contact details, and links to online portfolio and social media.

⬇ Establishing consistency This portfolio presents thumbnails in a unified, grayscale appearance. When the visitor interacts with the thumbnail, the thumbnail is replaced with the colorized version of the graphic.

⬆ ➡ Show what you know If you are presenting yourself as a designer who can code HTML and CSS, your online portfolio is a fantastic opportunity to demonstrate your expertise. In this example, the designer is presenting a responsive design.

UNIT 7: ASSIGNMENTS

○ WIREFRAMES

Revisit the sites that you view more frequently and create wireframes of their layouts. Look for trends in how content is organized. Take note of sites that break from established trends. Identify which factors, unique to the website, benefited from breaking from the trend. Measure the amount of white space—vertical and horizontal—that is used within layouts to separate content.

○ FLOWCHARTS

Select an existing website and document the pages in flowchart format. Pay specific attention to how links are named and how they are ordered.

○ CREATE A STYLE BOARD

A style board is a graphical representation of stylistic approaches that you would be proposing to your client. Designed elements are pulled out of the specific web layout so they can remain the focal point of the preliminary design consultations. Typically, designers present three style boards for a client to review: conservative approach; a wild approach; and an approach that falls between the two extremes.

Select a website that you visit often and create three style boards. Start with the styles used in the current website. Then create two variations, one conservative, one wild. Identify:

• Color palette: dark, light, midtones, accent colors
• Typography: headline, subhead, body text, text links, quotes, captions, etc.
• Textures: background patterns, gradients, drop shadows, etc.
• Buttons: button size, shape, color, corner radius, drop shadow, etc.
• Icons: icons as a button element, icons to define content, etc.
• Images: cropping (rectangle/square), border, padding/spacing, drop shadow, corner radius, etc.
• Adjectives: list out four adjectives for each of your style boards. These adjectives set the tone for each approach and will be used to pitch your overall concept to your client.

○ RESEARCH

Web design is constantly evolving. Regularly explore the following websites to review current trends and derive inspiration for your own web design projects.
www.Dribbble.com
www.SmashingMagazine.com
www.WebDesignLedger.com
www.aListApart.com
webdesign.tutsplus.com/
www.NNgroup.com/articles/

○ MOBILE APP ICON DESIGN

The app icon is the main branding element for a mobile app project. Select an existing app (or an app that you would like to create) and make an icon.

Successful app icons visually explain the utility of the app. Start by writing out a list of potential visual elements. Explore past the first visuals that come to mind and try to infuse a more unique perspective.

Assemble your icon in Adobe Photoshop (72ppi, RGB) Resize your app icon design for use on an iPhone at the following dimensions (in pixels): 57x57, 72x72, 114x114, 512x512.

Explore adjustments and modifications that may be required, so that your artwork can be presented clearly at the different display sizes.

● PREPARING TO DESIGN A SITE

Organizing a website's assets from content through imagery to hosting needs to be planned. Imagine you are creating a website for a small boutique specializing in designer sunglasses. Using the questions below, create a proposal on what will be necessary for you to complete the job and what you will need to get from the client.

• What must the website do? What is the goal?
• How many levels will the site have? How will the content be organized?
• What navigation conventions will you need to ensure that the user can easily move between pages?
• What images and techniques will need to be generated?

• Consider domain registration and hosting of the site, since this may affect how you build it.
• Do you have access to all relevant content to build your site? How much content will the client/you generate?
• Who is the audience and on what size screen will the site need to be seen? Widescreen HD or mobile?
• Does the client want Flash or Javascript-based motion?
• Are there any special requirements for larger font sizes?
• Consider the target audience and the browsers from which they will most likely be visiting the site.
• How will client information and purchases be collected? How will they contact the vendor?

● WEBSITE MAKEOVER

Most websites have a life span of only a few years, influenced by refocusing of client goals or in response to revised trends in presentation or user experience. Many web designers appreciate site revision projects for the simple fact that most of the content is readily available.

Select a website that would benefit from a new approach. Start by defining the flow chart. Move ahead to exploring different content presentations in the wireframing phase. Finish by inserting actual content into your composition design.

● EXPLORE: EVOLUTION OF THE WEB

www.evolutionoftheweb.com/
This website features a graphical timeline of innovations that have influenced the Web over the past 20 years, from various web browsers, to code and functionality improvements, to presenting global web traffic numbers.

Further Reading:
Mike Monteiro, *Design is a Job,* Happy Cog/A Book Apart, 2012
Smashing Magazine, eBook, *Redesign The Web (The Smashing Book 3),* Smashing Media GmbH, 2012
Jeremy Keith, *HTML 5 for Web Designers,* Happy Cog/A Book Apart, 2010
Dan Cederholm, *CSS3 for Web Designers,* Happy Cog/A Book Apart, 2011
Jennifer Niederst Robbins, *Learning Web Design: A Beginner's Guide to HTML, CSS, JavaScript, and Web Graphics,* O'Reilly Media; fourth edition, 2012
Patrick McNeil, *The Web Designer's Idea Book, Volume 3: Inspiration from Today's Best Web Design Trends, Themes and Styles,* HOW Books; third edition, 2013

8 EXPERT PATHS AND COLLABORATIONS

By now you should have a good idea of which career path excites you, and will be interested in discovering what it might be like to work in a specific design field. Although expert knowledge in any one of the highlighted disciplines in this chapter will serve you well in the marketplace, remember that design is a collaborative field, and that it is becoming increasingly interdisciplinary. In fact, many of the skill sets in each path should be part of your repertoire. Build your expertise in the area that excites you the most, but find out enough about all of them to collaborate intelligently.

In this unit, each branch of a discipline is highlighted with the skills needed, the ups and downs you might encounter on the job, and some examples of the best in the business. It will provide you with resources and options to help you develop a career path that best suits your skills and aptitudes.

> **"Design is thinking made visual"**
> *Saul Bass*

Logo design and brand identity

Based in the realm of symbology and sign, and originating in pre-Neolithic times, the logo, or ideogram, is no stranger to anyone these days. Instantly recognizable and distinctly memorable, a well-designed logo is versatile in multiple ways, but resilient enough to retain its identity instantly in the viewer's mind. It is both cornerstone and keystone for brand development. In logo creation, decisions on style, color, aesthetics, and typography set up a "Rosetta Stone" upon which a client's whole branding and marketing strategy will be based. Designers must research, then refract, the essence of an idea into a system of elements showcasing a singular icon and idea, which in turn creates identity.

"Logo," "corporate identity," "brand," "trademark"; no matter how you slice it, these terms all point to the creation of a cohesive defining symbol that represents a client in every piece of communication. Easy and effective translation of goals, values, and expertise is vital to build trust with potential customers and satisfy current ones. Business cards, letterheads, brochures, ads, websites, motion graphics, and promotional items can all be used to create a public identity, and each element stems from the initial mark developed by the identity developer.

The process can be a long one, often involving a committee with different opinions. By researching and collecting information from a client and their industry, the identity developer utilizes their creativity and marketing savvy to generate several different ideas from multiple avenues of approach for a client to choose from. Patience and understanding are then needed to survive the editing process, when a client mixes, changes, and makes requests as you work with them to get their logo just right. As the process unfolds, keep in mind the alternatives for different contexts and consistency across a variety of media. An accomplished identity developer is a paragon of refinement and service that can keep the client happy and the brand beautiful.

Identity, logo, and corporate identity designers

A great identity developer should be detail-oriented, flexible, and have well-developed design and problem-solving skills that employ clarity, simplicity, and communication. Organizations spend hundreds of thousands of dollars annually to keep identity and branding fresh, current, and innovative, and we know those clients are out there just waiting to find the right talent. Large companies employ in-house designers who develop and update their logos, but many turn to external graphic design firms, and individuals who specialize in this field, to develop their brand.

Whether you decide to work in an agency or a design studio or go out on your own, you will run across a request for a logo every now and again. Sticking to the concepts of simplicity, clarity, scalability, and innovation will provide a starting point for any successful logo.

The exciting part...

- Opportunities for visual creativity and clever communication, especially for those designers interested in identity, marketing, and sales.
- Accomplished identity developers are often independent freelancers who have spent many successful years in agencies and studios, making employment options versatile.
- Opportunities to engage interest in marketing, psychology, and business.
- It is always gratifying to see a brand you helped develop launch, expand, and succeed.

... Not so much

- Many have created their "perfect logo" only to have it modified beyond recognition, or trashed inadvertently by a visually uneducated client. Such is the life of a designer.
- Unless you are hired for a full branding development position with a company, you'll need to generate lots of clients who need logos and letterheads in order to pay the bills.
- Ultimately, the ability to be completely creatively present for the client yet let go enough to meet their needs, regardless of all your training and better judgment, is a quality that is hard for some. Remember: you are creating their identity, not yours.

Skills required

- A firm, creative understanding and love of typography, visual semiotics, symbolism, illustration, color theory, brand design, and marketing psychology.
- Knowledge of all pro-level software programs and printing systems, and familiarity with a variety of traditional and innovative marketing materials and campaign approaches.
- Great research skills.
- Great communication skills. Listening carefully to a client at the beginning and throughout the branding process is the only way to deliver the winning brand.

⚫ Best in the business

Paul Rand, Pratt Institute graduate, Yale University professor, and American graphic designer who will go down in history for his groundbreaking work with some of the best-known corporate logo designs. A strong proponent of the Swiss style of design, Rand developed the foundation corporate identities for Apple, IBM, UPS, Westinghouse, and ABC. He was touted as a consummate salesman who, through explaining the necessity of proper identity creation to clients and students, helped usher in a new era for marketing and design.

Paula Scher, Corcoran College of Art and Design doctorate graduate, began as a record cover art director at Atlantic and CBS Records and has developed a career and style that has won her many prestigious awards for her work and innovation in the field of design. Currently a partner at Pentagram in New York, she is best known for her identity and branding systems, promotional materials, packaging, and publication designs for such clients as *The New York Times Magazine*, Perry Ellis, Bloomberg, Citibank, Tiffany & Co, Target, the New York Botanical Garden, and *The Daily Show With Jon Stewart.*

Ivan Chermayeff, founding partner of Chermayeff & Geismar, a leading graphic design firm in the fields of corporate identity, brand development, and logo design. Chermayeff studied at Harvard University, Illinois Institute of Technology, and the Yale University School of Design. With partner Tom Geismar, whom he met at Yale, he has designed iconic marks for hundreds of companies, including Burlington Industries, Chase Manhattan Bank, Dictaphone, Mobil Corporation, Pan American Airlines, Xerox, and the Museum of Modern Art.

LloydNorthover, one of Britain's most successful consultancies, working internationally in identity, branding, and communication, prides itself in providing creative solutions to strategic problems. In giving companies a competitive market advantage by making them highly visible, clear, and compelling, they have created many successful campaigns for Comet, De Beers, Elizabeth Arden, HSBC, Infiniti, Lexus, Mitsubishi, Morgan Stanley, Orange, and Royal Mail.

Collaborators

Motion graphics, web designers and developers, typographers, marketers.

Career options

Logo and brand identity design is part of every designer's skill set, but if you specialize in corporate identity you can find a career in the following:

» In-house designer with a creative studio
» Ad agency brand development specialist
» Freelance designer
» Brand specialist for a web development firm
» Corporate in-house designer in any large company or institution

Career path potential

» Junior and senior designer > creative director > partner in a firm

➕ **See also:** Michael Beirut, Massimo Vignelli, Herb Lubalin, Armin Hoffman, Saul Bass, Gerard Huerta, Walter Landor

Motion graphics

The field of motion graphics has transcended its early beginnings in film and TV opening titles and is now vital to the new media environment, interactive applications, post-production, advertising, animation, and digital environments for the Web and broadcast.

The emphasis in the motion graphics industry is on speed of communication—how quickly you can appeal to either a specialized demographic or a wide audience and communicate the product, proposal, or information as clearly as possible. From corporations to production houses, web, digital, and interactive media, music industry, television, and film, this industry can be divided into three specializations.

• Business-to-business (B2B) takes the form of idea proposals and pitches, training seminars, and other info-graphics.
• Advertising encompasses everything from web banners and TV commercials to websites.
• Film/video specialization covers music promotion, film/TV opening and closing credits, and other animated visuals and effects.

As with many specializations, you are likely to start in a long-established studio, under a creative director, art director, or producer. Later you may freelance or set up a small studio of your own, although the brief structure remains the same. Occasionally clients will give you the creative freedom to push boundaries; many times they will have a specific aesthetic in mind. Motion is everywhere now and this industry demands a constant stream of new and fresh talent and ideas.

Skills required

• Knowledge of communication strategies and rhetoric.
• Excellent grasp of typography, 2D and 3D composition, and color.
• Good appreciation of pace, rhythm, and storyboarding.
• Good spatial awareness and geometry.
• An ability to work comfortably with complexity and layering, both literal and metaphorical.
• Advanced and up-to-date knowledge of Flash, After Effects, Maya, Illustrator, Photoshop, and some FinalCut.
• Diplomacy and a client-centered outlook.

The exciting part...

• Working in a fast-paced, cutting-edge environment.
• If your work really communicates client concepts in an innovative way, it will be sought after.
• Motion graphics designers are multi-disciplinary and know how to collaborate. They are also masters of word and image and of many facets of design, versed in all the core skills.

... Not so much

• Much of the initial concept work will be time-consuming. Clients may not know exactly what they want, and you will probably have to develop many versions to actually pull it out of their heads.
• Turnaround speed can be crazy fast. Be realistic on what you can achieve in the time available to avoid missing your deadline.

⊗ Best in the business

Saul Bass (1920–1996), the godfather of motion graphics, is best known for his iconic opening and closing credits on Hollywood films such as Alfred Hitchcock's *Psycho*, *North by Northwest*, and *Vertigo*, and on *West Side Story*, *Broadcast News*, *Goodfellas*, and *Big*. His animation styling set the standards for many who followed, and he was an accomplished poster and logo designer.

Maurice Binder, best known for his signature graphic work on the opening credits of 14 James Bond films, designed credits and animations for a wide variety of films from the 1950s to the 1990s.

Kyle Cooper studied graphic design under Paul Rand at Yale University. The multi-award winning Cooper has directed over 150 title sequences for film and television and has done much to have titling and motion graphics recognized as the art they surely are. He is the founder of Imaginary Forces and Prologue Films, and is best known for his work on the film *Se7en*, and most recent work includes *Argo*, *Sherlock Holmes*, *Mission Impossible*, *X-Men*, *Twilight: Breaking Dawn*, *Tree of Life*, *The Walking Dead*, *American Horror Story*, and *Iron Man II*.

Career options

- ⊗ Film and special effects studios
- ⊗ Broadcast stations and online content developers
- ⊗ Advertising agencies and design firms
- ⊗ Web development firm
- ⊗ Promotion designer for a large company or institution

⊕ **See also:** Angus Wall (Game of Thrones), Stephen Frankfurt (To Kill a Mockingbird), Garson Yu, R/GA Media Group Inc, www.momoco.co.uk, www.artofthetitle.com

Web design

In the early days of the Web, the original designers who took the first stabs at web development were print-based graphic designers. Now, over a few short years, there are students graduating from colleges across the globe with concentrations focusing solely on web design and development, online communications, interactive media, and web commerce. So what does a career in web design and digital media have in store?

Companies and organizations hire hundreds of web designers annually to help them create and perfect their online presence and identity. For the more interactive designer with a penchant for heavier coding, design studios and advertising agencies have teams of web developers, coders, and information architects to handle the contemporary online needs of their clients, such as interactive interfaces, e-commerce installations, content management systems, and social networking platforms. No matter where your intrinsic skills lie, the field of web design has quickly become a rich tapestry of varying disciplines and skills in which any designer can match their talents and interests.

Is it right for you?

Whether working freelance in a home studio or as an in-house developer at a creative firm, the current population of web professionals is made up of true devotees of emerging media. Countless personal hours are spent learning and mastering the latest HTML conventions, or JavaScript libraries, or CSS. Days are spent in a trial-and-error limbo as designers research and modify bits of coding to get the interface to react just as the client expects it to. During months of work, from initial thumbnails to final launch, developers and designers work together to create accessible sites that can be easily accessed and instantly understood by people all over the world. Millions of cups of coffee or tea are poured as these self-starters stay up into the wee hours learning digital languages that are never uttered nor seen, but experienced. All of this happens because there are always those who have the abilities and interests to see the possibilities in the enlarging world of the Web, and because they can see themselves within those possibilities.

Hierarchy

Some web designers work successfully from home, conducting a large portion of their client contact by phone and email. Most of the time these solitary designers have a very good command of a wider array of web specialties, such as HTML/CSS coding, content management systems (PHP), Flash, and Maya animation, as well as image correction and manipulation, and awareness of the user experience.

In larger work environments, a web designer may be the only professional on the team qualified to design and write a bit of code while working with a team of professional code writers/developers/producers, content managers, marketers, and executives. There may even be a variety of multi-disciplinary web designers and developers, or specialists that focus on one aspect of each project.

Skills required

- Firm understanding of typography, composition, layout, balance, color theory,

imagery creation and manipulation.
- Understanding of the user experience (UX).
- Basic understanding of HTML and CSS.
- Growing familiarity with the usage of JavaScript, Ajax, and PHP.
- Understanding of the concepts of user interaction (UI) and client goals and their relationship to the interface.
- Desire to discover and stay current in the latest web languages and innovations.
- Understanding of such principles as web standards, web accessibility, and search engine optimization (SEO).
- Eye for detail, to the pixel level for the visual, and the ability to write clean code.
- Familiarity with how color and devices work in regard to the Web and how that relates to the viewer.

The exciting part...

- Involvement in a constantly evolving technology.
- Near-immediate edits and updates to a body of work with little fuss, as compared to print design.
- More opportunities for freelance and home-based work situations for web designers.
- The excitement of cross-platform and multi-device design.

... Not so much

- The proliferation of amateur work on the Web, and the disregard of good design in favor of speed and ease of format.
- Projects are ongoing, requiring regular upkeep.
- Technology updates are time-consuming, but you must stay current with revised standards in the industry.

✪ Best in the business

Jeffrey Zeldman is a lecturer and author on web design. He also runs his own web design studio, Happy Cog, which has created influential web work for clients such as AIGA, Amnesty International, Mozilla, Warner Bros. Films, and Stanford University. His book *Designing With Web Standards* set the tone for modern-day semantic web design.

Hillman Curtis has spent a decade blending the Web, Adobe Flash, and film through his company Hillmancurtis, Inc. to design digital media for such companies as Adobe, Hewlett-Packard, Intel, Yahoo!, Rolling Stone, and MTV. Curtis and his company have been featured in many publications for their designs and have won many awards for their online work.

Molly E. Holzschlag is an award-winning lecturer and web designer, as well as author of over 35 books on web design and markup. She has worked with the W3C and WaSP, focusing on web standards, web accessibility, web sustainability, and related topics.

Career options

Here are the basic situations an emerging web designer may find when ready to enter the working world.

- ✪ Independent freelance web designer/developer
- ✪ Contract freelance web designer/developer
- ✪ Web designer/developer working with an agency
- ✪ Design, marketing, or advertising for a variety of clients
- ✪ Web designer/developer working within a company. With a focus on the main site or sites for the company; often in charge of the office intranet, email, etc.

⊕ **See also:** Chris Coyier, www.chriscoyier.net, who runs CSS-Tricks and writes the Shop Talk Show. He's more of the technical, front-end side of the web.

Editorial design

Modern editorial design arguably originates from the 15th-century printing press of Gutenberg, when pages of type were manually set in movable metal type. Each page was set in relation to margins, gutters, and borders, and printed in multiple copies—a huge leap from handwritten manuscripts. With evolutions in print-production methods and the influence of early 20th-century art and design schools such as the Bauhaus, the designer began to gain control over the page. Editorial designers now work in an unprecedented range of media and technologies. Many new forms of editorial design have been generated over time, and aesthetic considerations are wide ranging.

Editorial designers are key players in the production of books, print and virtual magazines, brochures, and catalogs, with the task of aesthetically transforming raw text and image to maximize legibility, impact, and communication.

Depending on the publication, there may be a need for flexibility in styling. In a publishing house a designer may work on a series of titles with different demographic target audiences: children, teen, young professional, special interest, parents, or families are just a few of many possibilities. Each needs a different style, emphasis, and direction. The aesthetic direction is generally agreed on by the upper production team, including the art director and design editor. It is the designer's role to implement these decisions, carry out instructions, and respond to changes in the market.

Editorial designers also work on larger web-based publications, such as news websites, corporate web presence, and advertising and webzines. Smaller websites usually do not have a specialized designer. There are different design issues on the Internet, such as legibility of fonts, and other considerations such as type in motion.

Wide ranging

Editorial designers are driven by and focused on content, and usually work within teams in medium to large organizations; they are rarely freelancers. They are often the focal point for many streams of material, such as raw text from authors, images from photographers and illustrators, and overall concept styling from art directors and development teams. They are expected to consider and combine these assets to create the finished publication.

There are endless stylistic choices in editorial design, from minimalist problem-solving aesthetics to complex contemporary juxtapositions. As an emerging editorial designer, you need to be aware of design possibilities and design intelligently.

Skills required

- Excellent appreciation and mastery of typography, hierarchy, and grid systems.
- Good spatial awareness and compositional skills.
- Strong sense of design history.
- Ability to work well with complexity and layering.
- Accurate eye for content correction—whether it's grammar, color, or mood.
- Advanced and up-to-date knowledge of InDesign, Illustrator, Photoshop, and, to a lesser extent, Quark.
- Team-focused attitude and diplomacy.
- Ability to negotiate extensive revisions to your designs, and to let your ego "slide."

The exciting part...

- You are the designer for the layout and composition of pages/spreads of the publication.
- You see your work in the bookstore or on the Internet.
- You work on a wide variety of content (especially in book design).
- Your interpretation of content can set the mood of the piece.
- Your editorial visuals can be thought provoking.

... Not so much

- As the focal point for many different information streams, coordination of deadlines and organization of work can become tricky.
- As with many specializations, design school rarely prepares you for the speed or amount of work involved in each project.
- There will inevitably be many corrections/revisions to the work on the way to the final product. You will need to be open to this process and respond well to feedback.

⭐ Best in the business

Alexey Brodovich, Neville Brody, and **Cipe Pineles,** known for their innovative magazine designs.

Jost Hochuli and **Jan Tschichold,** known for their book designs and contributions to modern typography.

Bradbury Thompson and **Piet Zwart,** known for their powerful and imaginative designs in many editorial contexts.

Also look at the work of **David Carson, Carin Goldberg, Herbert Bayer, Janet Froelich, Tibor Kilman,** and **George Lois.**

Career options

- Design assistant, junior designer
  Invaluable opportunity to learn the ropes by assisting on a wide variety of projects, but with limited room for creativity.
- Senior designer
  Greater opportunity to be creative, designing templates as well as working with them, and making image and direction choices.
- Art editor or creative director
  Managing the design of projects, overseeing freelance designers, and working closely with editorial and production staff.

⊕ **See also:** The Society of Publication Designers, www.spd.org, established in 1965 for international trade, corporate, institutional, newspaper and consumer editorial art directors.

Environmental graphic design

Environmental graphic designers work with architects and interior designers to create distinctive design works that visually define the built environment. These projects can include exhibition design for museums, galleries, and public art installations; wayfinding and architectural signage; pictogram design; mapping; complete branding and identity systems; and themed environments. Their work is in demand by the retail and entertainment industries, real-estate developers, and city planners, and is a critical factor in public facilities and transportation where clear signage and efficient crowd circulation are essential.

Environmental graphic designers are among the most collaborative in the design disciplines, and will partner with experts in many areas to research, and then deliver, functional design in an informative, entertaining way. They combine their skills with those of digital media experts to create sophisticated interactive communications, work with product designers and industrial designers on fabrications, with landscape architects, and with individual clients in hospitals, schools, and businesses. Large architecture firms may have environmental graphic design departments in house for signage, wayfinding, identity, and supporting print materials. Others consult graphic design firms that offer environmental design services for big projects that require complicated information visualization. Both types of firms may work with freelances on a portion or a complete project.

In the thick of it

As with any graphic design project, in the first stage of development—the programming phase—the environmental graphic designer determines the client's objectives and researches the potential needs of the building/space, users, or audience. This will enable the client and designer to determine the amount and location of signs and other fabrications for estimating. Then, the designer will begin the conceptual design process with a combination of sketches and 3D models or digital illustrations rendered in 2D or 3D. When the design is refined enough for estimates, the environmental graphic designer will supervise the bidding process for fabrication of the architectural elements, will work with the design team to select the fabricators, and is often on site for the actual installation of elements.

Skills required

- Strong design skills in composition, form, color, scale, and texture.
- Good drawing skills.
- Ability to visualize three-dimensional space.
- Familiarity with the codes and regulations for signage.
- Understanding of human factors, including visual and lighting requirements, color perception, and behavioral psychology.
- Understanding of symbolism and multi-lingual needs.
- Strong interpersonal and communication skills.

The exciting part...

- Your design work becomes a permanent installation.
- You will have a very hands-on research experience.
- You can see the effect your work has in public.

- You work with architects, structural engineers, industrial designers, and fabricators.
- You get to work in 3D.

... Not so much

- The process is long and complicated.
- Mistakes can be expensive and time consuming.
- Your deadlines are affected by the entire team and can make scheduling complex.

⊛ Best in the business

Environmental design is collaborative, and it involves graphic designers, architects, interior designers, fabricators and more.
Look at:

Ralph Appelbaum Associates
Pentagram Design Group (especially the work of **Paula Scher** and **Andrew Freeman**)
The Rockwell Group
Gensler
Local Projects
Deborah Sussman

Career options

Environmental design is collaborative and involves graphic designers, architects, interior designers, fabricators, and more. The designer should have excellent communication skills and the ability to work as part of a team. Areas of specialization for environmental designers may include:

- Exhibition design
- Wayfinding systems
- Architectural signage
- Interactive visitor experience
- 3D visualization

⊕ **See also:** www.thincdesign.com, www.segd.org, www.brandculture.com.au, www.p-06-atelier.pt

Advertising

The designer whose strengths lie in developing innovative and convincing concepts can play a pivotal role in this high-energy, fast-paced industry. Advertising designers can sway the public consciousness not only through commercial advertising campaigns, but also as part of promoting social change, and raising awareness of local and global issues such as health, sustainability, and politics.

Advertising is a very competitive field. Thoughtful, creative ads reach and influence more minds, attract more attention, and generate more sales. With a team, the freelance or in-house advertising designer creates a campaign concept for a client to present to the public. As the visual arm of a marketing team, the designer must call upon psychology, marketing, communication, and humor to create successful market penetration through media such as television, radio, newspapers, magazines, email, the Web, and social media. The goal is to be more innovative, more thought-provoking, and more memorable, so advertising designers keep ahead of the curve, are aware of emerging trends, and are continually connected to current events and ideas.

Advertising designers

Advertising probably still employs more talent to produce creative work than any other occupation, since everything is advertised in some way.

You can expect to work long, sometimes inconvenient hours, since the agency needs to meet the timing of clients who are often in other time zones. In a larger agency you're more likely to specialize in a certain area, such as pharmaceutical advertising, than in a small agency, where you're more likely to do a little (or a lot) of everything.

There are three main positions: graphic designers, art directors, and creative directors. These roles can sometimes be filled by freelance and contract workers, or they may be full-time as part of a creative department. Regardless of the position you may take, a good advertising piece has a way of sticking with you—whether it's a memorable jingle, a clever catchphrase, or a beautiful image. If you feel you have always had the eye for the perfect way to sell something to the world, advertising design provides a rewarding and exciting career for the up-and-coming graphic designer.

Skills required

- Artistic ability and a knack for good, clever visual thinking.
- Being artistic and being a good designer are two different things; both are desirable. Being able to capture and communicate a client's message within the current cultural style while keeping it clever, innovative, and graphically sound is a skill that will take you far.
- Research skills and knowledge of customer psychology and cultural tastes.
- Competitive edge—at times the advertising industry has been called cutthroat.
- The ability to work well to deadlines and under pressure.
- Knowledge of design and advertising history.
- Cultural currency.

The exciting part...

- Upward momentum and networking: great opportunities to meet other prospective employers and clients.
- You are involved in strategies to help clients make high-level business decisions.
- Great salaries if you move up.

... Not so much

- The larger the budget, the larger the possibility of failure.
- Advertising can create notoriously high-stress environments.

⭐ Best in the business

Grey Advertising, in all its forms, the giant ad agency that has been around for 95 years, and represents Volkswagen, 3M, Proctor and Gamble, Mars, Kraft, Marriot, Toshiba, E-Trade, Cannon, the NFL, among others.

Wieden+Kennedy has offices all over the world and has been at the top of their game for the last 30 years, with clients like Nike, Coca-Cola, Facebook, Converse, Kraft, Levi's, and Sony.

BBDO employs 17,200 people in 287 offices in 77 countries worldwide, and is an award-winning agency network, headquartered in New York, that opened its doors in 1928. BBDO has been recognized for amazing work for high-profile clients such as Pepsi, Ikea, FedEx, BBC News, General Electric, Campbells, Gillette, Motorola, Chrysler, Pfizer, Wrigley, Mitsubishi, and UNICEF.

Ogilvy was founded in 1948 as Ogilvy & Mather and is an international advertising, marketing, and public relations firm that operates 497 offices in 125 countries around the world. Opened by David Ogilvy, the company quickly became a leading worldwide agency by the 1960s as it helped build brands for American Express, BP, Ford, Barbie, Maxwell House, IBM, Kodak, Nestlé, Pond's, and Dove.

Droga5 is one to watch, named 2012 Agency of the Year by Adweek, Creativity's 2011 Agency of the Year, and number two on Advertising Age's 2011 Agency A-List.

Leo Burnett was opened in 1935, gained momentum in the 1950s, and is still the ninth largest agency in the world. The agency has undergone many changes, but has garnered many big-name accounts along the way, such as McDonald's, Coca-Cola, Walt Disney, Marlboro, Maytag, Kellogg's, Tampax, Nintendo, U.S. Army, Philips, Samsung, Visa, Wrigley, and Hallmark. Today the agency has 97 offices in 84 countries across the globe.

In addition to the agencies above, check out the work of these individuals: **George Lois**, **Joe Pytka**, **Lou Dorfsman**, **John C. Jay**, **David Droga**.

Career options

- Working in advertising usually means at an agency, which provides great opportunities for teamwork, networking, higher budgets, broader-scoped campaigns, awards, and unmatchable experience. Working for big-name clients is more common in bigger cities, and movement between agencies is an option for many designers as they graduate to head designers and art directors.
- Copywriter, marketer, account manager, production artist. The person who enters advertising design will often wear more than one hat.
- Interns and internships are in heavy rotation due to the fast-paced, low-attention-span nature of the public as it scans for the next big thing. Interns are temporary, like trends, and their work is creative, fresh, and usually free. Being at an agency offers interns a lot of benefits—contacts, clients, and projects—but teaches them only one thing they need to know about working in advertising: whether they love it or hate it.

See also: Adweek, Advertising Age, The Clio Awards

Information design and data visualization

Information design, sometimes called information architecture, is a fast-growing and deeply rewarding profession for the right kind of person. Perfectionists and innately curious people are frequently attracted to information design, along with those who want to produce useful design that serves society rather than selling products. Information design is user-centered, and research and analysis heavy.

Signage, computer-generated information systems, graphs/charts, visualizing scientific and technical data, digital control displays and computer interfaces, and the design of legal and technical documents are all part of information design, but the field is expanding. People drawn toward mathematics and science, but who are highly creative, are also drawn to information design. It requires all the skills of a designer, including problem-solving, the ability to communicate clearly, a high degree of typographic knowledge, image generation, and great research skills. However, the information designer must possess an additional level of rigor, be interested in resolving the tiniest details of a job, and be able to nail the relationship between form and content. Information designers frequently work with complex data, finding a way to visualize that information in the most direct and unambiguous way.

In addition to all the design skills mentioned, it's necessary for an information designer to understand how systems work and how they change in different environments (print/digital/3D/space). They need to have a strong grasp of how messages are perceived, how information is processed by readers/audiences (cognitive processing), and be prepared to spend many hours analyzing and bringing beautiful order to chaos.

Functional design

Information design is important, meaningful, useful, and functional. It is a powerful form of design that should speak to people in a clear, unambiguous language, putting the message first without sacrificing any of the innovation or beauty of design. If it works, it can illuminate a subject matter you previously thought nothing about. If it doesn't work, it can distort information, create confusion, or the information simply gets lost.

There's very little that's arbitrary or subjective in this profession, but the visualizations have become marvelously creative and are now in demand from every sector of the business world as full-page, or full-screen, illustrations.

Skills required

- Great typography skills.
- Ability to approach complex information logically and creatively.
- Understanding of systems and messages.
- Analytical mind.

The exciting part...

- Rewarding (meaningful and useful).
- Serves society (potential for good).
- Working with multiple content(s) and complex data.
- Combines design and scientific rigor.
- Witnessing your design functioning in society.
- Working with interdisciplinary teams.
- Many different media and contexts for design.

... Not so much

- Detail oriented (not for everyone).
- Content driven.
- Involves complex problem solving.

⭐ Best in the business

Eric Spiekerman Information architect, font designer, and author of books and articles on type and typography. Founder of MetaDesign agency, Germany's largest design firm.

Otto Neurath (1882–1945), Austrian economist and sociologist whose work for the Social and Economic Museum of Vienna led to the development of the Vienna Method, or Isotype, to convey complicated information to the Viennese public. His use of iconic pictograms looks just as current today.

Richard Saul Wurman, architect and graphic designer, first coined the phrase "information architecture" and is a pioneer in information design. Wurman has written and designed over 83 books, and is the creator of the TED conferences.

Edward Tufte, called "the da Vinci of data" by *The New York Times*, the American statistician gained his reputation through his outstanding presentation of informational graphics.

Career options

- Designer in a company with a specialism in information design, systems design, user documentation, or signage.
- Web designer in a company dealing with information architecture.
- Designer in government agencies that deal with delivering complex information to the public, such as health services, transportation, and weather.

➕ **See also:** Nicholas Felton (www.feltron.com), Toby Ng (www.toby-ng.com), Peter Grundy (www.grundini.com).

Resources

The International Organization for Standardization (ISO) "A" series is a system for sizing paper that was first used in Germany in 1922 where it is still called "DIN A" (Deutsche Industrie Norm). Each size is derived by halving the size immediately above it. Each size is the same as another geometrically as they are halved using the same diagonal. A0 is the first size and is 10 ¾ square feet (1m², approximately) in area. A series sizes always refer to the trimmed sheet. The untrimmed sizes are referred to as "RA" or "SRA." About 26 countries have officially adopted the A series system and it is commonly used everywhere in the world except Canada and the United States.

The "B" series is used when a size in between any two adjacent A sizes is needed, which is relatively rare. The British and American systems, unlike the metric A system, refer to the untrimmed size of the sheet. As quoting just the A or B number can cause confusion, both the A or B size and the size in inches or millimeters should be given when specifying paper.

ISO A series

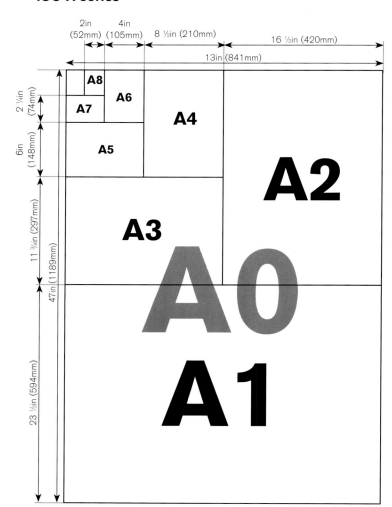

British standard book sizes

	Quarto		Octavo	
	in	mm	in	mm
Crown	9 ½ x 7 ½	246 x 189	7 ½ x 5	186 x 123
Large crown	10 x 8	258 x 201	8 x 5	198 x 129
Demy	11 x 8 ½	276 x 219	8 ½ x 5 ½	216 x 138
Royal	12 ¼ x 9 ½	312 x 237	9 ½ x 6	234 x 156

U.S. book sizes

in	mm
5 ½ x 8 ½	140 x 216
5 x 7 ⅜	127 x 187
5 ½ x 8 ¼	140 x 210
6 ⅛ x 9 ¼	156 x 235
5 ⅜ x 8	136 x 203
5 ⅝ x 8 3/8	143 x 213

North American paper sizes

Size	in × in	mm × mm
Letter	8 ½ × 11	216 × 279
Legal	8 ½ × 14	216 × 356
Junior Legal	8 × 5	203 × 127
Ledger[2]	17 × 11	432 × 279
Tabloid	11 × 17	279 × 432

ISO B series

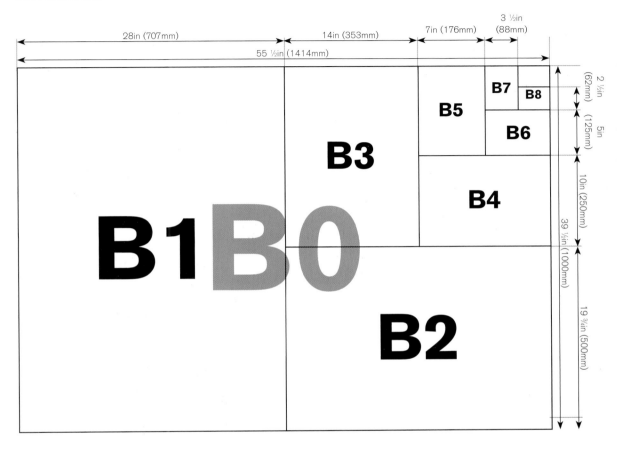

28in (707mm)   14in (353mm)   7in (176mm)   3 ½in (88mm)

55 ½in (1414mm)

2 ½in (62mm)   5in (125mm)   10in (250mm)   39 ½in (1000mm)   19 ¾in (500mm)

B1   B0   B2   B3   B4   B5   B6   B7   B8

Envelopes

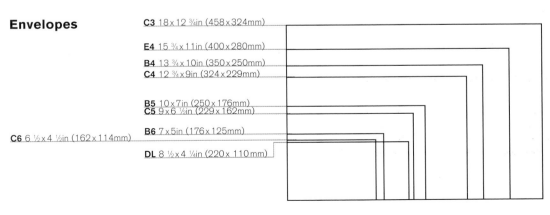

C3 18 x 12 ¾in (458 x 324mm)

E4 15 ¾ x 11in (400 x 280mm)

B4 13 ¾ x 10in (350 x 250mm)

C4 12 ¾ x 9in (324 x 229mm)

B5 10 x 7in (250 x 176mm)

C5 9 x 6 ½in (229 x 162mm)

B6 7 x 5in (176 x 125mm)

C6 6 ½ x 4 ½in (162 x 114mm)

DL 8 ½ x 4 ¼in (220 x 110 mm)

Glossary

AAs: "Author's alterations" are edits made to the content of a file by the client. Usually handled before sent to press, if the client makes edits while the job is at the printer—usually in the proofing stage—AAs can prove very costly.

Abstraction: An aesthetic concept describing something that is drawn from the real, but has been "distilled" to its barest minimum form, color, or tone, often removed from its original context.

Ad server: A web-based system for inserting advertising content dynamically into a web page.

Additive color: System used on monitors and televisions, based on RGB (red, green, blue). When combined, these form white light.

Adobe Acrobat: The family of Adobe programs that create and manage PDFs.

Ad server: A web-based system for inserting advertising content dynamically into a web page.

Advancing and receding color: Colors in the red spectrum appear to advance to the human eye, whereas those in the blue spectrum appear to recede.

Alignment: The setting of text relative to a column or page.

Analogous: Similar, comparable, alike; for example, two colors that are near to each other, such as grass green and leaf green, are analogous.

Anchor link: A navigational link that directs the user to a specific section of a web page.

Anchor point: In a design program, a point on or at the end of a curve or line that can be "grabbed" by the cursor and moved around the canvas, either to change the curve shape or to move the entire curve.

Artboard: In Illustrator, the virtual "ground" into which images are placed.

Associations: Connections between colors and emotions, culture, experience, and memory.

Asymmetry: A composition where elements are juxtaposed and do not mirror the other forms on the page.

Audience: In its broadest sense, the consumers, voyeurs, and occasionally participants of design work.

Balance: The deliberate placement of objects on a page.

Banding: Series of lighter or darker bands running across an area of solid color.

Baseline: The line on which the lowercase letters sit, and below which the descenders fall.

Baseline grid: Locks text onto consistent horizontal points.

Book jacket: Packaging that advertises both product and publisher.

Brainstorming: A visual aid to thinking laterally and exploring a problem, usually by stating the problem in the center of a page and radiating outward spokes for components of the problem. Each component can then be considered separately with its own spokes, so that each point, thought, or comment is recorded.

Calibration: Color settings that should be set to show color on screen as it will be in print.

Categories: A taxonomy structure for designating dynamic content (posts) to appear in similar, or different, news feeds within a website. Can be used as a search criteria for displaying similarly themed posts.

Clip: The name for a sequence of images or length of developed film or video.

Canvas: The virtual "ground" that images are placed onto in Photoshop.

Centered: Text that is aligned in the middle: symmetrical, with an even gap at the end of each line.

Closure: The ability of the human brain to observe an incomplete circle and to perceive it as complete.

CMS: Content management system. The structured framework of a dynamically driven website.

CMYK: Cyan, magenta, yellow, key (black): the four colors that make up the full-color printing process.

CMYK break: The computed percentages of C, M, Y, and K ink that make up a color.

Coated: A hard, waxy surface, either gloss or matte, and not porous (ink sits on the surface).

Coated one side: A paper that is coated on one side and matte on the other.

Collage: Derived from the French word for "to glue" involving the assemblage of elements of texture, found materials, and newspapers.

Colorimeter: Hardware that attaches to or hangs in front of your screen, allowing you to calibrate and profile your monitor.

Color modes: The expression of color in numerical values that enable us to mix them efficiently: CYMK, LAB, RGB.

Column: Vertical block of text.

Complementary color: Colors, such as red and green, that lie opposite each other on the color wheel.

Composition: The arrangement of elements or parts of a design (text, images) on the page.

Comps: Comprehensive sketch, a close approximation of the printed product.

Concertina folds: Folds in alternate directions.

Connotations: A color's broader associations, for example: green—jealousy, naivety, illness, environment, nature.

Consistency: The considered selection of design elements that have similar attributes.

Contextualization: The process of placing something within the interrelated systems of meaning that make up the world.

Contrast: Obvious differences in elements in a composition; size, form, color, and weight.

Critical pathways: Defining the desired route of a website's audience, as it relates to taking an action (purchasing, contacting, registering, etc.).

Crop mark: Vertical and horizontal lines at the corners of an image or page to indicate to a vendor where to trim off the bleed area.

Customer profile/profiling: The process of creating a series of parameters or set of information that defines the desires, trends, or interests of a demographic so that designs can be pitched or marketed to them.

Dashboard: The administrative back-end for a content management system (CMS).

Data: Facts or pieces of information of any kind.

Denotations: What the color means, or is; for example, a red rose is a green stem with red petals.

Depth of field: Distance between the object of focus and where the focus starts to blur. For example, a photographer may want a product to be in sharp, clear focus but the background to be blurred, so would choose a smaller aperture (f22), a slower film speed (ISO 100) for higher resolution, and have extra lighting and external flashes set up.

Diagram: Drawing or plan that explains the parts of something, or how something works.

Didactic: A pragmatic and unambiguous method of giving clear information.

Digital presses: Automate direct image transfer from digital file to paper without the creation of plates.

Digital printing: Method of printing that uses a plateless computer-controlled press.

Documentation: The recording in written, visual, or aural form of what is of interest.

Domain name: The web address for a website. It is renewed annually by the site owner for a nominal fee.

Dot gain: A printed dot that becomes bigger than intended due to spreading, causing a darkening of screened images, mid-tones, and textures. This varies with different paper stocks.

Downsampling: A form of compression that lowers the resolution of images by eliminating unnecessary pixel data.

DPI: Dots per (square) inch; the common form of resolution measurement. Designers typically use 72dpi-sized images for web images, and 300dpi-sized images for photo-realistic prints.

Drop-down (menu): A navigational element that is revealed when a visitor clicks a main navigational link to reveal related links (subsections) that are displayed below.

Earmark: Identifying or distinguishing marks or characteristics of a typeface.

Element: One small part of a composition, such as a point or line, an image, a letter, or a word.

Email client: An application used to review and compose emails.

Embedding: A PDF removes the need for multiple requisite files by including fonts and compressed imagery in one file.

Ephemera: Objects such as newspapers, bus and train tickets, and other found textures and typography.

F stop/Focal length and aperture: Size of aperture or "iris" inside a camera, which controls the amount of light that hits the film or pixel sensor; the range on a general camera is f4 (large aperture) to f22 (small aperture). A large aperture (f2, for example) brings more light into the camera and results in a softer image; a small aperture (f16, for example) allows less light into the camera but gives a sharper image.

Favicon: A small branded element that appears in the web browser's URL field, bookmark list, or favorites list.

Filter: Plates of glass or plastic attached to the front of the lens in order to accentuate different qualities. For example, a polarizing filter cuts down light glare; a color filter enhances different colors.

FLA: The uncompressed and editable file format from Flash. Make sure to keep your master copy safe.

Flexography: Method of printing that uses rubber relief plates.

FLV: Flash video, the file extension format for displaying video on the Internet supported by sites such as YouTube and news feed streaming.

Fly-out (menu): A navigational element that is revealed by extending out to the side of a main navigational element.

Font: One size, weight, and width of a typeface: Garamond Roman 12pt is a font.

Footer: The lower section of a web page layout, usually featuring navigation and copyright information.

FPO: For position only; the use of a temporary placeholder or low-resolution image in place of the high-quality counterpart during the design process.

French folds: Sheets of paper are folded in half, so that they are double thickness. The two folds are at right angles to each other, and then bound on the edge.

Gamut: The complete range of colors available within one system of reproduction, e.g., CMYK gamut or RGB gamut.

Gang-run printing: Printing many different jobs on one large sheet.

Gatefold: A way of folding paper so that the outer quarters of a page are folded to meet in the center. The result works like symmetrical doors that open onto an inner page.

Gestalt psychology: A theory that suggests that the mind perceives and organizes holistically and finds patterns in that which appears to be unconnected.

Gloss: A shiny form of paper, used for magazines, books, etc.

Gravure: Method of printing that uses plates with recessed cells of varying depths.

Grid: Series of horizontal and vertical lines on a page, used as a visual guide for lining up words and images.

Ground: The page, surface, or area in which the design will be placed.

GSM: Grams per square meter, or g/m2.

Gutter: The gap between two text blocks or spreads on separate pages either side of the book fold or binding.

Handle: An anchor point in a design program connected to the main vector path by tangential lines that can be manipulated to change the shape of the curve.

Harmony: Image with a balance of two or more colors that work together, for example taupe and gray.

Header: The top section of a web page layout, usually featuring branded elements and the main navigational structure.

Hierarchy: The different "weight" or importance given to type or image to emphasize different aspects.

Hyperlink (navigational link): A clickable navigational element that allows site visitors to navigate through the website.

Hyphenation: The point at which a word is broken at the end of a line in continuous text, and a hyphen is inserted.

IAB: The Interactive Advertising Bureau.

Identity: A unified, identifiable look for a product or organization.

Information Architecture (IA): A balance of the intrinsic naturec of a website and established user expectations, combined with your client's overall goals.

Inline text link (navigational link): Hyperlink within the body of a web page layout.

The Interactive Advertising Bureau (IAB): An organization that documents and works to define the standards for online advertising.

ISO: International Organization for Standardization. This sets a standard range for virtual film speeds in digital cameras: ISO 100, for example, works best in good lighting conditions for stationary objects; ISO 1600 works best in poor lighting conditions and for mobile objects.

Justified: Lines or paragraphs of type aligned to both margins simultaneously, creating different spacing in between words.

Juxtaposition: The process of putting two or more unrelated or opposite elements or objects together to create different effects.

Kerning: Adjustments to the spaces between two letters (used extensively for capitals).

Keyframe: Either the frame of an animation at a key stage, or a frame in a clip where a transition is due to start.

Laid: A paper that has lines on its surface from its means of production. Often used for stationery.

Lateral thinking: A form of research where the emphasis is on indirect, creative forms of inquiry and thinking.

Law of closure: The mind creates a solid object on the page from suggestions of shapes and placement and proximity of elements.

Layer Comps (Photoshop): A feature that allows the user to record which items are viewable in a complex, multi-layer document.

Layout: Placement of words and images on a grid or document to organize information.

Layout roughs: (See Roughs) Loose concept sketches for page design that organize space without showing detail.

Leading: The horizontal space between lines of type. Related to the historical use of strips of lead in letterpress.

Lens: Different lenses extend the capabilities of the camera.

- A normal lens on a digital or film SLR is 35mm, considered to be near enough to human vision.
- A macro lens captures sharp, extreme close-ups of objects.
- A wide-angle lens captures a wider vision, but with perspective distortion.
- A telephoto lens captures objects at distance.

Letterspacing (Tracking): The space between letters, which can be adjusted.

Ligatures: Two or more letterforms joined to create a single character.

Line: A continuous form of connection between two points ("___").

Linear reasoning: A form of thinking that implies strategic thought process, one in which step-by-step logic is employed.

Linen: Similar to laid, but finer lined.

Linguistic: Of, or relating to, language.

Lists (unordered/ordered): An unordered list is a bulleted list of similar concept. An ordered list is grouped in order, by using an alphanumeric sequence.

Lossy: A compression format that removes or "loses" certain areas to achieve a smaller file size, yet reopening the file causes the program to "guess" at the missing data, possibly creating a lower-quality version.

LPI: When printing halftones, such as in one-color newspapers and reproductions, the lines per inch is the number of lines that compose the resolution of a halftone screen.

Margin: The usually blank space to the top, bottom, and sides of a page between the trim and the live printing area. Headers, footers, and page numbers are traditionally placed within this area.

Market research: The process of collecting and collating data from questionnaires, interviews, and comments from the public regarding a concern, a problem, or a possible solution.

Matte: A dull, non-shiny quality of paper, used for newspapers, for example.

Measure: The length of a line of text on a page, based in inches, centimeters, points, or picas.

Metaphor: Word or image that sets up associations; for example, a "piece of cake" is a metaphor for easy.

META tags: Elements within the HTML code, used by the search engines to properly index websites.

Metrics: The strategy for measuring the success—or failure—of a project's goals.

Monetized: Earned revenue from online marketing activities, such as banner ad placement.

Montage: Derived from the French word for "assemble;" a picture made from pieces of other pictures.

Navigation (breadcrumb): A path-based navigation that identifies the user's location within the structure of a website.

Navigation (dropdown): A navigational element that is revealed when a visitor clicks a main navigational link to reveal related links (subsections) that are displayed below.

Navigation (fly-out): A navigational element that is revealed by extending out to the side of a main navigational element.

Negative space: The white or colored area around an element, e.g. a margin of a page.

Non-representation: The opposite of representation.

Offset lithography: The digitally produced printing plate is treated chemically so that the image will accept ink and reject water.

Onomatopoeia: In typography, the use of type to suggest the sounds of a spoken language, such as adding a large "o" to the word "open."

Optical adjustment: Making adjustments to letterspacing by eye, not mechanically.

Ordered lists: Typically a grouped list of items using an alphanumeric sequence.

Organic results: Search engine results based on the natural appearance of keywords within a site dialogue.

Ornaments: Typed characters that embellish the page. Also known as flowers.

Page plan/Flat plan: A document with a series of numbered thumbnails set out in an ordered grid that represents each page in a book.

Panel: Device used to highlight information. Also known as a sidebar.

Pantone Matching System (PMS): An international system to ensure reliable color selection, specification, and control.

Paper grain: The direction of wood fibers that make up a piece of paper.

Patch: The space on a bookstore's shelf occupied by spines of books from the same series.

Path: A drawn line in a design program, mathematically determined; also called a vector.

PEs: "Printer's errors" are mistakes and omissions found at the proofing stage by the designer or client that did not, for whatever reason, make it from the supplied file to the press. The cost of these errors is usually absorbed by the vendor as a matter of customer service.

Perfect binding: Method similar to paperback binding, where loose sheets are encased in a heavier paper cover, then glued to the book spine. Edges are trimmed to be flush with each other.

Photomontage: The assemblage of various fragments of photographs.

Pixel: The smallest element of a computer screen or printed image. The word "pixel" is an amalgamation of picture (pix-) and element (-el).

Placeholder: A temporary or low-resolution image in place of the high-quality counterpart during the design process.

Plates: Separate printing plates for separate colors that overprint to create color images in 4-color offset printing.

Plugin: A WordPress term for an element that adds a functional enhancement to the basic CMS structure. Also referred to as widgets and modules.

Poetic: A style that is less clear, but more artistic, more open to interpretation.

Point: A dot on a page, such as a period (.).

Point size/Pica: The relative size of a font. There are 72 points in an inch.

Positive space: A form, image, or word printed or formed on the page.

PPI: Pixels per inch or pixel density is interchangeable with DPI, but usually refers to the resolution of an unprinted image displayed on screen or captured by a scanner or digital camera.

Primary color: Red, yellow, or blue.

Primary research: Gathering material that does not preexist, such as photographing, drawing, making prototypes, interviewing people.

Proximity: The relationship of one object to another.

Quality control strip: Usually incorporated in printed sheets outside the grid to monitor the quality of plate-making, inking, and registration. Checking black sections helps point out color casting.

Quantitative: Related to quantities of things, or measurements (numerical).

Ragging: When text is aligned left some words at the end of the lines might jut out farther than the rest and cause uneven-looking paragraphs.

Ranged (or Ragged) left/Ranged (or Ragged) right: Text that is aligned to a column or margin, either left or right.

Raster: Assemblages of pixels on a 2D grid system that can be viewed on computer screens or print media.

Ream: Standard quantity of paper; 500 sheets.

Recto: The right-hand page in a book.

Registration marks: Hairline marks at the corners of a printed page to help ensure plates are lined up correctly and designate what will be cropped off at finishing time.

Relief: A printing process that uses a raised surface, such as letterpress.

Repetition: The repeated use of select design elements within the same composition.

Repetition with variation: The alteration of select aspects of a repeated element.

Representation: Something that looks like, resembles, or stands in for something else. In drawing, this is also known as figurative, since it deliberately attempts to mimic the thing drawn.

Resolution: The clarity of a digital image. A low-resolution image (30dpi, for example) will have clearly visible pixels; a high-resolution image (300dpi, for example) will not.

Responsive web design: The content of a website layout is coded to reposition itself in response to the specific devices on which the website is being viewed.

Return on Design Investment (RODI): The measure of receiving positive results for the client's investment in the project.

Rhetoric: A style of arguing, persuading, or engaging in dialogue. For a designer, it is a way of engaging the targeted audience.

RODI: Return on design investment indicates the success of a project in relation to the project's unique goals.

Rollover folds: A way of folding a page so that successive folds turn in on themselves and the page is folded into a roll.

Rotations: The number of times that an animated GIF file will play, from the first frame to the last.

Roughs: Loose sketches for concept and compositional development that do not include fine detail.

Saddle stitching: Binding method where sheets of paper are folded in the center, stitched together along the fold, then glued into the cover spine.

Sans serif: Without serif. Typefaces such as Univers, Helvetica, Aksidenz Grotesque, and Futura, characterized by their lack of serifs. Predominantly associated with the 19th/20th centuries.

Satin: A form of paper between matte and gloss.

Schematic: Simplified diagram or plan related to a larger scheme or structure.

Screen printing: Method of printing that uses stencils.

Screen resolution: The resolution of a file that will be viewed onscreen is 72 pixels per inch (PPI). When designing for high-density displays (i.e., Apple's "Retina Display"), the document's dimensions should be doubled, not the resolution.

Secondary color: A mix of any two primaries: orange, green, or violet.

Secondary research: Gathering material that already exists, such as design work, color samples, written texts, newspaper/magazine articles, archive images (e.g. historical samples of advertising).

Semantics: The study of meaning in language and elsewhere.

Semiotics: A system that links objects, words, and images to meanings through signs and signifiers.

Serif: Structural details at the ends of some strokes in old-style capital and lowercase letters.

Shift-scheduling: Allowing presses to run all day and night.

Simultaneous contrast: The human eye tends to differentiate between two neighboring colors by emphasizing their differences rather than their similarities—background colors affect foreground colors (the image).

SLR: Single lens reflex. These types of camera use a viewfinder and mirrors so that the photographer's sightline goes through the main lens and results in a what-you-see-is-what-you-get image.

Spot color: Any flat color, like Pantone or Toyo colors, printed as a solid, and not made up of CMYK.

Statistical: Related to the collection, classification, and organization of (often numerical) information.

Stock: A generic form or type of paper, such as tracing paper or matte coated.

Storyboard: A document similar to a flat plan, but with a sequence of thumbnails that specifically lays out the narrative for a comic strip or film.

Stress/Axis: The angle of the curved stroke weight change in a typeface. Seen clearly in letters such as "o."

Style board: A presentation of proposed website stylizations for review by a client, independent of the overall website structure.

Subtractive color: System used in printing, based on CMYK colors.

SWF: ShockWave Flash, the file extension format for displaying animated vector files on the web.

Symbolism: A way of representing an object or word through an image, sound, or another word; for example, a crossed knife and fork on a road sign means a café is ahead.

Symmetry: A composition where elements are balanced or mirrored on a page.

Syntax: The study of the rules for the formation of grammatically correct sentences.

Tag cloud: A keyword-based navigation element on a website, where keywords can be selected in order to refine search criteria to display similarly themed posts.

Taxonomy: A way to group related content in a structural format.

Theme: A collection of predesigned web page layouts, designed around a centralized concept, where the arrangement of the page's structure as been specified by the theme's author.

Thumbnail: Small, rough visual representation of a bigger picture or final outcome.

Timeline: The linear timeline in both Flash and After Effects in which keyframes can be fixed in order to designate animated milestones in a production.

Tool tips: A message that displays when a user hovers with a mouse over a linked element.

Type anatomy: The language used to describe the various parts of letterforms.

Typeface: The set of visual attributes (design or style) of a particular group of letters: Garamond is a typeface.

Typographic rules: Printed lines that direct the reader's eye.

Unordered list: Typically a bulleted list of grouped items.

Uniform Resource Locator (URL): The address of a website.

User Interface (UI): The space where humans interact with machines. It is a part of the larger user experience (UX) of a website or application.

User Experience (UX): The experience a user has with a website.

Varnish: A liquid sprayed or spread onto paper to give it a hard-wearing surface so that printed ink stays intact.

Verso: The left-hand page in a book.

Vibration: Complementary colors of equal lightness and high saturation tend to make each other appear more brilliant, and cause the illusion of motion along the edges where they meet.

Web hosting: A designated online storage space for hosting a website and related email accounts.

Weight: Colors differ in perceived "weight." For example, if a man was to move two large boxes equal in size but one pale green and the other dark brown,

he would probably pick up the green one because it appeared lighter. It is generally assumed that blue-greens look lighter whereas reds appear stronger, and therefore heavier.

White space: The open space surrounding a positive image that defines shape and directs hierarchy.

Widgetized areas: Locations within a CMS theme where plugins and widgets can be inserted into the physical layout. Typically, these are located within the side column and lower (footer) area of a web page.

Wove/smooth: A smooth, uncoated paper that is very porous (ink sits under the surface).

x-height: The height of a lowercase "x" in any typeface.

Bibliography

Eye: The International Review of Graphic Design (magazine)

J. Abbott Miller, Ellen Lupton, *Design Writing Research*, Phaidon Press Ltd

Philippe Apeloig, *Au Coeur du Mot (Inside the Word)*, Lars Müller

Phil Baines, *Type and Typography: Portfolio Series*, Laurence King

Gabriel Bauret, Alexey Brodovitch, *Assouline*

Russell Bestley, Ian Noble, *Visual Research: An Introduction to Research Methodologies in Graphic Design*, AVA Publishing

Michael Bierut, William Drenttel, Steven Heller, D. K. Holland *Looking Closer: Critical Writings on Graphic Design*, Allworth Press

Lewis Blackwell, *20th-Century Type: Remix*, Gingko Press

Robert Bringhurst, *The Elements of Typographic Style*, Hartley & Marks Publishers

Michael Burke, Peter Wilber, *Information Graphics: Innovative Solutions in Contemporary Design*, Thames & Hudson

Italo Calvino, *Invisible Cities*, Hyphen Press

Rob Carter, Ben Day, Philip Meggs, *Typographic Design: Form and Communication*, John Wiley & Sons

David Crow, *Visible Signs*, AVA Publishing

Department of Typography, University of Reading, *Modern typography in Britain: graphic design, politics, and society*, Hyphen Press

Geoffrey Dowding, *Finer Points in the Spacing and Arrangement of Type*, Hartley and Marks

Johanna Drucker, *Alphabetic Labyrinth: The Letters in History and Imagination*, Thames & Hudson

Johanna Drucker, *Figuring the Word: Essays on Books, Writing and Visual Poetics*, Granary Books

Johanna Drucker, *The Century Of Artists' Books*, Granary Books

Johanna Drucker, Emily McVarish, *Graphic Design History: A Critical Guide*, Prentice Hall

Kimberly Elam, *Grid Systems: Principles of Organizing Type*, Princeton Architectural Press

Alan Fletcher, *The Art of Looking Sideways*, Phaidon Press Ltd

Online resources

Friedrich Friedl, Nicolaus Ott, Bernard Stein, *Typography: An Encyclopedic Survey of Type Design and Techniques throughout History*, Black Dog & Leventhal Publishers Inc

E. M. Ginger, Erik Spiekermann, *Stop Stealing Sheep and Find Out How Type Works*, Adobe Press

Steven Heller, *Merz to Emigré and Beyond: Avant-Garde Magazine Design of the Twentieth Century*, Phaidon Press Ltd

Steven Heller, *Paul Rand*, Phaidon Press Ltd

Jost Hochuli, *Detail in Typography*, Hyphen Press

Jost Hochuli, Robert Kinross, *Designing Books: Practice and Theory*, Princeton

Richard Hollis, *Graphic Design: A Concise History*, Thames & Hudson

Allen Hurlburt, *The Grid: A Modular System for the Design and Production of Newpapers, Magazines, and Books*, John Wiley & Sons

David Jury, *Letterpress: The Allure of the Handmade*, Rotovision

Robin Kinross, *Modern Typography: An Essay in Critical History*, Hyphen Press

Robin Kinross, *Unjustified Texts: Perspectives on Typography*, Hyphen Press

Willi Kunz, *Typography: Macro and Microaesthetics, Fundamentals of Typographic Design*, Ram Publications

Ellen Lupton, *Thinking with Type: A Critical Guide for Designers, Writers, Editors, and Students*, Princeton Architectural Press

Per Mollerup, *Marks of Excellence*, Phaidon Press Ltd

Lars Müller, *Josef Müller-Brockmann, Pioneer of Swiss Graphic Design*, Lars Müller Publishers

Joseph Müller-Brockmann, *Grid Systems in Graphic Design*, Niggli Verlag

Alan Pipes, *Production for Graphic Designers*, Laurence King

Norman Potter, *What Is a Designer: Things, Places, Messages*, Hyphen Press

Paul Rand, *A Designer's Art*, Yale University Press

Paul Rand, *Design, Form and Chaos*, Yale University Press

Paul Rand, *From Lascaux to Brooklyn*, Yale University Press

Ferdinand de Saussure, *Course in General Linguistics*, Books LLC

Adrian Shaughnessy, *How to be a Graphic Designer, Without Losing Your Soul*, Laurence King

Paula Scher, *Make It Bigger*, Princeton Architectural Press

Bradbury Thompson, *The Art of Graphic Design*, Yale University Press

Jan Tschichold, *The New Typography*, University of California Press

Jan Tschichold, *Asymmetric Typography*, Cooper & Beatty

Edward Tufte, *Envisioning Information*, Graphics Press

Edward Tufte, *The Visual Display of Quantitative Information*, Graphics Press

Edward Tufte, *Visual Explanations: Images and Quantities, Evidence and Narrative*, Graphics Press

Wolfgang Weingart, *My Way to Typography*, Lars Müller Publishers

http://www.aiga.org/
http://www.artsandecology.rsablogs.org.uk/
http://www.baselinemagazine.com/
http://www.blog.eyemagazine.com/
http://www.coroflot.com/
http://www.design21sdn.com/
http://www.designandsociety.rsablogs.org.uk/
http://www.designcanchange.org/
http://www.designcouncil.org.uk/en/About-Design/Design-Disciplines/Information-Design-by-Sue-Walker-and-Mark-Barratt//
http://www.designobserver.com/
http://www.designersaccord.org/index.php?title=Main_Page
http://www.grainedit.com
http://www.greengaged.com/
http://www.hyphenpress.co.uk/books
http://www.ilovetypography.com
http://www.johnlangdon.net/
http://www.kateandrews.wordpress.com/resources/
http://www.lars-mueller-publishers.com/
http://www.logolounge.com/
http://www.lovelyasatree.com/
http://www.metadesign.de/
http://www.printmag.com/daily-heller/
http://www.re-nourish.com/
http://www.redjotter.wordpress.com
http://www.service-design-network.org/
http://www.segd.org/home/index.html
http://www.socialdesignsite.com/
http://www.spd.org/
http://www.sustainability.aiga.org/
http://www.sustainability.aiga.org/sus_reading/sustainable_design
http://www.ted.com/talks/chip_kidd_designing_books_is_no_laughing_matter_ok_it_is.html
http://www.thedieline.com/
http://www.typographica.org
http://www.typotheque.com/articles/my_type_design_philosophy.html
http://www.textmatters.com/
http://www.thersa.org/home
http://www.threetreesdontmakeaforest.org/
http://www.typotheque.com/site/index.php

Index

Acknowledgments

Quarto would like to thank the following for supplying images for inclusion in this book:

© 1996-2013, Amazon.com, Inc, p.164cl

© 2012 Johns Hopkins University, p.143c

© 2013 Apple Inc. All rights reserved, pp.21cr, 164tcl, 171cl

© 2013 ENVATO, p.174tl/cl/bl

© 2013 Nike, Inc. All Rights Reserved, p.22tl

© 2013 The New York Times Company, p.149tr

© Christie's Images/Corbis, p.35t

© Copyright 2012-3 SimsUShare, http://simsushare.commandsim.com, p.171tl

© Copyright Make it Digital 2013, www.makeitdigital.co.uk, p.171tcr

© Design Bridge, www.designbridge.com, pp.2bl, 6l, 9tc, 20cbl, 70b, 78t

© Frost*, http://frostdesign.com.au, pp.2c, 20tr/cr/br, 44b, 46t/c/b, 47b, 56c, 131cl/cr

© T&CO. 2013, p.164bl

Aloof, www.aloofdesign.com, pp.79t, 156t, 167r

Bach, Tran , Shutterstock.com, p.103tl

Bain, Kitch, Shutterstock.com, p.103b

Balaban, Nelson, http://www.behance.net/nelsonbalaban, p.157

Beck, Krissy, Drexel University, pp.81b, 95bl, 129tr

Bell, Vance, www.vancebell.com, p.177tl

Beltramo, Lauren, Drexel University, www.laurenbeltramo.com, pp.85tl/tr, 129br

Bessermachen DesignStudio, design and packaging; Stiig Helgens Binggeli, Brandhouse, for archetypes and the idea, www.brandhouse.com, pp.130tr/cr

Big Spaceship, www.bigspaceship.com, p.7r

Bird, Sean, Daredevil Creative, Design Executive, www.daredevil-creative.com, p.152tl, 153tr

Bloom, Jeremy, Drexel University, https://involvio.com, pp.63t

Bluehand, Shutterstock.com, pp.8bl, p.97cr

Bodanza, Chris, http://www.designguru.net, p.183t/r

Boenisch, Alex, Drexel University, p.93br

Bridgeman, p.39b

Bright Pink Communication Design, pp.151b, 160t/c/

Brolik Productions, www.brolik.com, pp.147br, 163tl/tlb, 166ctl

Cervo, Diego, Shutterstock.com, p.103br

Chi, Jenny, Drexel University, pp.88cl/cr/bl/br

Chipp, Kidd, Knopf Publishing, p.84

Cichowski, Aaron, Drexel University, http://aaronpauldesign.net, p.75

Coffey, Marcy Zuczek, www.wfgd.net, p.34c

Cohen, Shira, Drexel University, pp.44t, 93bl, 95cr

Cook, Kyle, www.kyleacook.com, pp.8c, 57bl, 117c/b, 119tr

Courtesy of The University of Michigan, Designer: Steif, Ariela, http://www.arielasteif.com, p.159t

Date, Philip, p.104cl/cr

DeMirjian, Brielle, Drexel University, p.129tl

Dillon, Hannah, Drexel University, www.hannahdillon.com, p.33

Dobryanskaya, Natalia, Shutterstock.com, p.103tr

Drexel University Graphics Group, p.124

Eckert, Julie, www.julieeckertdesign.com, p.166cbl

Edwards, Victoria, pp.63b, 83t, 85b

Elliott, Steven, Drexel University, p.76b

Émigré, http://emigre.com, pp.7c, 39t, 69tl/c

Flynn, Megan, Drexel University, pp.50tr, 83cl

Foster, Rebecca, www.rebeccafosterdesign.co.uk, pp.157tl, 161t/c/b

Gallagher, Erika, Drexel University, www.impartcreative.com, www.erikagallagher.com, pp.71b, 95tr, 132-133t

Germano, Frank, Man on Fire Design, pp.3l, 17tl/r/cr/bl/br, 22bl, 37tr

GINGERMONKEY, www.gingermonkeydesign.com, pp.9tl, 16t, 17tl, 55bl/br, 58b, 62t, 149tl

Goldberg, Carin, www.caringoldberg.com, pp.3cr, 8btl, 48tl/cl, p.53bl/br, 68b

Graff, Jody, Jo to Go Design, p.94l

Grand Union Design, www.grandu.co.uk, pp.28t, 29tl, 50tl, 51t, 117

Greene, Rachael, Drexel University, p.71cr

Gross, Phillip, Drexel University, www.philipgdesign.com, pp.22br, p.92tl, p.128t

Grundy, Peter, http://grundini.com/, pp.3cl, 59tl, p.85tr, 96tr

Gundelsberger, Caitlin, www.caitlin-g.com, Drexel University, pp.2tr, 8tc, 24t, 32t, 129bl

h2a s.a, www.h2a.lu, pp.43tl/tr, p.54bl/br, 59tr, 72t, 81t

Hale, Don, www.donhalephotos.com, p.149bl

Happy Cog, www.happycog.com, p.149cl

Haring Jr., Don, pp.18b-19b

Hart, Jennifer, Drexel University, www.jenniferhartdesign.com, p.97cl

Huerta, Gerard, www.gerardhuerta.com, p.69br

Huff, Priscilla, www.priscillahuff.com, p.147t/cl/bl, 181b

HUGE, www.hugeinc.com, pp.58t/c/bc

Hughes, Rian, www.devicefonts.co.uk, p.182t

Jia, Fan, Drexel University, p.91br

Johnnyraff, Shutterstock.com, p.103bc

Joy, Linda, Drexel University, p.22bc

Kenyon, Sally, Drexel University, p.114tl

Langdon, John, www.johnlangdon.net, pp. 8tr, 36br, 38btr, 69bl

Lareau, Alexa, www.alexalareau.com, pp.8br, 25br

Laschenski, Caroline, www.carolinelaschenski.com, pp.6l, 42, 77t/b

Lewandowski, Catherine, Drexel University, www.c-lewandowski.com, p.34tc

Luis Santos, Shutterstock.com, p.21tl

M.Gazarelli, Drexel University, p.68tr

Make it Clear, www.makeitclear.co.uk, p.171cr/br

Marques, Ana, www.anartworld.tumblr.com, p.6r

Massarelli, Nicholas, Drexel University, p.116t

Matter Strategic Design, www.matter.to, pp.131t/tcl/tcr/131b

Mattson Creative, http://mattsoncreative.com, p.182br

McCune, Sascha, Drexel University, www.sasha-em.com, pp.8tl, 83cr

McDaniel, Keri, Drexel University, pp.48tl/tc/tr

Molino, Dante J, www.dantemolino.com, p.166bl

Moralba, April, Drexel University, p.95tr

Mortal Muses, www.mortalmuses.com, p.149cr

Morton, Katie, Drexel University, pp.45tr/cr/br

Mortula, Luciano, Shutterstock.com, p.97br

Mousegraphics, www.mousegraphics.gr, pp.34tl/cl/bl/bcr/br, 39tl/cl/bl, 50b, 130tc, 133b, 134tr, 135t

Musical Offering, Tableware Icon, p.171tr

Neumeister, http://neumeister.se, pp.52b, 56tl/tc/tr

Octavo Corp/Source Library, www.octavo.com, p.45b

Ollin, Hannah, p.22br

p'unk avenue, http://punkave.com, p.167l

Park, Ran, www.ran-park.com, pp.9tr, 10t, 11tl/tc/tr/cl/r/bl/

Patel, Chandni, www.chandnipatel.co.uk, pp.9bl, 13tl/tc/tr

Potter, Kirsty, http://www.cargocollective.com/nogutsnoglory, pp.2br, 13bl/br

Queiroz, Dado, http://dadoqueiroz.com, p.181t

Quevedo, Luis, http://www.behance.net/luiseq, pp.3r, 9br, 57br, 80c, 113br

Raisner, Evan, Drexel University, www.evanraisner.com, pp.47tr/cr, 57tr

Ray, Fever, p.63c

RedPoint Design Direction, Art Direction, Design & Illustration: Clark Most, Design: Joe Rivard, www.designdirection.com, p.6cr

Rhode, Mike, www.rohdesign.com, pp.144-145t

Rice Creative, Images shot by Arnaud De Harven, http://rice-creative.com, pp.20tl/cl, 131cr

Robertson, Scott, p.146tl

SantiPhotoSS, Shutterstock.com, p.135b

Scher, Paula, Pentagram Design, www.pentagram.com, pp.6cl, 9bc, 69tr, 70t, 73t, 82b

SeanPavonePhoto, Shutterstock.com, p.97t

Segura, www.segura-inc.com, p.149br

Seimon, Holly, www.hollysiemon.com, p.15cr

Shutterstock, Inc p.177r

Simmons, Kirsta, Graphic Design, Star Halma portfolio page, www.kirstasimmons.com, p.180t

Sinisi, Danielle, Drexel University, p.48b

SMACK | Creative Digital Studio, www.SMACKagency.com, pp.49tl/cl/bl

Smikeymikey1, Shutterstock.com, p.104t

Soppelsa, Moreno, Shutterstock.com, pp.136tr, 137t

Stuber, Andrew, www.andrewstuber.com, p.183br

Syfert, Stephanie, Drextel University, 22bl

The Learning Grove, www.thelearninggrove.com, Visual identity and design: Louise Carrier, Development and Project Lead: Murray Longworth, Annatto Design, p.151cl

The Natural Rug Store, www.naturalrugstore.co.uk, Visual identity and design: Louise Carrier, Development: Koded and Annatto Design, pp.150t, 151tl,

Todd, Sarah-Jayne, www.sarahjaynetodd.co.uk, pp.14bl/bc/br, 15bl/br

Tollet, Cathy for New Scientist magazine, p.119cr

Tomczyk, Tom, Shutterstock.com, p.103tc

Wan, Cheng, Drexel University, p.91bc

Weinstein, Brielle, Drexel University, p.80b

Willie, Mark, Mark Willie Design, www.markwilliegraphicdesign.com, pp.24t, 82tl

WordPress, http://wordpress.org, p.173br

Yee, Karen, Drexel University, http://karenlyee.tumblr.com, p.91bl

Zuzceck, Marcy, Drexel University, p.92tr

All step-by-step and other images are the copyright of Quarto Publishing plc. While every effort has been made to credit contributors, Quarto would like to apologize should there have been any omissions or errors—and would be pleased to make the appropriate correction for future editions of the book.

With special thanks to Jessica Glaser for her assistance with images for Unit 7.

Author acknowledgements

Sandra Stewart: Thanks to Bill Rees of A+B Design for lending his expertise in production and for his contribution to the Practices unit.

Thanks to Josh Gdoven, Gdoven Design, for his help with After Effects and Flash.

Thanks to the Graphic Design faculty at the Antoinette Westphal College of Media Arts & Design, Drexel University, for their support and suggestions.

Thanks to Chip Kidd, Frank Germano, Carin Goldberg, Gerard Huerta, Paula Scher, John Langdon, and Mark Willie for amazing generosity in sharing their work with the next generation of designers.

Eric Zempol: Thanks to the students, faculty, and alumni of Drexel University's Graphic Design program for their contributions to this book.

Thanks to Kent Eisenhuth, Michael Estok, Bill Rees, and Kosal Sen for their wonderfully varying perspectives on website project development processes (Unit 7, module 1).

Thanks to Drew Thomas from Brolik Productions for their project example contributions (p. 147, 163, 166).

Thanks to designer Dado Queiroz for his design contribution and personal introductions to other international designers (p.181t).

Thanks to Jon Kaye, PhD for his expertise on topics relating to Adobe Flash (Unit 7, Module 3).

Thanks to Will Ackerman and Chris Bodanza for their contributions relating to Banner Ad Design (Unit 7, Module 11).

Thanks to John J. Errigo, MS; Leslie M. Curran, MBA; Fidel Taveras Sosa, and Donald Stockman for their ongoing support as sounding boards for various topics discussed in Unit 7.

Special thanks to Chris Bodanza for sharing his technical expertise and perspective throughout Unit 7.

Thanks to designers Rian Hughes and Carlos Segura for their generous contributions.